A. LINCOLN

HANDEL

SHAKESPEARE

CARTIER

CHARLES DICKENS

DANIEL WEBSTER

ROBERT E. LEE

THE CHILDREN'S HOUR

Volume One
FIRST STORY BOOK

Volume Two
FAVORITE FAIRY TALES

Volume Three
OLD TIME FAVORITES

Volume Four
CARAVAN OF FUN

Volume Five
BEST-LOVED POEMS

Volume Six
STORIES OF TODAY

Volume Seven
FAVORITE MYSTERY STORIES

Volume Eight
MYTHS AND LEGENDS

Volume Nine
FROM MANY LANDS

Volume Ten
SCHOOL AND SPORT

Volume Eleven
ALONG BLAZED TRAILS

Volume Twelve
STORIES OF LONG AGO

Volume Thirteen
ROADS TO ADVENTURE

Volume Fourteen
FAVORITE ANIMAL STORIES

Volume Fifteen
LEADERS AND HEROES

Volume Sixteen
SCIENCE FICTION–GUIDE

Leaders and Heroes

A BOOK TO GROW ON

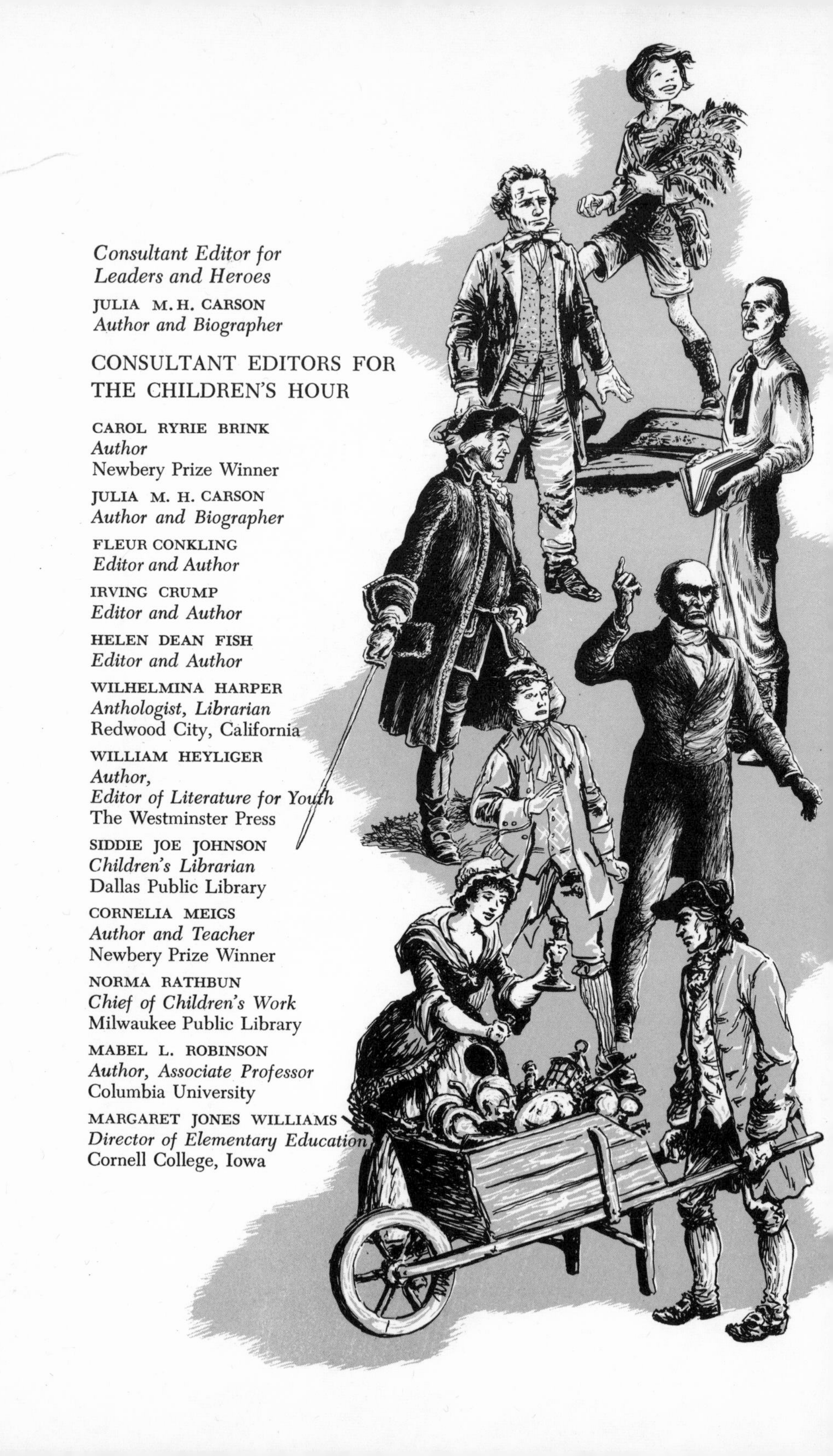

Consultant Editor for Leaders and Heroes

JULIA M. H. CARSON
Author and Biographer

CONSULTANT EDITORS FOR THE CHILDREN'S HOUR

CAROL RYRIE BRINK
Author
Newbery Prize Winner

JULIA M. H. CARSON
Author and Biographer

FLEUR CONKLING
Editor and Author

IRVING CRUMP
Editor and Author

HELEN DEAN FISH
Editor and Author

WILHELMINA HARPER
Anthologist, Librarian
Redwood City, California

WILLIAM HEYLIGER
Author,
Editor of Literature for Youth
The Westminster Press

SIDDIE JOE JOHNSON
Children's Librarian
Dallas Public Library

CORNELIA MEIGS
Author and Teacher
Newbery Prize Winner

NORMA RATHBUN
Chief of Children's Work
Milwaukee Public Library

MABEL L. ROBINSON
Author, Associate Professor
Columbia University

MARGARET JONES WILLIAMS
Director of Elementary Education
Cornell College, Iowa

THE CHILDREN'S HOUR

MARJORIE BARROWS, *Editor*

Leaders and Heroes

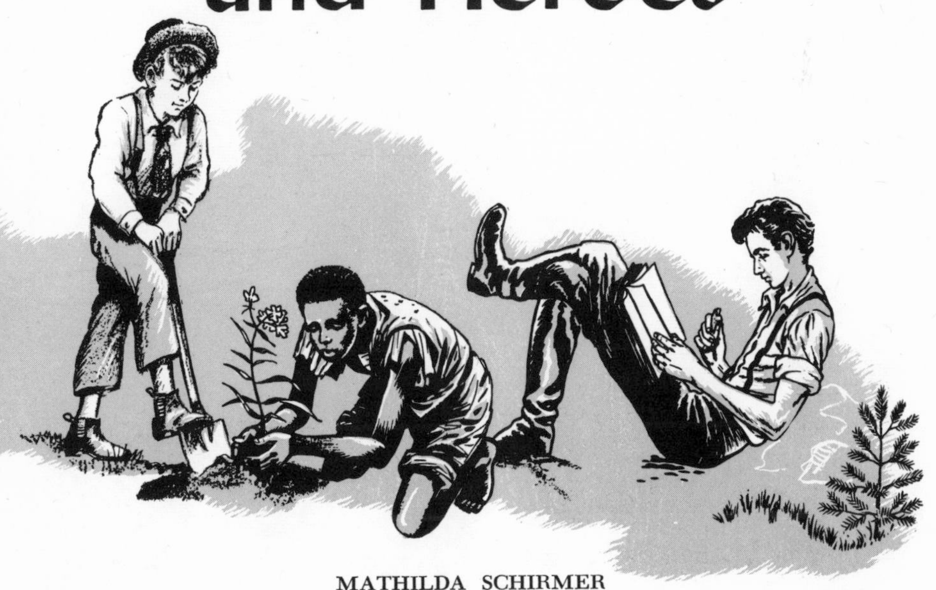

MATHILDA SCHIRMER
Associate Editor

DOROTHY SHORT
Art Editor

THE SPENCER PRESS, INC. • *Chicago*

153 N. Michigan Avenue
Chicago 1, Illinois

PRINTED IN THE UNITED STATES OF AMERICA

Acknowledgments

The editor and publishers wish to thank the following publishers, agents, authors, and artists for permission to reprint stories, poems, and illustrations included in this book:

APPLETON-CENTURY-CROFTS, INC., for "Charles Dickens: The Boy of the London Streets" by Rupert Sargent Holland from *St. Nicholas Magazine*, copyright, 1909, Century Company.

BECKLEY-CARDY COMPANY for "A Great Soldier: Robert E. Lee" by Margaret Thompsen Raymond, from *Leaders of the Frontier*, edited by Mathilda Schirmer.

THOMAS Y. CROWELL COMPANY for "Henri Fabre: A Place of His Own" from *Wide Fields* by Irmengarde Eberle, copyright, 1943, by Irmengarde Eberle; "Michelangelo and the Snow Man," "Titian's First Picture," and "Antonio Van Dyck and His Master Rubens" from *Stories of the Youth of Artists* by Mary Newlin Roberts, copyright, 1930, by Thomas Y. Crowell Company; and for "Georg Handel and the Duke" and "Wolfgang Mozart" from *Young Masters of Music* by Mary Newlin Roberts, copyright, 1931, by Thomas Y. Crowell Company.

DIDIER PUBLISHERS, New York, for "Ben Franklin's First Adventures" from *Franklin, the Life of an Optimist* by Andre Maurois.

DODD, MEAD & COMPANY, INC., for "Henry Wadsworth Longfellow" from *Famous American Poets* by Laura Benét, copyright, 1950, by Laura Benét; "Alexander Mackenzie: Hero of Canada" from *Knight of the Wilderness* by Maxine Shore and M. M. Oblinger, copyright, 1943, by Dodd, Mead & Company, Inc.; and "Jane Addams" from *Famous Women of America* by William Oliver Stevens, copyright, 1950, by William Oliver Stevens.

DOUBLEDAY & COMPANY, INC., for "My Struggle for an Education" from *Up from Slavery* by Booker T. Washington, copyright, 1900, 1901, by Booker T. Washington.

GARDEN CITY PUBLISHING COMPANY for "Thomas Alva Edison" from *Life Stories of the Great Inventors* by Henry Thomas and Dana Lee Thomas, copyright, 1946, by Garden City Publishing Company, Garden City, New York.

HOUGHTON MIFFLIN COMPANY for "Two Scenes from the Life of George Washington" from *American Hero Stories* by Eva March Tappan; "A Journey with Dickens" from *My Garden of Memories* by Kate Douglas Wiggin, copyright, 1951, by Helen K. Bradbury.

ALFRED A. KNOPF, INC., for story and illustrations for "Columbus Discovers America" from *They Put Out to Sea* by Roger Duvoisin, copyright, 1944, by Alfred A. Knopf, Inc.; and story and illustration for "Galileo" from *Album of the Great* by Rolf Klep, copyright, 1937, by Alfred A. Knopf, Inc.

J. B. LIPPINCOTT COMPANY for "The Boy Who Liked Puppets, Hans Christian Andersen" and "The Boy Who Loved Birds, John James Audubon" from *Tell Me a Birthday Story* by Carolyn Sherwin Bailey, copyright, 1931, 1932, 1933, 1934, 1935, by J. B. Lippincott Company; "Kings' Daughter, Queen Elizabeth of Great Britian," with illustrations by Margaret Ayer, and "Seeing-Eye Girl, Helen Keller" from *A Candle for Your Cake* by Carolyn Sherwin Bailey, copyright, 1952, by Carolyn Sherwin Bailey Hill; and "Thomas Jefferson" from *Ten Brave Men* by Sonia Daugherty, copyright, 1951, by Sonia Daugherty.

LITTLE, BROWN & COMPANY for "Guglielmo Marconi" and "The Wright Brothers" from *Heroes of Civilization* by Joseph Cottler and Haym Jaffe, copyright, 1931, by Joseph Cottler and Haym Jaffe; and "Early Days with Invincible Louisa" from *Invincible Louisa* by Cornelia Meigs, copyright, 1933, by Cornelia Meigs.

LONGMANS, GREEN & CO., INC., for a few pages from *Son of Thunder, Patrick Henry* by Julia M. H. Carson.

NEW YORK WORLD-TELEGRAM and THE SUN for "Lindbergh Flies Alone," editorial which appeared in the New York *Sun*, May 21, 1927.

G. P. PUTNAM'S SONS for "New York to Paris" from *We* by Charles A. Lindbergh, copyright, 1927, by Charles A. Lindbergh.

RINEHART & COMPANY, INC., for "Daniel Webster" by Stephen Vincent Benét and "Theodore Roosevelt" by Julian Street from *There Were Giants in the Land*, copyright, 1942, by Rinehart & Company, Inc.

RALPH FLETCHER SEYMOUR for "Shakespeare" from *New Lyrics* by Agnes Lee.

MARGARET FORD ALLEN for "Lewis Carroll" and "When Mark Twain Was a Boy," first published in *Child Life Magazine*.

WALTER RANSOM BARROWS for "Robert Louis Stevenson" and "Leonardo da Vinci."

CONSTANCE BUEL BURNETT for "Marian Anderson: A Voice in a Hundred Years" reprinted by permission of *The American Girl*, a magazine for all girls, published by the Girl Scouts of the U.S.A.

JULIA M. H. CARSON for "Patrick Henry Enters Public Life."

MARCHETTE CHUTE for "A Life of William Shakespeare."

RAGNA ESKIL for "Jacques Cartier" and "Louis Joseph, Marquis de Montcalm."

MARJORIE GORDON for "Ludwig van Beethoven."

MABELLE E. MARTIN for "George Washington Carver," first published in *Highlights for Children*.

HELEN NICOLAY for "Abe Lincoln's Boyhood," first published in *Child Life Magazine*.

NICHOLAS NIRGIOTIS for "Marie Curie: Discoverer of a Hidden Treasure."

MABEL L. ROBINSON for "Louis Agassiz."

MATHILDA SCHIRMER for "Albert Schweitzer: The Doctor in the Jungle" and "Howard Pyle: Great American Illustrator."

ELSIE SINGMASTER for "Benny and the Cat's Tail."

JOHN GEE for illustrations for Mary Newlin Roberts' "Michelangelo and the Snow Man," "Titian's First Picture," and "Antonio Van Dyck and His Master Rubens."

ALEXANDER KEY for illustrations for Joseph Cottler and Haym Jaffe's "The Wright Brothers" and "Guglielmo Marconi."

KEITH WARD for illustrations for Elsie Singmaster's "Benny and the Cat's Tail."

DOROTHY WILDING and The British Information Services for Command Portrait by Dorothy Wilding of Her Majesty Queen Elizabeth II.

Great pains have been taken to obtain permission from the owners of reprint material. Any errors that may possibly have been made are unintentional and will gladly be corrected in future printings if notice is sent to the Spencer Press, Inc.

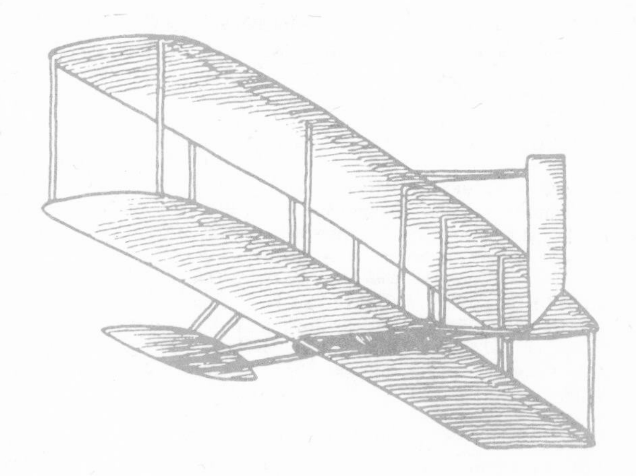

Contents

Part I: FOR YOUNGER READERS

MICHELANGELO showed a talent for drawing at an early age, and attracted the notice of Lorenzo de Medici, ruler of Florence, who helped him with his art studies. During his long career, Michelangelo lived in Florence, Venice, and Rome. Among his best works are the "Pieta," a statue of Mary with the dead Christ in her lap; the great statues of Moses and David; and the paintings of the Sistine Chapel in the Vatican. These decorations were painted on the ceiling of the chapel, and he had to paint many of them while he was lying on his back, with the paint splashing down on his face. Michelangelo was not only a sculptor and painter, but also a poet and architect. The great dome of St. Peter's Cathedral was his design, and the sonnets that he wrote are among the best in the Italian language.

Mary Newlin Roberts

MICHELANGELO AND THE SNOW MAN

ILLUSTRATED BY *John Gee*

YOUNG MICHELANGELO stood looking out on a new world. The snow had fallen all night upon the roofs of Florence, that most beautiful of all Italian cities—and in his short life he had never seen the low roofs and tall towers, the churches and palaces so mantled with white. He thought it made the whole city into a marble city, and although it was beautiful it made him sad. All the world seemed rather a cold place to the boy, because he had lost not long ago a wonderful, kind, and powerful friend, the great Duke and ruler, Lorenzo de Medici. In the garden of the Duke the young Michelangelo had learned to carve and chisel with other young boys; and because he had carved out of stone a remarkably fine mask of a faun's head, the great Duke had noticed him and befriended him and had him sit at his right hand on feast days in the palace. There had been purses of gold, too, and beautiful velvet doublets and, best of all, tons of marble for the gifted young sculptor to carve and hack at to his heart's content.

But now that was all over, and in the palace the son of the great Lorenzo, the young Pietro, ruled. Poor Michelangelo no longer sat at the long and magnificent table and no longer worked and was happy in the fine old gardens of the palace. Pietro was little more than a boy himself, but a proud, tall, handsome, reckless youth who cared more for his horses and his athletes and his feasts than anything else, and it amused him to cast away the boy his father had treated with such consideration. In the old days of old Florence there were many cruel things done with a laugh that nobody nowadays would laugh at at all. And so because it was old Florence young Michelangelo had to suffer in silence and be content to build more airy statues in his young brain than out of actual marble.

He stood at the narrow, long iron-grated window of his house and watched the white flakes drift down upon the beautiful tall tower that Giotto had built. He could see it rising above the roofs and he could see, too, the gateway to the Medici palace gardens and the snow deep and white on the familiar path and bushes.

"Ah," he sighed, "everything is changed now." And his deep-set eyes were far graver than they should have been at his age. A sound of merriment and laughter suddenly drifted up to him, for although this was over four hundred years ago the Italians were as vivacious and gay as they are now, and the novelty of the snow had roused the young and old, rich and poor alike, to laughter and pranks. Michelangelo was after all only a boy, and his eyes lit with a quick, fine spark of life as he leaned out between the bars to see what was going on.

Here a group of musicians had cast aside their instruments and were pelting each other with snowballs; and there, two servants in the blue and gold livery of some fine old family chased each other about, flinging white handfuls at one another till their splendid coats were like flour bags.

Today was a feast day—a fiesta—and Michelangelo, with a better view now of the city, could see the banners hanging from the Medici balustrades and towers. He knew that tonight the long table in the great hall would be lined with guests down its sides and that young Pietro would sit at the head in the great carved chair with some youthful favorite at his right—probably that swift young runner whom Michelangelo knew to be his great pride.

He was startled from his dreams by a rapping below and, leaning still farther from the window bars, his face turned first red then pale at what he saw. A page in the Medici livery was beating upon his own front door.

The messenger, glancing up, saw the boy and called in his full Italian voice.

"Aha, my young sculptor. His Magnificence, the great Medici, wishes you to come and build a statue for him at last!"

Michelangelo's hands tightened on the bars, and his heart beat such a gallop he could not answer.

"Dost thou not hear? Fear not—this is no jest. Speed thee now, and follow fast, lest the great lord grow weary of waiting."

"Art thou truly in earnest?" asked Michelangelo. "For I have never been sent for since the great Lorenzo lived in the palace."

"Aye, truly am I, lad, and there is much fine marble for thee to work with."

Something in the man's tone caused an uneasiness to the young artist. He hesitated a moment and then with a proud straightening of his thin young shoulders, he called out, "I come!" and flinging a cloak about him he descended with rapid steps into the narrow, snow-filled street.

His companion was inclined to chatter to him in a vein of mocking encouragement, as they hurried toward the great iron gateway of the palace, but Michelangelo set his lips in a firm, straight line and kept his eyes before him.

"Aha, proud boy," laughed the messenger as they turned into the snow-filled park, "this is a great day, is it not, for thee? To work in marble again for the great lord of Medici?"

They passed now in through a small side door and up a winding stairway, each curve and each stone of which was as familiar as his own name to the young artist. His heart had not ceased to gallop in his breast, and the hands that kept his cloak about him were clenched, but the fiery gleam of defiance in his eyes burned brighter than before. In an upper hallway they came soon upon Pietro surrounded by a group of boys and men, standing at a long window opening upon a stone balustrade that overhung the gardens. There was laughter and loud jesting amongst them, but when Pietro turned to the serious, waiting figure of Michelangelo there was a slight pause.

"Aha," cried Pietro, looking him up and down. "So once more we have sent for you to honor our house with your great talent, young Michelangelo. They tell me that thou art a master sculptor even at thy age."

Michelangelo's deep eyes blazed. After a slight bow he stood erect with chin in air.

"So thy great and good father was wont to believe, my lord," he answered with his direct gaze fixed upon the laughing face.

Pietro flushed and turned to one of his companions.

"Take this lad to the gardens below us here," he commanded.

"There thou wilt find tools, my young friend, and all the whitest marble in the world. I am giving a feast tonight, and thy statue will be finished for my guests to enjoy. Tomorrow our warm Italian sunshine will melt thy great work. Aha, why startest thou, my lad? The work will be as beautiful in snow!"

There was much laughter now. Michelangelo had turned very pale. He, who had been so honored, to build a man of snow!

He was very young and very proud, and he knew that he possessed a great and wonderful talent. For a few moments his anger rushed over him wave upon wave, making the mocking faces of the Duke and his followers grow dim. He fought with himself fiercely, for he knew that he would have to do the bidding of this son of his former great patron.

It occurred to him that he might fashion a portrait of Pietro in the snow to show that all power passes and fades away, and

there would come a time when even Pietro himself would be forgotten. This was a hard moment for a boy to face, but Michelangelo was no ordinary young person. Something noble and strong seemed to come to his aid, and suddenly his heart beat more steadily, and he found his voice.

"I will build thee a statue in snow, my lord," he answered in his strong, rough young voice. "Thou art the great Lorenzo's son, and mayhap thou, too, will honor my work before it melts away."

Pietro laughed, but not so merrily as he had before. He drew aside the great curtain from the window and pointed to the white garden below.

"There is space and plenty of material. There is thy studio, then, lad. Put thy great skill to work, and none shall disturb thee. I will tell my guests tonight the name of the snow-man builder."

Michelangelo was glad to feel at last the cool air on his burning forehead—glad to be alone again in the gardens that he knew and loved so well. He stood quite still a long time, thinking of the great, kind man who had often talked with him here, striving to set aside the pain of the interview he had passed through. Then he looked at the sky and drew a long, deep breath.

"My art will win," he murmured. "Even in snow it will win." And with swift hands he set to work.

All day he worked, putting into the growing white figure all the power and skill that he possessed. Slowly it grew under his fingers in all its strength and life, beautiful and true.

The snow limbs seemed ready to leap into action, and the snow lips ready to speak. It was the figure of a youth, noble and strong, and the gardens seemed infinitely more beautiful for the presence of this new lovely white figure in their midst.

From time to time the young Michelangelo would stand away and look up at what he had done, for even though his snow youth was seated on a pillar of snow he was far larger than the youthful sculptor himself, and to put the delicate finishing touches to the parted snow lips and modeled snow brows he had need of a stone jar turned upside down to raise him to his work.

At last the beautiful snow man was finished, and Michelangelo, forgetful of everything but his art, stood lost in a deep dream of delight.

It was done and it was good, and he had forgotten that tomorrow the cruel, warm sun would shine down upon his statue and melt it into nothing but a puddle of water.

A shout from above brought the truth all back to the poor, enraptured Michelangelo.

"I will come down to thee, lad, and see thy work if it be done," called Pietro from the balcony.

"It is done, my lord," answered Michelangelo, but his voice shook, for he remembered that he had worked in the snow.

He stood aside and waited and soon he heard them coming with laughter and jest into the snowy courtyard. Then they were there—gay in their scarlet and gold and velvet and satin against the pure white of out-of-doors.

"Ah-ha," cried Pietro, leading the way. "Where is this famous snow man, my little sculptor?"

Michelangelo remained silent and erect, with serious eyes fixed on the young Duke's face. There was a kind of prayer in the boy's heart that Pietro would be noble and worthy of his great father who had so often in these very gardens paid tribute to true art. He waited, very still and very eager.

Pietro stood and stared, and his companions formed a bright group of color behind him.

Michelangelo did not notice the others—he looked only at Pietro's face. The mocking smile slowly faded from the young noble's lips, and gradually a look of awe stole into his eyes and then a look of sorrow.

"Not in *snow,*" he suddenly cried. "Ah, tell me it be not made of snow. Alas, that anything so beautiful should ever fade!"

He turned to Michelangelo who stood with a hand pressed to his heart to ease its happy beating.

"Nay-nay. This is no longer a jest. Never in marble have I seen such beauty as thou hast wrought in snow. Come back to the palace, thou marvelous youth, and build true statues for me. Would to heaven I could keep the sun forever from its shining."

At the feast that night Michelangelo sat at the right hand of Pietro, and he knew that there were proud and wonderful days ahead for him.

Today if you go to lovely old Florence you can see the mask of the faun's head that the boy, Michelangelo, carved for the great Lorenzo, and you can see many powerful and glorious statues carved in marble by Michelangelo when he grew to be one of the greatest sculptors the world has ever known.

But the beautiful snow man no longer stands in the gardens, for the sun shone in Florence in spite of the proud Pietro.

Margaret Ford Allen

LEWIS CARROLL

ILLUSTRATED BY *Esther Friend*

TEN small brothers and sisters, with hands unclean, followed Charles around the house, hunting for the creamy white letter. Of course the letter, the first one Charles had ever received, was in his pocket. Mother had sent it to him, and Charles intended to keep it. He would hide it until he grew to be an old man, and then he would take it out to read again. But where could he hide it? Where in all the house was there a box or drawer or closet in which the brother of ten dirty children could bury his white treasure safely? No, he decided, he would not hide it; perhaps there was a craftier way to keep his brothers from destroying the letter. On one side of the envelope he printed, "No one is to touch this letter; for it belongs to Charles Lutwidge Dodgson"; on the other side, "Covered with slimy pitch so that they will wet their fingers."

Charles had lived on a farm, one mile and a half from the English village of Daresbury, since 1833, the year of his birth. It was an "island farm, 'mid seas of corn," so far from the bustle of life on the main road that a wagon driving by the gate would cause the Dodgson children to run to the hedge and watch curiously. So quiet were the first ten years of Charles' life that they might almost have been a dream. Life was a sort of Wonderland where people and animals were to be treated alike. Once Charles supplied three earthworms with small pieces of pipe in case they might like to fight each other. He made friends with a family of blinking toads. One of his particular pets was a mysterious snail. (Whenever Charles picked her up to talk to her, she hid.)

The boy's father was the rector of Daresbury. The bargemen,

who worked on the neighboring canals, were unable to attend church on Sunday mornings, so that Rev. Dodgson held a service for them on Sunday evenings. An old barge on the canal was made over into a floating chapel. In the Sunday evening dusk, drifting upon a path of water which gleamed mysteriously from the shadow, Charles would listen to his father preach. Between the pauses of the deep voice, Charles could hear the soft lapping of water under the floor. Thus life at Daresbury not only taught him to live in a sort of Wonderland, but it taught him a serious love of the church.

When Charles was eleven years old, the family moved to Croft on the River Tees. Here, his father's new church was a very old one. There was a raised pew, reached by winding stairs, which had belonged to the Milbanke family, and which was covered in, so that the children thought it looked like a four poster bed. The village school was a sort of barn, standing in one corner of the churchyard. The Dodgson's new home, the brick rectory, stood in the midst of a beautiful garden. Here elegant gentlemen, and ladies in hoop skirts, came to visit his parents and played croquet. Here too, Charles and his brothers and sisters built wheelbarrow trains with stations, where small passengers could stop for refreshments. It was in this garden that Charles, in a brown wig and white robe, became a conjuror, taking eggs out of an empty hat before a round-eyed audience. And here, once in the winter, when new snow on the ground gleamed as smooth as frosting, Charles tracked a maze on the lawn which none of his brothers could solve. But, best of all, here the village carpenter helped Charles make a set of wooden dolls, which moved upon strings, and a toy stage for these marionettes to act upon. Now, in the garden, Charles presented stirring plays. He wrote them all himself; the most exciting was "The Tragedy of King John."

When Charles was twelve years old, he was sent away to school at Richmond, and later to the famous English school of Rugby. Charles was a good student, in mathematics particularly, and seldom returned home from school without having won one or more prizes. At eighteen, he went to college at Christ

Church, Oxford, where, when he graduated, he remained to teach mathematics for twenty-five years.

The dean of Christ Church, Reverend Liddell, had three little daughters, Lorina, Edith, and Alice, whom Charles Dodgson often took rowing upon the river. One summer afternoon, when the sun was hot upon the water, the four landed in a meadow beside the stream and sat down in the shade of a hayrick.

"Tell us a story!" begged the three children.

"And I hope," said little Alice, "that there'll be nonsense in it."

And so Charles Dodgson began to make up a story about Alice and an elegant White Rabbit. Just when Alice had kicked Bill the Lizard out of the chimney so that the people below shouted, "There goes Bill!" Mr. Dodgson leaned back against the hay and pretended to go to sleep.

Later, Alice asked Mr. Dodgson to write the story down for her. One day, a visitor saw the book which he had made for Alice, and persuaded Mr. Dodgson to have his tale published. They called it *Alice in Wonderland.* At once it was so popular that is was soon translated into five languages. But Mr. Dodgson did not want people to know that a serious mathematician had written a nonsense book, so he named himself "Lewis Carroll." (Carroll means Charles.)

Mr. Dodgson played with children at the seashore, took little girls to the theater in London, and wrote child friends many funny letters. Here is one:

"My dear Agnes: About the cats, you know . . . I lent them the portfolio for a bed—they wouldn't have been comfortable in a real bed; they were too thin—but they were *quite* happy between sheets of blotting-paper—and each of them had a penwiper for a pillow. Well, then I went to bed; but first I lent them the three dinner bells, to ring if they wanted anything in the night.

"You know I have *three* dinner bells—the first (which is the largest) is rung when dinner is *nearly* ready; the second (which is rather larger) is rung when it is quite ready; and the third (which is as large as the other two put together) is rung all the time I am at dinner. Well, I told them they might ring if they happened to want anything—and, as they

rang *all* the bells *all* night, I suppose they did want something or other, only I was too sleepy to attend to them.

"In the morning I . . . shook hands with them all, and wished them all good-bye, and drove them up the chimney. They seemed very sorry to go, and they took the bells and the portfolio with them. I didn't find this out till after they had gone, and then I was sorry, too, and wished for them back again. What do I mean by them? Never mind.

"How are Arthur, and Amy, and Emily? Do they still teach the cats to be kind to mice? . . .

"Give them my love.

"Who do I mean by them? Never mind.

"Your affectionate friend,

"LEWIS CARROLL."

You see, half of Charles had grown up to be the solemn preacher and mathematician, but half of him remained the person who made trips to Wonderland and in his own mind turned the world upside down to make a funny picture.

Roger Duvoisin

COLUMBUS DISCOVERS AMERICA

ILLUSTRATED BY THE AUTHOR

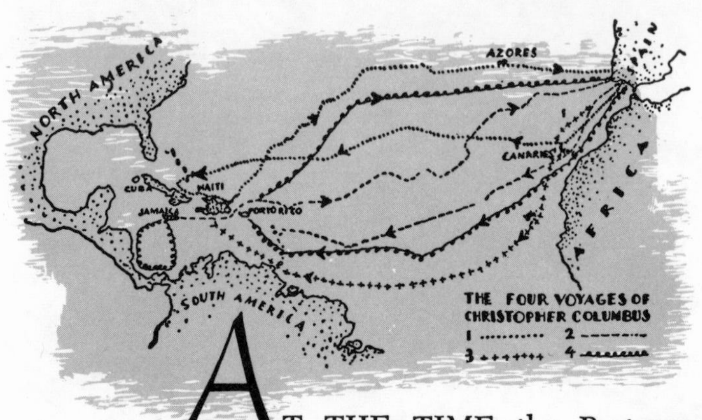

AT THE TIME the Portuguese seamen were still looking for the southernmost end of Africa there came into Lisbon a young Italian named Christopher Columbus.

Columbus was much interested in everything which had to do with the sea and ships, and faraway islands and kings. In Lisbon, where everyone talked of all these things, Christopher Columbus helped his brother Bartholomeo to paint maps and sell books. He loved to watch the mariners unload from their sailing ships the monkeys, the bright parrots, the elephant tusks, and the other wonderful things which they had gathered in the new land of Africa. When, sometimes, he sailed on a Portuguese caravel, he liked to hear the sailors tell stories about the adventures they had met with in trying to sail to Asia, around Africa.

After a time, Columbus himself began to dream that he was sailing to Asia too, that great Land which he was trying to paint on his brother's maps. He read Marco Polo's book and other books which tried to show where China and India lay, and he pored over Ptolemy's very small map of the world.

Now, very strangely, the two biggest mistakes Ptolemy had made on his map gave Columbus an idea. As we have already said, Ptolemy had drawn the world smaller than it really is.

He had made Asia much too big toward the east, so that there was little room left on his world between the east coast of Asia and the west coast of Europe. There was only room for a small ocean.

"Ptolemy was a learned man," Columbus said. "His map must be right. Then, since the world is round, if one sails straight toward the setting sun from the west shore of Europe, one will reach Asia in a short time. And it is silly for the Portuguese seamen to try to get to India by going south round Africa and then east. It would be very much simpler to sail west from Lisbon."

"If it is true," said his brother Bartholomeo, "good caravels could, in a few days' sailing, come to Japan, for Marco Polo says that Japan lies to the east of China."

"And I will be the admiral commanding these caravels," exclaimed Columbus. "I am going to tell the King of Portugal about all this; surely he will give me the ships."

The king, John of Portugal, was amazed at Columbus' idea.

"Hum! I never thought of that," he said. "How can you be sure that Japan lies so near, across that mysterious Atlantic Ocean which we can see from any window of my palaces?"

"I have studied Ptolemy's map," answered Columbus. "I have also sailed to Iceland, the foggy isle of the north, where I heard sailors tell about a land not far to the west. I have sailed to Madeira where I was told of pieces of carved wood and strange hollow canes which the west wind had blown onto the beach. These could not have come from very far away."

"Yes, I know about the canes," the king said thoughtfully. "I have seen them."

"The sea has also brought dead pine trees of a kind we have never seen in our countries," continued Columbus. "There is land not far across the Atlantic, I know. Truly if you give me some ships I'll find the countries Polo told about—Japan, where the king's palace has roofs of gold; China, from whence comes our silk, and where there are so many rich and busy cities; India and the islands of the East from which come spices and precious stones.

"Of course, it is only fair that I have my reward for doing

all this. I want to be made a knight with golden spurs; and great admiral of all the oceans; and governor of all the countries I will find. I also want the tenth part of all the riches I bring back to Lisbon."

"All that!" exclaimed the king. "Well, maybe your idea is good; maybe it is not. I am not sure. I shall call the most learned scholars of Portugal to hear what they have to say."

The old scholars came, listened, looked scornful, and finally said: "No, no! This young man, Columbus, is just a dreamer. Only God knows how large the Atlantic Ocean is, and what lies beyond. Only a fool would try to sail across it, and he would not return. Our sailors are now busy trying to sail to India and China round Africa; it is a good way. It would be unwise to try to find another one."

Columbus went home broken-hearted.

"There are other kings who will like your idea," his brother Bartholomeo told him. "Go and see the King of Spain, Ferdinand, and his Queen Isabella. They are not trying to sail round Africa and they will like to get to China before the King of Portugal does."

So Columbus took his dream into Spain and was heard by the queen and the king.

"I think there may be something in your idea," said the king.

"So do I," said the queen. "But we are very busy now chasing the Moors out of Spain, and we have no time to study all that ourselves. Let's get together some learned scholars of Spain, so they can hear what you have to say."

The Spanish scholars met but could not make up their minds at once. So they went home to think it over, and Columbus waited.

From time to time, the scholars met again but still they could not say yes and they could not say no; and again Columbus waited and waited. He talked of his dreams. He became desolate and penniless.

"Look at this man in tattered clothes," people began to whisper, "offering our king islands and continents and mountains of gold. He must be out of his mind."

Finally the scholars decided. They said no. But they added: "Wait until the Moors are out of Spain, then come back. Perhaps we will have changed our minds by then."

"No more waiting," said Columbus. "I am going to see the King of France."

And he departed for France.

But then, some of his friends went to Queen Isabella and they talked so well about Columbus that she called him back.

"Perhaps you are right, after all," she said to him. "Perhaps you can bring us the spices and silks and precious stones of the East."

"I know I can."

"Then if I give you the ships, what will you ask in return for yourself?"

Columbus repeated what he had asked the King of Portugal.

"That's too much," exclaimed the queen, her eyes big with surprise. "Much too much."

"I would not do it for less," declared Columbus.

"Then we won't give the ships."

Columbus was quite angry now. He said good-bye to his friends and again took the road to France.

However, the treasurer of the king and queen, who was a wise man, said to Isabella:

"I think you should give Columbus what he wants. What can you lose? It does not cost much to give him the golden spurs and make him a knight. If he comes back from China with his ships full of treasures, wouldn't you rather give him one tenth and keep all the rest than have the King of France have it?"

"I would," said Queen Isabella. "Go after Columbus and catch him before he gets into France."

This second time, when Columbus came back to King Ferdinand and Queen Isabella, he was granted the ships and the rewards he asked for. And it was all written down on parchment and signed by the king and queen.

It was in the port of Palos in southern Spain that Columbus made his caravels ready. There were three of them: a large one, the *Santa Maria,* and two smaller ones, the *Pinta* and the *Niña.* On a misty summer dawn, in August 1492, the three caravels spread their sails with the painted cross, and sailed away.

"Now," thought Columbus, standing on the high stern of the *Santa Maria,* "every minute that the wind blows, I am nearer Japan, China, and India. Soon I will be the great admiral of all the seas."

Columbus' sailors knew the Atlantic Ocean from Spain to the Canary Islands, which belonged to King Ferdinand. They were sure they would not meet horrible sea monsters until they arrived there. But beyond, it would be another story. And so even though their delay made Columbus unhappy, they were glad to remain many days in the safe islands, to repair the rudder of the *Pinta* which had broken on the way.

As soon as the rudder had been repaired, it was with a sad heart that they put out to sea again and sailed west. It was the very first time that ships had ventured straight onto an unknown sea with no land on either side.

"How can our captain be so sure that this ocean has an end?" wondered a young Spaniard. "For my part, I fear that we shall never return. Look, the wind blows steadily toward the West. We won't be able to get back with this wind always at our bow."

"In my time," said an old sailor, "I have heard many stories of ships swallowed by sea serpents; of ships falling off the

earth at the end of the sea. I believe they are true stories."

"They *are* true," said many sailors together. "And so are many others, just as bad."

While they frightened one another in this way with strange sea tales, the three caravels sailed on and on. The sailors thought of Spain, behind them. Columbus thought of Asia ahead of him. Sometimes birds flew in the blue summer sky, and that made the sailors happier, for they imagined that land could not be far away. But they were sadder than ever when more days passed and the man in the crow's-nest never cried, "Land!"

One day they saw that the sea was green with seaweed. Another day, a black whale swam by, puffing white vapor about. Then they were cheerful again. "Seaweed and whales," they said, "do not go far from land."

One morning, they climbed the masts and riggings with joy after Captain Pinzon, master of the *Pinta,* had cried "Land! Land!" But the next morning was like all the mornings before, nothing in sight but the blue waves which never tired of running after one another.

"If we go on, we are lost," growled the men. "Our place is in Spain with our wives and children, not on this awful sea with a captain who lives in a silly dream, full of Japans and Chinas."

"We shall not go on another day," they all said menacingly.

"Let's throw him overboard," an angry sailor cried. "Then we can turn 'round."

Columbus came out of his small cabin on the high aft castle, and looking at them without fear, said:

"There is no use complaining. I have come to seek Japan, China, and India, and with the help of God, I will find them. Do not be afraid. You will go back to your families, with your hands full of gold."

Seeing that Columbus was so resolute, the seamen went back to their posts though they still grumbled. They kept their eyes on the blue horizon, hoping for a sight of land.

As the days went by, there were many signs that land was not far off. Once, all night long, great flights of birds flew over the ships. One afternoon, a reed and a carved stick floated by. At the end of that same day, as Columbus stood on the aft castle, watching the night ahead of him and listening to the waves as they broke on the sides of the *Santa Maria,* he suddenly saw a little light. "Look!" he cried to his sailors, "before us, at the bow. Do you see that light?"

"I see it," said one man.

"I don't!" said another.

"Perhaps it is another mistake, then," sighed Columbus.

But it was not, for soon after that, a sailor on the *Pinta* shouted: "Land! Land! It's land, for sure."

Among cries of joy, Columbus ordered his ships to lie at anchor. Few sailors slept that night; most of them stood on the decks, their eyes peering into the dark, like people in a theatre waiting for the curtain to rise.

"What shall we see in the morning?" wondered Columbus. "The gold roofs of Japanese palaces, no doubt, for this land lies just where I thought Japan was—to the east of China. It must be Japan!"

At dawn, as darkness began to lift, a small island slowly took shape; a cool white beach: tall green palm trees, still wet with dew. All was quiet. Then a bird, hidden among the leaves whistled, and others answered it. Some naked brown men came down to the water's edge, talking and yelling among themselves in a strange language, pointing to the big sailing vessels which the night had brought. Some of them had painted their bodies red; others had blue faces; a few had dipped their noses into yellow paint.

America lay before Columbus' eyes. It was October the twelfth, fourteen hundred and ninety-two.

"I don't understand!" murmured Columbus. "There are no gold roofs. In his book Marco Polo does not say that the Japanese and the Chinese go naked and painted. He does say that they wear rich robes of silk; and he also says that the seas around Japan are full of islands. That must be one of them."

Columbus now put on his most beautiful clothes and his coat of green velvet and landed on the shore, holding in his left hand the banner of the King of Spain. Behind him came the captains of the *Niña* and the *Pinta*, carrying the flag with the green cross.

"From now on," Columbus declared, "this island will belong to King Ferdinand, and it will be called 'San Salvador' on the map." His scribes wrote that down, and Columbus and his officers scratched their names below it.

The painted brown men stood around them and wondered what it was all about. They would have been sad had they known that the greedy white men would soon chase them out of their fairy-like islands.

They smiled, showing all their teeth, when the sailors gave them some glass beads, tinkling bells, and red bonnets. As they, too, wanted to be generous, they brought presents of cotton balls, green parrots, fruits, and arrows.

Although grateful, Columbus planned to deceive these kind, confident islanders. He ordered his men to take seven of them by force and put them on board his ships. He wanted to show them to the king, on his return to Spain.

"There is nothing much in this small island," he said. "It is time to leave it, for I am impatient to go and look for Japan and China. All aboard!"

There were many islands in these seas, all very green and beautiful. They were full of new kinds of flowers and fruits, with birds of all colors flying among the palm trees. But nowhere did the gold roofs of the palaces of the King of Japan glitter above the trees. There were but the straw huts of the naked men. Nowhere did Columbus find the rich cities, busy with hundreds of laden ships, which Marco had seen in China.

When he came to the island of Cuba, it looked so big to him from the sea, that he was sure it was China, the country over which the great Khan ruled.

"I see only green forests and yellow huts, but that's all right," he thought. "The great Khan lives somewhere in the middle of that country. I haven't time to look for him now. I'll come back later to give him King Ferdinand's letter."

The Spanish seamen saw no gold in Cuba but they noticed that the brown men rolled large dried leaves, and made smoke with them in their mouths. It was tobacco. The sailors could not know that men would become richer by growing tobacco in America than by looking for gold.

After Cuba, Columbus came to the great island of Haiti. As it lay east of Cuba he thought it was Japan. It was like a rich garden in which grew all sorts of trees, vegetables, and flowers the Spaniards had never seen. It, too, was peopled by the kind and peaceful Indians who went about naked, with gold rings in their noses.

Since Columbus thought he had come to Japan and China, these brown men might have been called Chinese or Japanese. But they were called Indians for Columbus was also looking for India. And Indians they are still called.

"Where are those rich palaces, those people clothed in silk and precious stones?" asked Columbus. "Where are they? It is time to sail back to Spain and I have not found them. I shall have to come back and look some more."

Before they were ready to sail, while the helmsman of the *Santa Maria* went ashore one evening, instead of remaining at his post, the currents carried the ship onto the rocks where it was wrecked. As there was not enough room on the two smaller ships for all the sailors to return to Spain, forty-four of them had to remain in Haiti, where they built a fort with the beams and boards of the *Santa Maria.*

When the *Pinta* and the *Niña* made their way back across the Atlantic Ocean, they did not carry embroidered robes of silk and satin like the ones Marco Polo brought back to Venice. In their place were Indians, a few noisy green parrots, balls of cotton, fruits, arrows, and some bits of gold jewelry.

After landing in Palos, Columbus went to see King Ferdinand and Queen Isabella in the city of Barcelona. He entered it to the sound of trumpets and drums, amidst flying banners.

The king and the queen were pleased with his discoveries, for Columbus told them that he had found Japan and China, although he had not seen the richest part of these countries. Then he showed the Indians, parrots and other things which he had brought back. Everyone gazed in wonder, for no men, birds, and fruits like these had ever been seen in Europe before.

Columbus' fame spread all over Europe. He was now a knight, Don Cristóbal Columbus, great admiral of all the oceans, with golden spurs, as was written on the parchment. As proof that he was a great gentleman of Spain, the king gave him a fine escutcheon with a castle, a lion and five anchors painted on it.

So now, on the west side of the Atlantic were lands which Spain claimed as her own, and on the east side were the newly found parts of Africa, which belonged to Portugal.

"That is all very well," said the Pope in Rome. "Spain claims lands in the West; Portugal in the East. But I very much fear that these two countries are going to put their flags on the same island and fight a war over it. That would not be so good. I must do something about it."

Just like a mother who cuts an apple in two and gives one half to each of her two children, he took the map and drew a line down through the Atlantic Ocean to the South Pole and up on the Asia side. And he said: "One half of the world, that which has in it the countries found by Columbus will belong to Spain. The other half, where Africa and India lie, will belong to Portugal." And that was that.

But Columbus was not interested in that. Amidst all his glory, he thought, and worried, and thought again about one thing:

"Where can the great Khan be? Where can the gold roofed palaces of Japan be? Where?"

He was impatient to be again on the deck of a good caravel, sailing westward across the Atlantic. The king, who was also anxious to find the treasures of Asia, gave him seventeen ships. They were filled with soldiers, craftsmen, and farmers; with horses, cows, and sheep; for cities were to be built, and farms started on the green islands.

Upon arriving on the other side of the Atlantic, Columbus discovered two more islands which he had not seen during his first trip—Guadeloupe, and Puerto Rico.

"There are as many islands in these seas as there are flowers in a June meadow," thought Columbus. "But I don't care for them; I want the riches of Japan and China and India."

In Haiti, Columbus found that the forty-four sailors he had left there had all been killed, and their fort burned. No doubt they had done something which had angered the Indians.

It was in this island that the masons and the carpenters of Columbus built their first town: the very first white man's town built in America. Columbus named it Isabella for the Queen of Spain whom he liked very much.

Again Columbus sailed on, searching and searching for the things Marco Polo had told about, but all he discovered was the big island of Jamaica.

He went back to Spain with nothing more to tell about than more islands and still more islands, all with green palm trees, naked Indians and yellow huts on them.

A third time Columbus crossed the ocean, to the West. He found more islands, and he also found the continent of South America, and the great Orinoco River. He thought that this big continent was just another island, so he named it *Santa Isle.*

The fourth time he went, he saw the shores of Central America.

But nowhere did he see the big ships, the rich cities, and the silk-clothed Chinese, the jewel-covered kings of India, or the gold-roofed palaces of Japan!

When he returned to Spain, after this last trip, he was broken in health and very unhappy. But he was sure that somewhere among his islands lay the countries of Asia, although by that time travelers already suspected that his islands had nothing to do with Marco Polo's land of the East, but were entirely new lands.

Columbus died soon after his fourth voyage without knowing that he had added to the map one of the biggest and richest continents of the world.

Helen Nicolay

ABRAHAM LINCOLN'S BOYHOOD

ILLUSTRATED BY *James Ponter*

IN KENTUCKY, about fifty miles directly south of Louisville, stands a little log cabin that was never beautiful, or even comfortable to live in. Its windows are so small that most of the light which enters has to come through the door, and the chimney built on the outside at one end is not of brick or of stone, but only of sticks laid up "log cabin fashion" and liberally plastered with clay to make it less likely to catch on fire.

Yet people make pilgrimages to this little house from all parts of the world and think it more precious than many a marble palace. Not only that, people flock to a copy of it that has been carefully built on an estate in Milton, Massachusetts, coming literally in thousands on the two days of the year when the lady who owns this place opens her gates and invites the public to enter. One of these days is the fourth of July; the other is the twelfth of February, the birthday of Abraham Lincoln.

On February 12, 1809, Abraham Lincoln was born in the little cabin in Kentucky. At that time even the children of the very rich did not have many things which we now consider necessities, and the parents of this child were far from rich. The farm on which they lived was as poor as the house itself. His father found it impossible to raise good crops on such land, and when the child was four years old the family moved to another farm nearer Louisville. Perhaps Abraham never saw his birthplace again; but he had a retentive mind, and all through life he must have carried a pleasant if not very distinct memory of the fine spring of clear water surrounded by trees, beside which he had played from the time he had learned to walk. Because of this spring, the one really attractive feature of the place, it was known in the neighborhood as the Rock Spring Farm.

Water and mud delight any small child as playthings. These were almost the only playthings Abraham had; so with the birds and bugs and small furry creatures who found the spring as useful as human beings did, the spring must have afforded him his principal amusement during those earliest years. He had a sister, Sarah, two years older than himself, but we hear of no near neighbors or other playmates.

It is hard to realize how many things people did without in those days. Radios and airplanes and movies would not even be dreamed about for almost a century to come. Automobiles and telephones and telegraphs had not been invented; nor were there any railroads. There was no known way for a human being to travel faster than horses could carry him; and in a newly settled country like Kentucky, roads were so few and so bad that a man with useful long legs could take short cuts and reach his journey's end just as quickly as a horse could carry him over the uneven ground.

There were no cookstoves or ranges. The boy's mother cooked their simple meals in pots that stood in the hot ashes or hung from an iron crane over the blaze in the clay-lined chimney. If the fire went out it was almost a calamity, for a spark had to be kindled and the blaze coaxed into being by means of a flint and steel. Matches, even the sulphur matches that blazed and spluttered and gave forth such an evil smell, had not yet come into use; and of course, there was neither gas nor electricity. After nightfall the only light in the cabin's room came from that same fire on the hearth.

Often there were no books in frontier cabins; in others the whole library consisted of a Bible and an almanac. It is unlikely that Lincoln saw a picture-book made especially to please and amuse little children, or indeed a picture of any kind printed in colors, until after he was grown. In those days the books written for children were rather dismal affairs, not at all likely to encourage a love of reading. He did not have even these.

Doubtless the Lincolns owned a Bible, for all his life Lincoln showed a familiarity with its words and phrases that was unusual even in a day when it was read more often than it is now. Very likely Nancy Lincoln taught her little boy his letters from the big book. We know that she was better educated than her husband, who had been a wandering laboring boy, and that after they were married she taught him how to sign his name. With that achievement Thomas Lincoln appears to have rested content, so far as he was concerned; but he had distinct ambitions for his son—nothing less than that the boy should be able to "cipher clean through the 'rithmetic."

Abraham took kindly to study. We can imagine him spelling out the exciting Bible stories of Joseph and his jealous brothers, and of the strong man Samson, as soon as he was able to find his way among the TH's and S's and Z's that strew the pathway of young readers with pitfalls. Samson must have interested him particularly, for even when very young he was tall and strong for his age and proud of his strength.

In Kentucky at that time it was easier to find a hoe or an axe than a schoolbook to put into the hands of such a boy; and when Abraham was only seven the matter of educating him became harder still. Thomas Lincoln was overcome once more by the pioneer's urge to move westward; and giving up his home in Kentucky, took his wife and children to live in the deep woods of southern Indiana, in what is now Spencer County. Here, on Pigeon Creek, at a point about sixteen miles from the Ohio River, they and the half dozen families that made up the new settlement endured great hardship. For almost a year the Lincolns did not even have the protection of a cabin, their only shelter being what was called a half-faced camp, a shack of three walls and a roof, entirely open to the weather on the fourth side, where a fire, built on the ground, was supposed to make up for all that was lacking. Almost everything was lacking. The nearest doctor lived thirty miles away.

"It was a wild region, with many bears and other wild animals in the woods," Mr. Lincoln once wrote, describing this region. "There were some schools, so-called, but no qualification was ever required of a teacher beyond readin', writin' and cipherin'

to the rule of three. If a straggler supposed to understand Latin happened to sojourn in the neighborhood, he was looked upon as a wizard. There was absolutely nothing to excite ambition for an education."

Thomas Lincoln still hoped to see his son make his way triumphantly through the arithmetic; but the need to cut down trees and fence fields and raise crops was pressing, and strength such as young Abraham had in his long arms was not to be despised. He tells us that from the time he reached Pigeon Creek until after his twenty-second birthday "he was almost constantly handling that most useful instrument," an axe.

Before leaving Kentucky, Abraham had attended two schools, for the Lincolns did the best they could by their children in this regard. To reach one of them, held in a cabin very like that in which he had been born, the boy of seven had to walk four or five miles. The scholars had no textbook except *Webster's Elementary Spelling Book*, and no paper or ink or slates; and it is probable that neither of these teachers had had as much education as falls to the lot of an average twelve-year-old boy today.

In Indiana, Lincoln's opportunities to attend school were scarcely better. The last one came when he was sixteen; and again he had to walk four or five miles to reach the log schoolhouse. All these terms of instruction were very short. The names of five different men have been preserved in history for the sole reason that at one time or another they numbered this boy among their pupils; but of his schooldays Lincoln once wrote: "Abraham now thinks that the aggregate of all his schooling did not amount to one year. He was never in a college or an academy as a student, and never inside a college or academy building till after he had a law practice. What he has in the way of education he has picked up. After he was twenty-three and separated from his father he studied English grammar—imperfectly, of course, but so as to speak and write as well as he now does. He studied and nearly mastered the six books of Euclid since he was a Member of Congress. He regrets his want of education, and does what he can to supply the want."

People marvel that a man who had so few opportunities as Lincoln became so well educated; especially that he became so skilled in the use of words, for besides being a great president Abraham Lincoln was also a great writer, little as he himself may have realized the fact.

He was fortunate in the stepmother who came to rule over the home after Nancy Lincoln had died of privations and a pestilence that swept over the Pigeon Creek settlement. The new mother was Sarah Bush Johnston, a kindly widow who had known Thomas Lincoln from the time they were both young. She brought with her, in addition to a four-horse wagonload of furniture and comforts the like of which Abraham and his sister had never known, three children of her own who were amiable and companionable if not remarkably gifted. The best of all, she brought understanding and sympathy that gladdened the lives of her stepchildren.

It did not take her long to recognize Abraham's unusual qualities, and she saw to it that after his day's work in the fields or forest, he had time for study. The other young people complained good-humoredly that she was partial in assigning the household chores; but they were really as proud of Abraham's love of reading as she was, and helped rather than hindered her efforts to leave him undisturbed. A cousin who lived with them has told how, when they came in from the day's work, "he would go to the cupboard, snatch a piece of corn bread, take a book, cock his legs up as high as his head, and read." Another member of the household remembered that "when he came across a passage that struck him he would write it down on boards if he had no paper and keep it until he did get paper. Then he would rewrite it, look at it, repeat it. He had a copybook, a kind of scrapbook in which he put down all things and thus preserved them."

A few stray leaves from this precious book are the only objects owned by Lincoln in his boyhood that have come down to us. The care with which he copied tables of land measure and long measure and examples in multiplication leads to the belief that he did not even own the arithmetic from which he studied. Paper was far too scarce to waste in doing sums merely for practice or in copying anything he already had in print. Light from the open fire was still the only illumination at night; and in place of iron fire shovels, which were a rare luxury, the pioneers used broad, thin pieces of board narrowed at one end to form a handle. It was on such a shovel that young Lincoln worked his sums in the firelight, using a bit of charcoal until both sides were covered with figures, when he would take a drawing-knife and shave it clean again.

Yet for all his fondness for study, we must not think of him as a bookworm. He liked people and practical jokes and took a leading part in all the frontier merrymakings—such as corn-huskings, and wrestling matches and "raisings," when the pioneers gathered and made a frolic out of helping a newly arrived settler put up his cabin. There was only one frontier sport in which young Lincoln took no interest. That was hunting. The time other boys spent lying in wait for game he preferred to give to reading.

"He read every book he could lay his hands on," his stepmother said. The books that chance cast in his way were few, but short as the list is, it could scarcely have been bettered if it had been chosen solely with reference to his future needs. First of all there was the Bible with its stately English. Then there was that book beloved by all boys, "Robinson Crusoe." Out of his own experience of living in the deep woods young Lincoln might have given Man Friday himself good advice. Another book was Aesop's "Fables," from which he learned an art that was invaluable to him in his political life—that of telling in a few vivid words, and almost humorously, a story which carried

a serious moral. He read "Pilgrim's Progress," and Weem's "Life of Washington" and a "History of the United States"; and last but by no means least, there was a volume of the "Revised Statutes of Indiana," not the kind of book the ordinary boy would find interesting. But he was not an ordinary boy, and printed in this book were the Declaration of Independence, and the Constitution of the United States, and the Ordinance of 1787, documents of immense importance to him in his after career.

He accepted help in his studies gladly, whenever and wherever he could find it. In New Salem, the town to which he went at the age of twenty-three to make his own way in the world, he did not go to school, but it was the schoolmaster Mentor Graham who encouraged him to study English grammar and also helped him to a practical knowledge of surveying. In the same town was Jack Kelso, whose reputation was not of the best, and who drank far more than was good for him. But he loved Shakespeare and the poetry of Robert Burns, and taught young Lincoln to love them too.

But Lincoln's real unfailing teacher was his own honest, direct mind, which went straight to the heart of a matter and disliked anything that fogged or clouded it. His interest in the value and right use of words, and his self-training in this regard, began almost in babyhood. He did not often talk about his childhood after he became a man, but one day he said to a friend, "I remember how, when a mere child, I used to get irritated when anybody talked to me in a way I could not understand. I don't think I ever got angry at anything else in my life; but that always disturbed my temper, and has, ever since." He would lie awake at night puzzling over the sayings of men who came to talk with his father, and after he thought he had caught their meaning would repeat it again and again in simple words until he was sure he had put it in language plain enough for any boy to understand.

In this bit out of the far-off past, when the great President was only a child living in a log hut on the edge of the wilderness, we have the secret of his self-education.

Carolyn Sherwin Bailey

KINGS' DAUGHTER

ILLUSTRATED BY *Margaret Ayer*

THE STORY of a fairy-tale princess always begins with her christening; the Royal cradle, the lace christening robe, the good fairy and the wicked one who casts a spell over the baby. So, except for the bad fairy, does the story of Princess Elizabeth of Great Britain begin.

She was born in London, that city of history and story. She was christened at the ancient Lily Font brought for the ceremony from Windsor Castle to the private Chapel in Buckingham Palace. Kings and queens, princes, and princesses surrounded the golden-haired, blue-eyed baby. The good fairy was her mother, the gracious and beautiful Duchess of York. But Elizabeth had something on her name day which fairy tales omit. She had a tall christening cake of many layers frosted in designs of flowers and leaves. On the top of that cake there was a small silver cradle and in the cradle lay a tiny silver doll. Until she was grown, Princess Elizabeth kept that cradle and doll in her cabinet of toys in Windsor Castle.

The stories of fairy-tale princesses always leave out the most interesting details of growing up, usually beginning when the prince arrives. Princess Elizabeth is no exception in having a prince, but the years before he came were filled with work and play, dogs and horses, everyday and Royal doings. There is a story of Elizabeth's visit to a penny shop in Scotland near Glamis

Castle where her Grandmother Strathmore lived—that castle of fountains and the ghost of Macbeth; of hundreds of stone rooms in one of which there was a fearsome stuffed bear; of gardens and beehives; of good times for a child and plenty of ghosts as well. It is told that at that time Elizabeth had a shilling a week as her allowance. The shop was probably like the one in *Through the Looking Glass*, with striped candy sticks in glass jars, small toys, cakes, and wool for knitting. The shopkeeper welcomed them, "What would the little lady like?" she asked Elizabeth. Dignified, and at that time feeling important, Elizabeth said, "I am not a little lady. I am a Princess."

The grandmother put a light hand on the little girl's shoulder, apologizing. "Ah, no, she is not at the moment a lady," she said. "But she will grow up to be one."

And so she did. Elizabeth was only five years old when this story was told. Almost at once her education as a Royal child began, and it meant being deprived of many delightful doings that you enjoy. In the first place, when she was nine years old, Elizabeth's father and mother became King George VI and Queen Elizabeth of England. That meant that Princess Elizabeth had to give up all hope of going to a regular school; of having the fun of meeting school children and playing with them in a friendly give-and-take way. Her parents were sorry for this. In every way, they tried to make up to Elizabeth for the loneliness of Royalty. But the family was obliged to live the greater part of the year at Windsor Castle.

Windsor is a true castle out of the fairy books, with ramparts, battlements and turrets, hundreds of rooms, and a gold dinner service of so many pieces that more than a hundred dinner guests may have several plates apiece. It still seemed to the King and Queen a sad place for a lively little girl to grow up in. Elizabeth had become a vivid, kind, little girl, who wore Stuart tartan skirts and sweaters, called jumpers in England, for everyday; for best only, flowered silk frocks and white socks, and always very sensible shoes. She had her own sitting room at Windsor, a sunny room with white furniture with a raised-gold design, upholstered in pale pink brocade. Cream-colored cushions and draperies with a pattern of flowers, cream-colored walls and pictures of country scenes made the sitting room a cheerful place. The schoolroom where Elizabeth and her sister Margaret, four years younger, studied, was a happy room also. Light walls, a fawn-colored carpet, a big oak table, white apple-wood chairs and pink chintz made it unlike the usual schoolrooms. And all of one wall space was taken up with a model toy farm that Elizabeth had arranged with small animals and buildings that she had bought at Woolworth's in London. But there were only those two girls to study there in the Royal schoolroom.

Windsor Castle stands in centuries-old, acres-wide Windsor Great Park. Forest land, soaring birches, squat and moss-hung oaks, bracken glades and a sea of leaves, make it possible for one to lose oneself there. One can hardly count the years, the number of kings and queens of Britain, whose footsteps could be followed along the paths. At a distance from Windsor Castle there stands a home known as Royal Lodge. It was a shooting box for George IV, and has a large drawing room, bed and living rooms less austere and formal than those of the Castle. Queen Elizabeth had Royal Lodge painted pink, because as a child she had once lived in and loved a pink house. She furnished it with simple, comfortable things. There she and the Princesses kept house, and with the King gardened, trimmed trees, and lived the plain life they loved.

One might see the Royal family there, in country clothes, the King with his sharp clippers, the Queen trimming the lower branches, Elizabeth gathering up brush in her small cart, taking care of the forest where the trees truly seemed to them like relatives. Trailing the Princess would be her dogs. There have been so many Royal English dogs since Princess Elizabeth was old enough to love them that their names would fill a canine *Who's Who*. Chee-Chu, a Tibetan lion dog, and his son Ching; Golden Labradors and their puppies; the beloved Welsh Corgie named Dookie; and Jane, a Labrador, with her twins, Crackers and Carol.

At Royal Lodge, Elizabeth's flower garden bloomed with daffodils, tulips and forget-me-nots in the spring; poppies, stock, sweet william and pansies in the summer. Flowers were her favorites, but the King insisted that she raise vegetables, a necessary kind of gardening when the war came on. Elizabeth became a potato expert. She carried big, fancy spuds about in her apron pockets to show what could be done in raising better kinds.

The schooling of a princess is somewhat different from yours. Elizabeth, when she was eleven, had to study ancient and modern history, the theory of government, foreign languages, geography because of Britain's far-flung Empire, and grammar. She helped her father in keeping the intricate accounts of the Royal housekeeping. She learned music, fine sewing, and knitting. The latter proved very useful, for during World War II the Royal family had to retire often to a bomb shelter, and Elizabeth knitted innumerable pairs of socks and jumpers for soldiers. But her schooling was fun, too. She learned to draw from small colored models of animals and houses, dolls and trees, filling in the backgrounds with paints. On rainy afternoons, covered with a large apron, she painted what she liked and made paper dolls. She dressed up and gave pantomimes, always planning the best part for her sister, and inviting the children of the Castle's Ladies and Gentlemen, the children of the village and her Royal cousins. *Cinderella, Aladdin* and *The Sleeping Beauty* were her favorites. Usually these pantomimes were given at Christmas, and were great treats for everybody.

English children live almost until their teens in a nursery, not exactly as we know the word, but a place where they may have their own belongings separate from those of grown-ups, their own meals, and their own young life. This was true of Elizabeth, except that she had a suite of rooms, including bedroom, her sitting room, the schoolroom and the old day nursery. She never cared as much for dolls as for horses. All her toy horses, from big hobby-horses of wood to small models, lived in the day nursery until there was no more room; then they stood in a long row in the hall outside. Every day she fed them and brushed them. As soon as she could sit up on a saddle, Elizabeth had horses to ride, trotting for miles among the trees of Windsor

Forest. She said once, "If I ever become Queen of England, the first thing I shall do is to make a law forbidding people to ride or drive on Sundays. Horses must have a holiday." And Elizabeth had an odd and historic French pony cart that she drove. It had been built years before in Paris for Queen Alexandra, and was drawn at Windsor by a horse famed for his gentleness and his love of sugar, Old Hans.

In the day nursery, until she grew up, Elizabeth kept her Palace of Playthings. This was a large cabinet with glass doors within which was a great collection of gifts sent by all the countries of the British Empire to the Princesses: miniature tea sets, tiny soldiers and ships, china cottages and castles, small cottage furniture for dolls, beasts, birds and fish in blown-glass, that silver cradle and doll from the christening cake, and costume dolls in historic and modern dress. But in almost every room where the Princess worked and played, set out prominently, were a floor brush and dustpan. These were to be used daily by Elizabeth; they were so used.

Not alone because she was a Princess of England, but because of their love for her simple and family-loving father and mother, British subjects have always wanted to do their utmost for Elizabeth. The greatest delight of a girl's life came to Elizabeth in the gift of the Little House, from the people of Wales, a complete, small thatched cottage, the right size for a girl but a trifle low for grown-ups. It was placed in the grounds of Royal Lodge, surrounded by well-tended gardens; its thatch was renewed when damaged by jays and mice, by the Welsh thatchers, the most skilled in that craft in the world.

The Little House is a model of an English cottage. It has white-curtained diamond-paned windows, an oak dresser with buttercup-yellow china, and in the drawer a complete set of initialed linen. A complete set of Beatrix Potter's books; a kitchen with every possible pot and pan, and a stove that bakes; canned goods, brooms, dry groceries, and everything for housekeeping are included. In addition there are a radio and a complete set of monogrammed flat silver. A small portrait of Elizabeth's mother painted in miniature and showing her when she was the young and lovely Duchess of York, hangs over the mantelpiece in the drawing room. Here in her Little House, Elizabeth learned the art of being a good housewife. Silver had to be polished, housecleaning done in the spring, everything must be in order and spotless; all good fun when it is your own house.

So Princess Elizabeth grew from a little girl to a gracious and lovable teen-ager. Her mother taught her that the first attributes of Royalty, as they are for us all, are kindness, friendliness, and understanding. From her father she was to learn that "The King's daughter should be all glorious within." She had few friends until she was allowed to organize a Girl Guides Troop that met in the grounds of Buckingham Palace, one of the Royal homes. That was fun, to meet other girls, make war dressings, and cook sausages outdoors. She had an old friend at Windsor in the clock-winder whose duty it was to wind daily the hundreds of clocks that sat, stood and hung in those many rooms. He had known other princesses and queens of England and told her stories. He helped her to feel what it meant to be the daughter of Royalty, with Royalty's cares and duties. She listened to her radio, sat beside a grate fire in her sitting room and sewed or knitted. She read her favorite books: *The Odyssey*, *Alice in Wonderland*, *The Rose and the Ring*, *Goblin Market*, *Little Women*, *The Wind in the Willows*, *Doctor Dolittle*. She tried to bring up her little sister to be a princess, as she knew what it meant in work and responsibility.

Because Elizabeth had so few intimate friends, a visit away meant ever so much in the way of excitement. There is a Royal Naval College at Dartmouth, England, and King George was called there for an inspection on board a training ship. Elizabeth went too, and was invited to visit a boy and a girl who lived at the Captain's house there, with the Dalrymple-Hamilton family. The boy was Prince Philip of Greece, soon to be a cadet in training, fair like the blue-eyed Elizabeth, and as handsome as the Vikings whose stories he loved to read and act. Philip was still in the stage of schoolroom living, a few years older than Elizabeth. The Prince's sitting-room floor was covered with a mechanical railway, all kinds of trains, switches, everything

DOROTHY WILDING

Queen Elizabeth II

complete and steaming away at his touch. Philip was a polite boy and allowed Elizabeth to run his railway. They had ginger cookies and lemonade and then Philip suggested that they go out to the tennis court and jump over the net. This was so he could show off. They next went to the swimming pool. And that evening Elizabeth was allowed to stay up later for games and dancing. It all seemed to her enchanting, and Prince Philip the nicest boy she had ever met. She remembered and dreamed about that visit for a long time.

War meant more responsibility, work and tragedy for England than we can know. When she was sixteen Princess Elizabeth felt that she should enroll in the Auxiliary Territorial Services, an organization of women war workers that would take her away from home, and into public service as no other Royal Princess in the history of England had entered. There was a good deal of family objection, but Elizabeth insisted that times had changed, that it was her duty to join other girls in real and useful war work. So she was put in the care of a commandant, measured for a khaki uniform and given the job of taking apart and putting together again a very greasy and complicated automobile engine. She worked at a bench, under cars, and handled engines until she knew their every part and was finally detailed to drive a motor lorry in the maze and hazards of London wartime traffic. The King and Queen were deeply anxious; so were the English people, for Elizabeth did not spare herself.

She slept at Windsor, but her days were spent inspecting, learning all about car maintenance, doing air-raid watching, getting as smudged and oil-stained as any mechanic. She drove a big Red Cross van, transported her commandant to his depot outside of London. It was a time of constant bombings but Elizabeth was unafraid and happy. She was seeing London as she had never before hoped to. Policemen waved to her, traffic slowed to let her through. She was one with the people of England in service and defense.

On Thursday, November 20th, 1947, all England thrilled with expectation. War was ended and London was bravely rebuilding. The Welsh people had sent Princess Elizabeth a lump of

gold, their most precious gift, for gold is scarce in Wales. Scotland had woven by hand some beautiful white fabric for London designers to embroider with jewels. Elizabeth was to have a new gown. Never had she seen so enchanting a dress, ivory satin embroidered with pearls, crystals and garlands of York roses and silver ears of corn. There was a long lace veil with starflowers, vines and orange blossoms, also shimmering with jewels.

Buckingham Palace overflowed with Elizabeth's presents. The King and Queen gave her a necklace of diamonds and rubies and two strings of pearls. Her sister gave her a picnic basket equipped with plastic dishes for four, quite as welcome as jewels to this outdoor-loving girl. President Truman sent a vase made of our Steuben glass. There was a silver-gilt dressing-table set of twenty-seven pieces. There were homemade tea cozies and kettle holders, a fur coat from Canada, hand-knit jumpers from girl friends, a vacuum cleaner, a sewing machine and a frigidaire. All these gifts, lavish or humble, and hundreds more, the Princess loved, and she wrote letters of thanks for all. The day and night before the 20th of November, 1947, from the countryside, the counties and all of London, the British people gathered. They brought small stoves, food, and camp chairs. They camped along the route from Buckingham Palace to Westminster Abbey, London's church of the centuries. It rained that night but the great day brought the sun. Cheers filled London as a procession left the gates of Buckingham Palace and wound slowly along Whitehall, Parliament Square, on, on in a pageant that Elizabeth's people had anticipated all her life.

Lorries and jeeps were put away and the ancient Royal coaches of painted wood, with glass windows and drawn by white horses, were brought out. In her jeweled dress and veil, Princess Elizabeth waved and smiled from the first coach. Flags floated all the way. The House cavalry on black mounts were the outriders. Foot guards in gold and crimson marched in precise formation. When the procession reached the Abbey the bells of London rang and trumpets sounded. There were more than two thousand waiting in the Abbey—royal relatives, lords and ladies, kings and queens from other lands. The Abbey glowed with color—dress uniforms, flowers, the gala dresses of queens and princesses, the Tudor colors of the Yeomen of the Guard, the red vestments of choir boys. Elizabeth and her father, King George VI, walked up the long aisle, the King in the uniform of the Royal Navy. Eight bridesmaids and two small page-boy cousins followed.

At the high altar, where the Bishop of Canterbury waited, Philip of Greece, newly created Duke of Edinburgh, met Elizabeth. He put a wedding ring, made from the lump of Welsh gold, on her finger. Thus a princess, loved for her simplicity and kindness, was married to the prince she loved. In the course of time they became the parents of Prince Charles and Princess Anne.

In the fall of 1951, Elizabeth and Philip traveled to Canada and the United States, making friends everywhere. While in South Africa, in 1952, the British Commonwealth of Nations church bells and Big Ben of London tolled. After more than a hundred years, again in English castles and cottages the formula was spoken: "The King is dead. Long live the Queen."

Thus, on February seventh of the year nineteen-hundred-and-fifty-two, the girl who had been taught queenship, but had not anticipated it so soon, was proclaimed Queen Elizabeth II, Head of the Royal Family, Ruler of Britain and the Commonwealth, Keeper of the Faith.

Elizabeth II occupies the greatest and most enduring of thrones. Nine centuries old, that throne has seen wars and peace, the Golden Age of Elizabeth and England's present ruins and austerity. But her country is undaunted and looks toward the restoration of another golden era in the reign of this twenty-five-year-old Queen. The British crown is heavy. It glitters with diamonds, rubies, emeralds; gold *fleur-de-lis* and crosses, also jeweled, add to the weight. The Crown of England had to be refitted to the girl's head. It is the first time in over a century that a woman has worn it. It is a rigorous future, but Elizabeth said:

". . . I shall always work, as my father did throughout his realm, to uphold constitutional government and to advance the happiness and prosperity of my peoples, spread as they are the world over. . . . I pray that God will help me to discharge worthily this heavy task that has been laid upon me so early in my life."

HANNIBAL, MISSOURI, where Samuel Clemens was born was a little frontier town of less than five hundred people located on the Mississippi River. Being a market town, it attracted all sorts of people—steamboat men, travelers, circus performers, and showboat actors. Hannibal and the people that young Clemens met there were destined to figure in many of his books, especially in *Tom Sawyer* and *Huckleberry Finn.*

His restless spirit led him to become one of the most skillful pilots on the Mississippi River and to work for newspapers in St. Louis, Cincinnati, Philadelphia, and New York. After prospecting for gold in the West and traveling to the Hawaiian Islands and to Europe, he settled in Connecticut and devoted all his time to writing and traveling. As storyteller and humorous writer, Clemens has no rival in America. His humor is characteristically American, for it is clean, good-natured, and shrewd.

Besides his boys' classics, *Tom Sawyer* and *Huckleberry Finn,* he wrote *The Prince and the Pauper, A Connecticut Yankee at King Arthur's Court, The Celebrated Jumping Frog of Calaveras County, Roughing It, Innocents Abroad* and *Life on the Mississippi.*

Margaret Ford Allen

WHEN MARK TWAIN WAS A BOY

ILLUSTRATED BY *Walter R. Sabel*

THIS IS the story of the real Tom Sawyer, a boy who wanted to be a pirate. Instead, he grew up to be a famous writer honored by statesmen and kings. He was born in a little cabin in Missouri (which was then a slave state). He never went to school after he was eleven years old, and he never saw a railroad until he was almost grown. If you had met him then, roaming the woods barefooted with Huckleberry Finn, "the Red Handed" (whose true name was Tom Blankenship), and if you had told him, then, that one day he would become a famous writer and put himself and his chum into a book, which boys ever after would read, he would have stared at you. Huckleberry Finn would have stared at you. They would have said that you were telling a "stretcher."

The real Tom Sawyer came to live in the little white town of Hannibal, Missouri, when he was four years old. He came in a wagon, surrounded by furniture and all the worldly goods of the Clemens family. For the boy's true name was not Tom Sawyer but Samuel Clemens. A wild, mischievous boy he was—small for his age, with a large head and thick hair which he had to brush continuously if he kept it from curling. Sam was more of a trial, his mother often said, than all of the other children put together. If you have read *Tom Sawyer* and remember Aunt Polly, you will know just what Sam's mother was like; for Aunt Polly in that book was Mrs. Clemens—a woman stern and at the same time so tender-hearted that she used to punish the cat for catching mice. Sam had a large family. There was his oldest brother, Orion, a boy of fourteen; his sister Pamela (the Mary of *Tom Sawyer*), a gentle girl of twelve; Benjamin, seven; then Sam; and last of all, Henry, the baby. There was also a slave girl, Jennie, whose duty it was to pull small Sam out of the river whenever he ran away. The father of this large family was a poor and struggling lawyer, who had wandered from town to town with his family looking for better fortune but had never quite succeeded in making both ends meet. It was in search of a better future that he had quit the little cabin in Florida, Missouri, where Sam was born, and taken his family by wagon to Hannibal.

Afterward Sam always remembered Hannibal as a "white town drowsing in the sunshine of a summer morning . . . the magnificent Mississippi, rolling its mile-wide tide along . . . the dense forest away on the other side." As a playground it could not have been improved. For there was not only the river front, where one might watch the puffing steamboats stopping to let off freight and passengers and loaded rafts floating by on their way to New Orleans, but also two miles or so below the town there was a wonderful cave, full of winding passages, which a boy might explore all day and still not have reached the end.

And north of the town, a daring swim's distance, there was an island, three miles long and uninhabited, where boys could hunt turtle eggs to their hearts' content and build a fire and talk.

Of all the boys in Hannibal, as Sam grew older, he especially admired a ragamuffin, dressed in fluttering patches, named Tom Blankenship. (This, of course, was Huckleberry Finn.) He was the only boy in the town who didn't have to go to school, or even church. He could sleep anywhere he chose—in an empty hogshead, if it suited him—and he didn't have to obey a single soul. All the mothers in town hated Tom Blankenship, and all the boys in town wanted to be like him. As for Sam, he adopted Tom on sight.

Many an evening, as Sam grew into boyhood, he would leave his bed in answer to a faint "meow" from below. Out of the window he would climb to the roof of the shed beneath, and so down a trellis to join Tom Blankenship. Usually John Briggs was waiting there, too, in the dark—a boy whom you will remember as Joe Harper in the story of *Tom Sawyer*. Then the three companions would set off in search of some adventure.

One night Tom Blankenship had a dream. He dreamed that a chest of gold was buried near Hannibal. When Sam and John Briggs heard about it, they were excited and bargained for a share in the treasure in return for helping Tom dig. Armed with a pick and shovel, the boys set out through the woods. When they reached the spot, Tom Blankenship sat down under the shade of a pawpaw bush and gave directions, while Sam and John dug mightily. Of course, Tom wasn't expected to do any digging; he had had the dream and that was his share.

The real treasure hunt did not turn out as well as the one in the book, where Huck and Tom Sawyer finally located the box of gold in the haunted house. For by late afternoon the real treasure-hunters had about given up hope. Though they had laid bare many holes, they had not unearthed anything but an endless succession of rocks. It was a hot day and Sam was almost exhausted. At last he threw down his shovel and vowed that his days of treasure hunting were over forever.

But that night Tom Blankenship had another dream. It ap-

peared that the boys had not been digging in quite the right place. The treasure was directly beneath the pawpaw bush where Tom had been sitting. This sounded so reasonable that the boys dug again. But they never did find the treasure. Tom Blankenship said he guessed it was because the boys hadn't dug just right.

Another episode that happened in Hannibal was used in the story *Huckleberry Finn.* In that tale, Huck found Jim, a runaway slave, on an island and helped him to escape. But in real life it was not Huck (Tom Blankenship) but his brother Ben who had this adventure.

Ben was older than the boys and teased them so that they were afraid of him. The townspeople thought him just another of the disreputable Blankenship family. Yet Ben was to prove that he was capable of great generosity.

One day Ben, who used to live by hunting and fishing, rowed across the river to the Illinois side. There, in the swamps, when Ben was looking for birds, he found a runaway slave hiding there. The man was almost starved; he had had nothing to eat but fish he had managed to catch. Ben knew that there was a reward of fifty dollars for this slave—a lot of money for a boy who had nothing. He knew the town would approve of him if he should turn the man in. But instead of that Ben helped the man hide in the swamps all summer; he shared food with him out of his own poor larder. Some weeks went by; then people began to grow suspicious. Some woodcutters set off to hunt for the runaway. Trying to escape these hunters, the Negro fled to a wild part of the marsh and was drowned. It was this incident that Sam Clemens later used as the basis of *Huckleberry Finn.*

The adventure of Sam and his gang would have filled many books. You remember, in the tale of *Tom Sawyer,* how that hero saved Becky Thatcher from a whipping in school by taking the blame for something he did not do? Tom's sweetheart, Becky Thatcher, was a real little girl—Laura Hawkins, by name—a neighbor and playmate of Sam's in Hannibal. Whether or not he saved her from a whipping is not recorded; but it is remembered in Hannibal that once in the Friday spelling bee in school Sam did leave the "r" out of "February" purposely so that he would lose and she could win the medal. Sam hated school and was a poor pupil in almost all subjects, but he *could* spell. There was scarcely a week that Sam didn't wear the medal for the best speller in school. And Sam could always be counted on to be kindhearted and brave.

Mr. Cross's school in Hannibal, which Sam attended, stood on the Square in the center of town. There were two long benches on opposite sides of the schoolroom—one for the girls and the other on which all the boys sat. Up in front at a pine desk sat Mr. Cross, the teacher, who kept order—with the aid of a hickory stick.

It was here that the future author, biting his slate pencil, composed his first poem. When he had finished, he shoved his slate over to John Briggs—Joe Harper, "the Terror of the Seas." John Briggs snickered as he read:

"Cross by name and Cross by nature,
Cross jumped over an Irish potato."

"Write it on the blackboard this noon, Sam," he begged. And when Sam refused, "Why *I* wouldn't be ascairt to do it!" said John.

"I dare you to!" hissed Sam.

"The Terror of the Seas" prided himself on never refusing a dare. When the pupils and teacher returned to school from their noontime meal, there in large round letters on the blackboard was the rhyme.

A titter went up from all the pupils, and suddenly Mr. Cross's eyes were peering straight into John Brigg's. He had recognized the handwriting. The teacher arose, stick in hand, and John Briggs paid with aching shoulders for Sam's first attempt at literature.

During the summer time Sam and John and Tom Blankenship played pirate in the cave down the river. It was a favorite pastime for excursionists and Sunday school picnickers to explore that part of the cave near the known door. But Sam possessed a secret entrance of his own, which led to an unused section of this maze-like cavern. As it is described in *Huckleberry Finn*, the would-be pirates climbed up to a thick clump of bushes which covered a hole in the hill. After all the boys had sworn to secrecy, they were allowed to crawl on their hands and knees into the hole. After two hundred yards the cave opened up. Sam lighted candle stubs, and led the way, ducking among passages, to a narrow opening in the wall. There was "a kind of room, all damp and sweaty and cold." This is where Sam's gang held their meetings and took the pirate's oath.

The real cave where Sam Clemens and Tom Blankenship played pirate in every detail is like the cave described in *Tom Sawyer*, where Tom and Becky got lost. There is the chamber that Tom and Becky called the "drawing-room." There is the room where the bats hung which put out Becky's candle. If you visit this cavern today near Hannibal, you can see the chamber with the cross formed on the ceiling, where Tom saw Indian Joe's hand holding the candle.

The Indian Joe in *Tom Sawyer* really lived in Hannibal. He was a bad character and the boys were afraid of him, but he was not so bad as the Indian Joe in the book. In real life Indian Joe was lost once in the cave, but he did not die there as is told in the book. However, he was very weak when they found him.

The boy Sam Clemens had another side to him than these

madcap experiences would indicate. He did not spend all his time seeking adventures with his gang. Often he would wander off by himself along the river. He would lie dreaming for hours on some hilltop overlooking the Mississippi—his river—and watch the steamboats pass. And then he would change his mind about being a pirate or an Indian or a trapper-scout. When he grew up, he would be a steamboat pilot instead, high up above the deck in a glorious glass cage—a lordly creature, whom everyone in the world, even the captain, had to obey.

Sam did become a river pilot when he grew up, and a very good pilot, too. For several years he led a happy, hard-working life, taking steamboats up and down the Mississippi River. That is how he came to choose the pen name by which the world knew him so well in later years. As a young man, when he began to write, nobody paid any attention to his real name, Samuel Clemens; so he adopted a name taken from a river term—"Mark Twain." The term means two fathoms of water—a welcome sound to any pilot. For if the depth of the river is two fathoms, the steamboat can make a safe passage and the pilot knows that all is well. It is as Mark Twain that he was known in later years, when he became one of America's best beloved authors.

One almost wishes that in those early, care-free days of his boyhood, Sam could have looked ahead and seen the wonderful career fate had in store for him. The good people of Hannibal used to shake their heads and predict that Sam and his gang would come to no good end when they reached manhood. But their prophesies were false. For Sam was an industrious boy and when he grew up he became in rapid succession a printer, river pilot, gold miner, newspaper writer, lecturer, famous humorist, and author. Sam—Mark Twain—was probably the most famous American of his day.

"And what became of his friends, John Briggs and Tom Blankenship?" you wonder. "The Terror of the Seas" grew up to be a prosperous and widely respected farmer, while "The Red Handed" went west and became a justice of the peace.

Carolyn Sherwin Bailey

THE BOY WHO LOVED BIRDS

ILLUSTRATED BY *Frances Eckart*

JOHN AUDUBON had a stepmother, not the cross stepmother one reads about in fairy tales, but one who loved him so much that she came close to spoiling him. The family lived in the small town of Nantes in the Loire Valley of France. John and his father had been travelers nearly all of John's ten years. Santo Domingo, with its jungles, clipper ships, spices and coffee plantations; New Orleans with its beautiful gardens, soft-voiced Creole children, and tinkling guitars; sailing ships that crossed the Atlantic Ocean with cargoes of tea, indigo and silks; France in the period of 1790—all these had been experienced by the boy, because his father was a trader and later an officer in the American Navy. But when we see John first, he is in the breakfast room of the house in Nantes and with him is Mignonne, his pet parrot.

Mignonne was a wiser parrot than most. Perched on the back of John's chair she plumed her gold and green feathers and talked in French. She always had her breakfast with the boy and that morning, she ordered in her sharp voice, warm milk, a roll, and some sugar. John's good stepmother hurried in with the breakfast tray, but before she could set it down a flying ball of fur dropped from the top of a chest of drawers in the corner of the room. Before the boy could do anything, John's pet monkey, who had also been waiting for breakfast, had caught poor Mignonne about the neck and choked her to death.

This is a sad way to begin a story, but Mignonne's death started a deep love of birds in John's heart. When his jealous little monkey killed Mignonne in a fit of temper because the parrot could ask for breakfast and the monkey could not, John made up his mind that no other bird should die if he could help it.

At this time Mr. Audubon, John's father, was away at sea. Before sailing he had entered John in a day school in Nantes, where he would be taught the lessons that were thought best for a boy in those days: drawing, arithmetic, geography, music and fencing. John loved his drawing lessons and soon showed that he could paint and sketch better than any of his classmates. But he liked to escape from his hard school bench into the forest and follow the banks of the River Loire, looking for birds. John's stepmother understood his restlessness and she felt that he needed the schooling of outdoors. When he wanted to spend a day in the woods watching the ways of birds and rabbits, his mother packed a large basket of lunch for him. Long days when he should have been in school were spent outdoors. Soon John's room looked like a museum. The walls were covered with paintings of birds, and the shelves with birds' nests. All the drawers held birds' eggs, pressed flowers and pebbles, each one carefully labeled. John was teaching himself to be a naturalist, but this helped him very little in his schoolwork. And after awhile his father came home from his sea trip.

On his first evening at home, Mr. Audubon called John and

his sister into the drawing room to test them in their school work. The little girl played a piece on the piano without the music notes. She read some French stories, repeated the arithmetic tables and danced all the figures of a minuet. But, alas, John failed very badly in everything that he should have been learning at school. His father did not scold him, but the next morning John's trunk was packed and his father took him in a carriage to the depot where horses for Paris were waiting. John James Audubon was sent to a boarding school, far away from the forests of Nantes.

The change, though, was for the better. The lessons John had at his new school helped him in his study of outdoors. Geography taught him how climate controls the growth of plants and flowers, how it affects the habits of birds and animals. Painting was added to drawing. John Audubon made two hundred drawings and paintings of birds and animals before he was sixteen years old, and his school marks were so high that his father gave the boy a trip to America as a reward. That was Mr. Audubon's native land, although John had been born in Santo Domingo.

Mr. Audubon had a business friend in the United States, Miles Fisher, the Quaker. Mr. Fisher owned the Mill-Grove

Farm, not far from the city of Philadelphia, a place of wide fields, avenues of trees, thick orchards, an old mill and a delightful cave in which the peewees built their nests and sang. There Mr. Audubon left John. Mill-Grove Farm was almost as pleasant a place as Nantes, but its only drawback in John Audubon's eyes was the stern rule of Mr. Fisher. After what he considered a sufficient vacation, he sent John to school, had him work on the farm every day after school, and allowed him to spend only his spare time studying nature.

John thought of running away, but one day he met Lucy Bakewell, who lived on the next farm. Lucy was an outdoor girl and loved birds and flowers almost as dearly as John did. Together they skated in the winter and had picnics in the summer. John watched and listened to one bird every day, learning its song, nesting ways, and coloring. Lucy helped him with the schoolwork that he disliked, and John taught Lucy how to paint and draw. When John's schooling was over he decided to go to our West where the plains were covered with different kinds of flowers, and there were strange birds and animals to study. Lucy Bakewell promised to take care of John's collection of birds' nests, eggs and drawings, and wait for his return.

That was the beginning of John James Audubon's adventurous life. He traveled through the entire United States, walking, riding horseback, following the rivers in a flatboat. After awhile he came back to Mill-Grove Farm and married Lucy. They went West and opened a general store in Louisville, Kentucky, where the blue-grass country was kind to the cardinal bird, and many other brightly colored birds nested. But John Audubon found standing behind a store counter as tiresome as school had been. He made his way to the Mississippi Valley to study water birds. After that he found work in the new museum of Cincinnati, stuffing and arranging the museum's collection of birds. Soon he traveled on again, always following bird and animal life and making such paintings of them as the world had never known.

Several times John Audubon's paintings were destroyed. He had trouble finding a publisher who was willing to spend the money that would be needed to print his large collection of colored pictures of birds and the descriptions he had written about them. But he knew that he would be successful sometime and his wife, the Lucy of his boyhood good times, helped him write, waited patiently for him to return from his nature-study trips and had the same love of their little feathered brothers that he had.

He went back to France and studied for a time with David, the famous painter. Back in the United States again, he took up his loved work of naturalist and woodsman. There was hardly a forest of all our United States that did not feel the footsteps of this great naturalist. He wrote once in his diary:

"I never for a day gave up listening to the songs of birds or watching their ways or drawing them in the best way I could. During my deepest troubles I would often take myself away from the people around me and return to some hidden part of the forest to listen to the wood thrush's melodies."

On the banks of the Hudson River in New York State there are some acres of land set apart and known as Audubon Park. It was there that Mr. Audubon had his last home. He lived in a roomy house with a wide porch on which all kinds of birds were at home. The grounds were alive with small, wild creatures. Squirrels, rabbits and chipmunks joined Mr. Audubon at his outdoor meals. A little river crossed by a rustic bridge ran through the grounds. A robin built her nest above the doorway.

In many states the birthday of John James Audubon is celebrated as Bird Day, and Arbor Day comes close to this date. But Mr. Audubon liked children to keep every day, winter and summer, autumn and spring, as a chance for watching and loving one bird, one small wild creature or one flower. He was our great discoverer of birds. He taught us their beauty, their usefulness in helping the farmer, and their music. He was the greatest bird painter we have ever known. His pictures fill the many volumes of "Birds of North America" and the "American Ornithological Review." Because of his story which began with Mignonne, the parrot, boys and girls all over our land, and in foreign countries as well, have banded together, to keep wild birds safe and happy.

TITIAN, whose real name was Tiziano Vecelli, left his mountain home when just a little boy of ten and went to study painting in Venice under the famous master Bellini. For a time he was official painter for the city of Venice and decorated several public buildings there. Later he became a portrait painter, and not only painted the portraits of popes, princes, and celebrated men, but was their friend. The Emperor Charles V was so pleased with the portrait Titian painted of him that he made Titian a knight and gave him a pension for life. In his later life, Titian painted chiefly religious mythological works. He is considered the greatest color artist of all time.

Mary Newlin Roberts

TITIAN'S FIRST PICTURE

ILLUSTRATED BY *John Gee*

THERE WERE two things little Titian Vecelli wanted very much. The first, and the one he wanted the most, was to put down somewhere, somehow, with his own hand, the beautiful forms and colors that were always in his mind. There was a soft, dim, old fresco in the little village chapel, and it was a favorite dream of Titian's to imagine other frescoes on other bare walls, and when he looked out from the hilltop in northern Italy where he lived and saw the trees and rocks and the small figures of people far below, and the changing lights and shadows, it seemed that his heart would burst if he could not somehow put all this into some bright, beautiful painting.

The other thing he wanted, and which seemed somehow part

of the first, was to see Venice—Venice so beautiful, down by the sea, with its domes and towers and streets of water, with its richly-decked nobles and ladies and its gliding gondolas and carved palaces. He would stand on the wild, rough hillside, and shading his eyes with his brown fingers, he would look toward the sea until he fancied he could almost see the gilded domes and hear the deep bells of Venice.

Sometimes, if you wish hard enough for worth-while things—wish with all your heart and soul—it helps to bring them about. Little Titian, no matter how busy he was, or how lively about all the everyday things, never ceased to long and hope that the time might come when he should paint a picture and see Venice.

One hot day in spring on his way from school, he clambered up the rocky slope of the hill where he lived and gathered great bunches of wild flowers. This was long, long ago, but wild flowers bloomed in Italy then, just as they do now. There were the tall Flowers-of-the-Angels (Fiori-di-Angeli) and the lovely little blue harebells; there were flowers like our foxgloves, and purple lilies, and a myriad of tiny, bright flowers that Italians have a myriad of bright little names for, and I dare say Titian Vecelli knew them all. Some of these small flowers grew close to the ground and were flat and many-colored like a soft, bright carpet; others were tall and swaying, and Titian bent and rose, plucking and gathering, holding them tightly in his small, hot hands. A cicada sang in a tree near-by, which meant summer was coming. A cicada is a kind of grasshopper and locust and cricket and katydid rolled into one, with a dry, hot song that begins soft and gets louder and louder and then dies away, and Titian liked to hear it while he gathered the flowers in the hot sun.

He climbed higher and higher and when he reached the shade of the walls of his home, he threw himself down with a grateful sigh and said, "Phew!" just like any hot boy on a hot day anywhere in the world nowadays. He put the flowers down carefully in the shade and then he noticed his hands and sat up and stared. His brown fingers and palms were stained with every kind of color—purple and yellow and green and red and blue.

Now it would be interesting to any boy to see that the stems of some Italian wild flowers and blossoming weeds hold juices that stain when they are squeezed hard by strong fingers on a hot day, but to little Titian Vecelli it meant far more, for the sight of the colors sent him dreaming at once. The tints on his hands reminded him of the fresco in the chapel, and he rose slowly to his feet and glanced about with eager, wistful eyes. Nobody was at home, and it was very quiet on the hilltop, and the bit of cottage wall near-by seemed waiting for something.

"Now I must paint a picture for myself," he thought. "The flowers have come to help me," and he stood very still for a few moments, very grave and thoughtful for so young a boy.

Then Titian Vecelli set to work, all by himself in the shadow of the cottage wall, squeezing and staining any way that he could with his fingers and a little stick, painting his first picture so many years ago.

The cicada sang, unheeded, and the beautiful flowers drooped, and the family came home and, because they did not see him busy in the shade of the wall, they wondered where he was.

Very slowly on the dull, bare wall, a picture came to life. Figures seemed to spring out by magic under the small deft fingers of the boy. His cheeks grew hot and his eyes brilliant with the joy of accomplishment. Inside there was bread and cheese and chicken and probably macaroni, but although Titian was a boy, and a very real boy, he forgot to be hungry and forgot everything but the delight of a dream come true.

He was so very busy that he did not see his father come up behind him and stand with hands upraised in amazement, nor did he see another figure climbing up the hill. This was no other than Signor Rostelli, the teacher of the school where Titian went each day, and neither did the busy young artist know that Signor Rostelli had come to talk seriously to Signor Vecelli about nobody else but Titian himself.

At the top of the steep hill the teacher came to a sudden standstill, folded his arms with a wide sweeping up of his black

cloak and stared at the picture growing on the wall, at the boy at work, and at the father watching.

"Aha!" he murmured, "this pleaseth me. This is well. This will help to show his father more clearly all that I have come to say." And he nodded his head and stroked his beard with an air of relief and satisfaction. Then he stood as quietly as Signor Vecelli and watched in silent amazement the picture on the wall growing bit by bit. That held as much beauty and soft color as the wild, bright flowers the boy had gathered on the hillside earlier in the afternoon.

At last when the sun had set, and the cicada was taking a twilight nap, little Titian found that he could squeeze no more stains from the juicy, aromatic stems, and so with a sigh he backed away to look with rapture at the transformed wall.

"Had I the true colors of a painter, 'twould have more depth," he breathed. "But even so I am happy." And backing farther still he collided into his father and Signor Rostelli who had drawn nearer and nearer. It was like a rude awakening from some glorious dream to Titian, to find his father and the teacher standing there, and to hear their voices bursting forth at once in exclamations and questionings, and much talk about himself that he did not want to hear. By degrees the teacher quieted Signor Vecelli and began to talk alone, holding Titian kindly by the arm and pointing from time to time to the work on the wall.

"It is true," he went on, "that he is not at all a student, that he must always be drawing and that this distracts his fellow students. I came to tell you how it is, but you have seen here for yourself, far better than I could tell it, that he is capable of doing great things. Here with nothing but a rude wall and the pale juices of flowers and weeds, he can do what no other boy can do."

"Aye," interrupted Signor Vecelli with a puzzled frown. "That is all true indeed, and all very well, but to be idle at school is not good, and artist or no artist it displeaseth me."

"But his strength lies here," cried the teacher. "It is well and wise to encourage a talent. Idleness will be left behind when the true powers are allowed to grow."

Titian stood listening to them as they discussed him, but because they were so much older and because he was looking at his picture which his heart and mind were still absorbed in, he did not heed the deep voices very much.

"I have painted a picture, and now nothing matters at all," he thought, and it seemed to him that the whole world had changed. Then suddenly he did listen. Signor Rostelli was speaking of Venice.

"It is really your duty, dear Signor Vecelli, to send him to

Venice to study painting. There are many artists and studios there and the lad will soon prove to you and to his masters of painting all that he is capable of."

Little Titian became all life and eagerness.

"Father!" he cried, springing closer to him and clasping him by the arm. "Father, I pray and beseech thee, let me go to Venice. I know not why but, there in Venice, I know that I will work and study. I will become a true artist. Only let me go to Venice!"

"Thou art a strange lad," answered his father gently. So standing there in the gathering dusk on that rough hilltop, it was arranged that he should go.

It was a moonlight night when little Titian Vecelli first saw Venice and that was another wish come true. The towers and the domes and the gliding gondolas were flooded with the light that only an Italian moon can give, and the nobles and the ladies were there, and the deep chiming bells, and beyond it all the wide lagoon—and beyond that the wider sea. It was all as he had hoped it would be.

"Here I shall always live," he whispered to himself, and Signor Rostelli, who had come with him to his new life, watched it all with the same air of satisfaction.

The soft tints of the picture on the cottage wall have long faded and gone as completely as the armful of flowers the dreaming boy gathered so many, many years ago, but to this day in Venice, in its old carved palaces and in its stately churches, stand the great works that Titian painted when he grew to be a man—glowing, strong and powerful works, that will never die. And Venice still stands, with its domes and its bells, and remembers Titian forever.

Elsie Singmaster

BENNY AND THE CAT'S TAIL

ILLUSTRATED BY
Keith Ward

BENJAMIN WEST was born in Springfield, Pennsylvania, of Quaker parents. At the age of seven, he surprised everyone with his remarkable talent in drawing, and although he received no encouragement from his parents, by the time he was sixteen he had taught himself to paint with great skill. It is said that his first colors were made from leaves and berries. West became a portrait painter in New York, and finally settled in London, where he painted many famous historical pictures and scenes from the Bible. He was president of the Royal Academy until his death at eighty-one. Keith Ward, the illustrator of this story whose other fine pictures you will find in these books, is a direct descendant of this famous American painter.

SEVEN-YEAR-OLD Benjamin West came downstairs very early in the morning. He lived in a pretty stone house in Pennsylvania near a settlement which is now the town of Swarthmore. There were only a few other houses and a little Quaker meetinghouse in sight. But in every direction, even between the settlement and Philadelphia, which was only ten miles away, there were tall forests. The Quakers lived very quiet, peaceful lives, and they loved forests and everything else in nature that was beautiful.

Before the house lay a meadow, which was a meadow and not a forest because the Indians had cut down the trees so that they might plant corn and beans. There were still Indians about, but they lived chiefly by begging and by weaving baskets for sale. They had made a treaty with William Penn, he and they agreeing always to be friends. So far the promise had been kept.

At the edge of the meadow stood a group of ancient oaks, and Benny thought of them while he went downstairs. He had seen them often, and each time they seemed entirely new. In the spring the young leaves covered them with rose and golden lace; in the fall they turned a deep maroon. At night they looked like a solid black wall and in the morning their tops seemed to float on the mist like balloons. That was the way they would look this morning.

He tiptoed on, carrying his shoes in his hand. You would think his shoes very heavy for a little boy of seven, but they were the only kind that boys had two hundred years ago.

It was necessary to be careful. If Father or Mother or any of his brothers or sisters woke they might go to sleep again, but there was one person, who, if roused, would refuse to close her eyes. This was Baby Sallie, whose mother, his oldest sister, had brought her to visit. If she woke, then the whole family would be awake in a jiffy, and that would mean good-bye to adventure.

Benny stood still in the kitchen until each object became plain in the faint light of dawn. It was not tiresome to stand still because he could see more than most people could. He said to himself, "What a graceful shape that pitcher has!" and "I can see the golden luster on Mother's honey jar!" He saw the deep black fireplace, all the utensils and vessels hanging in a row before it, the settle, worn by use to a smooth brown, and the red in the braided rug on the scrubbed boards on the smooth, dark floor.

Certain, at last, that no one stirred upstairs, he lifted the iron latch, and stepped out and closed the door behind him. Sitting on the step, he put on his shoes. He felt a little touch on his leg and looked down.

"Well, Pussy, is it thou?" he said in his Quaker speech.

The light was brightening; he could see the black arch of Pussy's back and the fine bow of her tail, which had an unnaturally long and thick bunch of hair at the end. He bent over and stroked her, letting the tail slip through his fingers. At the

tip his fingers closed, not because he wished to pinch her and hurt poor Pussy but because a brilliant, lovely, startling idea came into his head and his hand closed automatically.

"Why, thou dear thing!" he cried. "I know what I'll do with thee!"

Puss was alarmed but not hurt. She said, "Wow!" loud enough to wake all the sleepers and ran toward the barn.

Benny's idea made his heart jump so that he could scarcely walk, but he got to the middle of the meadow and stood there in the deep grass. Mooley, the cow, came toward him, her bell tinkling softly. The sun, rising behind him, tinted the mist with rose and brightened the trees to a brilliant green. The mist lifted, revealing more and more of the great trees. "Here we are," they seemed to say. "Look your fill, Benny!"

Benny gazed until he could look no more; it seemed to him that his heart would burst, the sight was so beautiful. It was not, however, to see the oaks that he had come out so early. He started to run through the tall grass. Mooley's bell sounded as though she were running after him, but she was not; she was only shaking her head.

The shade under the oaks in the forest was so thick that there was no undergrowth, only fine dark grass. His grandparents who came across the ocean in the same ship with William Penn said that walking here was like walking in an English park.

"I'm not afraid," said Benny, over and over to himself.

He walked on, now stopping to listen, now nervously rubbing one hand with the other. The trees seemed presently to move apart and enclose a glade walled by foliage. In it stood a circle of wigwams. In the center was a fire and over it hung a black pot, and round it walked a squaw with a baby tied tight to a board on her back. Another squaw sat holding a bowl in her lap. In the bowl was a mass of red clay which she was manipulating with her fingers, and beside her stood another bowl holding yellow clay.

Benny caught the eye of the woman handling the clay and said a little tremulously, "Good morning to thee!"

"Ugh!" said the squaw, by which she meant, "Good morning, Benny; how are you?"

It was almost impossible to hurry a squaw, but Benny's intense longing for the gift she had promised him made him impatient. "Dost thou have clay for me?"

The squaw looked toward one of the wigwams and uttered another "Ugh!" This "Ugh" meant: "My man might not like me to give you any clay; he fetched it a long distance and he wants it all to put on his face, but I don't care. Anyhow he won't know anything about it because he's asleep, the lazy creature!"

Benny took from his pocket an extremely unpleasant looking object which had been one of his mother's neat and savory patty-pan taffy cakes. Now, melted into shapelessness, it darkened the piece of printed paper which wrapped it.

The squaw grinned, seized it eagerly, held it up behind her so the baby might have a lick at it, and then licked it fervently herself. She handed Benny lumps of clay, both red and yellow.

"Thank thee! Thank thee!" cried Benny and ran.

When he reached home the house looked bright in the early

sunlight. He went round to the back of the barn. Beside and partly under the barn-hill a stone had fallen, leaving a dry and secret niche. Here he deposited his clay. There were other objects there—pieces of black and white and red chalk, a little green housepaint in a bottle, a little lump of dark blue substance which was part of his mother's bluing stick—everything, one might say, which an amateur painter might need, except palette, canvas, and brush.

Suddenly Benny laughed excitedly, "Oh, Pussy!" he called.

Pussy's failure to appear made him frown. "I'll get thee, never fear!" he said.

All was quiet in the house. The sun was up, but it was still very early. His heart thumping, he ran to the springhouse and dipped from a shallow pan in which cream was rising a good cupful of rich milk and carried it to the barn.

"Come, Pussy!" he called. "Come, Pussy!"

Pussy needed no coaxing to make up; she had a friendly and unresentful disposition. She was supposed to depend upon field mice for her menu, but this morning the field mice seemed unusually alert. A pan of rich milk was to her like roast turkey to a hungry boy. She purred, she lapped, she rested, she lapped again, she lay down to dream in the straw. She didn't realize that Benny had left her and that when he returned he carried his mother's scissors. "Pussy," he said. "I won't hurt thee!"

"Clip, clip!" went the scissors.

And in Benny's hand lay the beautiful long bunch of black hair which had formed the tip of Pussy's tail. He took a little piece of string from his pocket and with a shaking hand tied the bunch together. "I'll get one of Mother's skewers, then I'll have a brush," he planned. "Cat's hair should be as good as camel's hair any day."

When he opened the door, he heard Sallie crowing. His mother came in. She wore a soft, gray dress with a kerchief folded across her breast, and she had a lovely, gentle look.

"Why, thou art up early!" she said.

"Yes," said Benny, flushing a little. He knew how to mix red and blue to make purple, and blue and yellow to make green;

if he could be alone, or if he had time, he believed that he could make a picture of a tree or a house, perhaps of a person. But the Quakers did not approve of pictures and he felt uneasy. Suppose Mother should ask where he had been!

Then Benny held his breath. His sister carried little Sallie downstairs and laid her in the cradle in which all ten Wests had been rocked. As she lay there, he seemed to see her for the first time—the curve of her cheeks, the bow of her rosy lips, the outline of her tiny nose. Fire seemed to run through his body; he felt a queer itching in his fingers.

"If I had my paints and a brush I could make a picture of her," he thought excitedly. "But I'll never have a chance."

But he did have a chance. His father went to work, the older boys and girls went to help him on the farm or to the school for little Quaker children. Having crowed herself tired, little Sallie slept.

"Oh, I could easily paint her!" thought Benny. He looked around frantically. He couldn't get his clay and indigo very well, but there was ink in the stand on the table—two kinds, red and black. "I could draw her with ink!"

"I'm going to the garden," said his mother when the dishes were done.

"But Sister's here," thought Benny, in despair.

"Benjamin will look after Sallie," continued Mother in her placid tone. "Come with me, Daughter."

Benny sat down at the table and looked at Sallie; then he drew the lovely curve of her cheek on a sheet of paper. He took another look and drew the tiny button of her nose. He forgot how the Quakers felt about likenesses; something in his mind and soul made him draw. He took a third look and with the tip of his pen held sidewise laid Sallie's lashes on her cheek.

It would take too long to draw her ringlets with the fine pen. "Oh, dear Pussy!" he thought and pulled out Mother's knife-drawer to find a skewer. To it he tied the little bunch of hair and dipped it into the inkwell.

He believed that all this took only a few minutes, but when he looked up the sunlight, which had formed a rectangle on the floor, now formed a square and the hands of the clock had moved round a full circle. Sallie's picture was finished, though black and red were not Sallie's colors. She should have had her picture painted in rose and cream and gold. But mouth and cheek and nose and ear were Sallie's.

At least this had been his opinion a moment ago; now in a sharp reaction he could see no resemblance.

"Oh, dear!" he thought, then suddenly he turned his head. Beside him stood his mother and sister. Sister was a Quaker, too; both she and his mother stared. It seemed to him as though he had done a great wrong. He tried to hide the paper, but Sister's long arm was too quick.

"Why, Benny!" she cried. "See, Mother, what he's done!"

Mother looked over Sister's shoulder, then at Sallie, then back at Sallie's picture. Puss came and stood beside her, waving her abbreviated tail, but Mother saw only Sallie and the paper shaking in Sister's hand. She could not foresee that Benny was to become America's first great painter and the teacher of young men even more famous than himself, but she was convinced that God had given him his talent.

She did not reprove him; she praised him. She put her arms round him and kissed him. "Why, Benny!" she said. "Thou hast made a good likeness of dear little Sallie!"

Carolyn Sherwin Bailey

THE BOY WHO LIKED PUPPETS

ILLUSTRATED BY *Ruth van Tellingen*

MORE THAN a century ago, in Odense, a town of Denmark, there lived a shoemaker, his wife, and his young son Hans. The family was very poor. The shoemaker had a great longing to make dancing shoes for princesses. In fact, he once made a pair from a bit of gold brocade, but no one bought them. They lived in only two rooms in a poor part of the town and no princesses ever came by that way. Yet they did not allow this to interfere with their happiness.

The shoemaker's bench filled most of the space in the small front room, but all the rest of the furniture, even Hans' little bed, had been carved by hand by the father, and the walls were made beautiful with pictures. Above the shoemaker's bench there was a bookcase filled with well-worn books. The kitchen fairly glittered with its rows of shining brass and copper pots and pans. Someone was always singing, and on the roof of the small house where Hans could reach it by climbing a ladder up from the kitchen, there was a garden. The street was paved with stones, and the house had no land about it, but Hans's mother had carried earth up the ladder and filled boxes on the roof. In these boxes vegetables grew, and flowers blossomed. It was a gay and useful roof garden.

In the evening when the tap, tap of the shoemaker's hammer was stilled, young Hans began to have the best time of the whole day. All the leather, the tool, nails, and needles were cleared off the bench, and his father made him toys. They already had a puppet theater built from an old box, with the curtain cut from cloth scraps. Little puppets made of paper, leather, and tinsel acted there in the light of a candle as the shoemaker told Hans stories. He also made Hans scenery for the many plays given in the toy theater. He had made him, too, a magnifying glass and a tin case in which to bring home the wild flowers they gathered on Sundays.

Oh, those happy Sundays! Then Hans would take his father's hand, and they would start out for a long walk. There was very little green grass to be seen in the town, only stone-paved streets crowded with the workers on Sunday, the weavers, bakers, butchers, and builders. But at the end of the town there was a small bridge that crossed a stream and led straight to the moor. Flowering bushes, trees, and wild flowers grew there, and on summer evenings long-legged storks could be seen. Hans's father told him stories as they walked over the moor. They picked wild strawberries and strung them on long grasses. Hans made garlands of flowers to take home to his mother and they brought also beautiful branches of greenery to fill the wide cracks of the little house through which the rain sometimes came in.

The puppet theater became quite famous in the neighborhood, and Hans gave shows for the other children. He and his father made more scenery, churches, public buildings, and castles like those of the great near-by city of Copenhagen. They made and dressed many puppets, dancing princesses, soldiers in uniform, fairies and story-book characters. All these puppets needed clothing, from their tiny shoes to their crowns, caps, and cloaks. It was hard for the shoemaker to spare Hans even scraps, for they were a family of patches; every bit of cloth and leather left from the shoes had to be used to keep them covered. Still, the toy theater managed to costume its actors.

One day in the spring a splendid parade came down the narrow street where Hans lived. It was the annual spring parade of town workers. At the head marched a jester with bells. Then came the weavers. The bakers, the herders, the builders, and the candle-makers paraded. Even the town butcher marched, driving before him a great white ox, wearing a garland of flowers

His little theater was the delight of all who saw it

upon his horns. Up and down, and in and out of the streets of Odense the parade went and Hans followed, losing one of his wooden shoes in the mud, but what did that matter? He had an idea, and in a few days he put it to work.

Not long after this, when the looms were clacking noisily in a cloth factory of Odense, the weavers were surprised to hear a clear voice singing village songs so sweetly that they could be heard above the din of the looms. When the foreman looked to see who this singer was, there was Hans, the shoemaker's boy, going up and down among the weavers, and singing as merrily as a bird. His music made the work go faster. Hans had been very much afraid when he entered the factory, but as he sang he lost his fear.

Hans wanted some scraps of silk, lace, tinsel, anything bright in which to dress the puppets for his toy theater. That was why he had formed this plan of singing in the factory. And the weavers gave him all the scraps of cloth he could carry home, to pay for his music. Hans returned and sang again and again for the weavers. Soon his puppets were better dressed than any others outside of Copenhagen, and his little theater was the delight of all who saw it.

Presently Hans began to earn money through his singing. He also began to write plays for puppets and for the real theater. When he had earned about thirteen dollars, he decided, although he was still young, to go to Copenhagen and try to earn his living. His father and mother still lacked comforts and Hans wanted to make their later years easier. So he packed his puppets and toy scenery, and said good-bye to the shoemaker's shop, the storks, and the town he loved so dearly.

It was not long until all Denmark began to talk about a new poet and playwright, who had gained high fame in Copenhagen. Not only were his plays acted and his poems read widely, but he had become a much-loved storyteller. He had been invited to tell stories to Charles Dickens, to Jenny Lind, to the Queen of Denmark, Queen Alexandra of England, to King George of Greece, and to the Empress of Russia. The stories these great people liked best were "The Fir Tree," "The Flax," "The Snow

Queen," "The Little Match Girl," "The Red Shoes," "The Faithful Tin Soldier," "Ole-Luk-Oie," and "The Old House." He was a rather shy man, more at home with children than adults, but the whole world knows him now as Hans Christian Andersen.

This famous storyteller always carried about in one of his pockets a toy soldier made of tin, which a little boy had given him. He did not seem to realize what a great man he had become, but when he entered a Court and began, "Once upon a time," troubled kings, queens, and emperors forgot everything but the colors and scents of the moor flowers, the call of storks, and the dreams that dropped from the umbrella of "Ole-Luk-Oie," as Mr. Andersen told his stories. Children came in hundreds to listen to these tales. As he told them he cut out pictures to illustrate them. Before one's very eyes there grew paper shepherds, fields of flowers, dancers and forests. So great became the fame of Hans Christian Andersen that his home town of Odense asked him to come back for a celebration.

The shoemaker and his wife now lived in quite a grand house in Odense, which their son had bought for them. But Hans Christian Andersen was still a very humble man. He was always at his ease when he was telling stories, but he disliked being made a fuss over. It is said that he had a very bad toothache when he returned to Odense for the celebration and tried to stay at home instead of appearing in the public square to review the parade in his honor, but his neighbors would not let him.

When he at last overcame his shyness, he discovered that this return to Odense as the town's most honored citizen was really the greatest event of his life. Schools were closed, and the children marched before him and sang and danced. Flags were flying. There was another parade of the workers, and in the evening a torchlight parade. A carriage was sent for Hans Christian Andersen, and his toothache disappeared with the coming of his happiness.

For almost one hundred and fifty years children have been loving the stories which began in Hans Christian Andersen's childhood, and found their way as far as thrones. Denmark is proud of being the land of Hans Christian Andersen's birth. Wherever there is a story hour he sits among boys and girls in company with "The Ugly Duckling," "The Faithful Tin Soldier," "The Nightingale," "The Emperor Who Wanted New Clothes," and "Thumbelina."

Rolf Klep

GALILEO

ILLUSTRATED BY THE AUTHOR

THE NEW ITALY which grew up a few hundred years after the fall of ancient Rome made high offerings to the world in music, in art, in exploration, in science. Her most famous scientist was Galileo. His family had been one of the wealthy, influential families of Florence. They were poor now, but were people of distinction nonetheless.

Galileo was very observant of simple facts, and from them he worked out significant conclusions. He noticed that a swinging lantern in the cathedral took the same length of time to complete the sweep of a long arc as of a short one. He noted that, contrary to the usual belief, a light weight fell through the air with the same speed as a heavy one. He took various weights to the top of the Leaning Tower of Pisa and dropped them to prove this latter contention to those who disputed it. These demonstrations led to new beliefs and new ways of measuring and figuring.

The first thermometer was constructed by Galileo.

When the invention of the telescope was rumored, Galileo immediately figured out how such an instrument could be made, constructed one, and perfected it rapidly, thus making many new astronomical discoveries possible. Some people who until now had been unwilling to believe that the earth revolved about the sun, gave in when they were shown, through the telescope, that Jupiter's satellites revolved about that planet. The new instrument served to convince them.

His writings had been widespread and were destined to start the world toward valuable mathematical and physical discoveries which would give it new instruments, new scientific theories, and new ways of thinking.

Galileo was one of the most brilliant thinkers who have ever lived.

GEORG FREDERICK HANDEL was born the same year as the great composer Johann Sebastian Bach, though the two were destined never to meet. In spite of his father's opposition, Georg taught himself to play the clavier, an early form of the piano, practicing secretly in the attic of their house. His determination to receive a musical education was so great that his father finally relented, and the boy became the pupil of a fine organist. When eleven he could already play the violin, the clavichord, and the organ. In compliance with his father's wishes, Handel studied law for a time, but after his father's death he found employment as a violinist and harpsichordist in a symphony orchestra. When he was twenty-five years old, Handel visited England and it was there, at the height of his fame, that he composed many fine operas, oratorios, anthems, chamber music, concertos, and his great *Messiah* with its wonderful Hallelujah Chorus, his most famous work. He continued to compose and play in public for the rest of his life.

Mary Newlin Roberts

GEORG HANDEL AND THE DUKE

ILLUSTRATED BY *Clarence Biers*

ABOVE EVERYTHING little Georg Handel wanted to see the Duke, so when he heard that his father was going to the Court, he went at once to his aunt, who was a round-faced, kind young aunt, and said, "Aunt dear, do beg my father to take me with him to court."

His aunt shook her head.

"But please," begged Georg. "The Duke is fond of music, and I shall play for him the tunes that are always in my head, and mayhap he will help me to buy an organ."

"Nay, nay," sighed his aunt. "He is too great to notice a little lad like thee, and thou knowest thy father forbids thee to think any more of music."

"Truly, great people love music and children too," cried her little nephew.

"That is true, little one, but this Duke is great in worldly duties and fashion. Canst thou not be content with the little silent spinet in the attic, which I bought for thee instead of a new silk dress for myself?"

"Aunt dear, I love the spinet and you for giving it to me, but it has only a soft faint voice, and I want to hear my music loud and beautiful as it is meant to be."

"But thou canst play on the organ in the Town chapel now and then, while I keep watch for thee so that thy father should not know, and oh me!" sighed his aunt, "very beautiful thy music is to hear."

But Georg pleaded and, like all loving aunts, she finally did what he asked.

After a little while, Georg's father sent for him.

"What folly is this?" asked the big man.

He was a kind, good man, but he did not approve of music. He was a surgeon and a barber, which seems to us a strange combination, but all this was more than two hundred years ago in the faraway town of Halle in faraway old Germany.

"Thou art too young to go to court, Georg," he said in his deep voice. "Thy head is full of nonsense. Thou must grow up into a worthy lawyer or carpenter. I fear thou art spoiled by thy aunt and that thou hast listened too much to the jigging tunes of those idle fellows who travel by playing on silly instruments, from village to village."

"Oh please, Father. I cannot help loving music, but I work hard and try to be good and please you."

His father did not like to disappoint him, but he shook his head.

"Nay, lad, I know best, and a court is no place for a child."

At this, little Georg flung himself upon his father and begged and argued until the big man lost his temper and bade him, with a swing of his stick, to be off to his room.

That night Georg slept little and, early in the morning, he put on his best suit and slipped outdoors where he hid behind a bush.

Before long he saw the coach, newly painted and gay with

the horses in new harness and red feathers, draw up before the door, and presently his father, very grand in court clothes, sprang in. Away then went the coach with a crack of the whip, and away went Georg helter-skelter after it.

On and on they went in the dust, up and down hill, over a bridge, around a curve and on. Little Georg was nearly exhausted and choked when, by a lucky chance, the fine horses slowed up on an especially long hill, and his father, looking out the back window, uttered an angry exclamation, and the driver pulled in his team. The dusty little figure scrambled in without a word, and on they went again in a silence that boded ill for Georg. All day strange hills and fields and woods rattled past and little Georg, afraid to look at his father, kept his nose pressed to the window. At dusk they drew up before a small house that stood close to a beautiful church.

"Here, thou naughty one, I shall leave thee with my friend, the choirmaster. He will keep thee out of mischief till I can take thee back to home and punishment."

Georg felt his heart sink when he found himself a prisoner, and no nearer the Duke than if he were back at Halle, but the choirmaster took a fancy to the dusty culprit, and Georg soon began to prattle, tired as he was, of how very, very much he wished to see the Duke.

"But thy father is angry with thee and has asked me to shut thee up," said kind Herr Volstead.

"My father does not love music, and to me it is my life. The Duke loves music, and so I must, must see him!" cried Georg.

The choirmaster looked at him curiously and stroked his brown beard.

"Well, well," he muttered, "we shall see. I love music myself."

Little Georg spent all the following day sitting sadly in his room, and at dusk he leaned on the window sill and watched the lights being lit in the chapel beneath him. Presently, to his surprise, an old woman in a big white cap came with a candle, and washed his face, and brushed his clothes, and led him downstairs. She took him to a side door of the chapel and, with a whispered caution to "be good" pushed him in. Coming sud-

denly into the church from the darkness, Georg was struck dumb by the lights of hundreds of candles and the scent of flowers, by the hanging banners and crowds of courtiers in rich attire. He was glad when a choirboy took him by the hand and led him to a dark corner by the organ.

"Sit quiet now," said the choirboy, "for the Duke is coming."

With a volley of chords from the organ, played by Herr Volstead, and a burst of song from the choir, the big doors of the chapel swung wide, and the Duke walked slowly in between the bowing courtiers and passed gravely to the altar. He was a noble-looking man, tall and fair and richly dressed in scarlet. Little Georg gasped with admiration and delight, and his heart beat with pride and joy.

But after the beautiful service was over, the Duke was surrounded by his lords and passed down the aisle again, and Georg all at once felt very hopeless and small in his dark corner. Then through the tears that sprang to his eyes he saw the great organ which was now deserted, and with a low cry he ran to it and, unnoticed, climbed with difficulty to where he could touch the keys with his strong little hands.

"This is the way I can tell the Duke about it all," he thought. "I am only a little boy, but if he is good, he will understand."

Then it was that the tall figure of the Duke paused with hand upraised, and the whole band of courtiers fell silent.

For a burst of beautiful music filled the church and floated higher and higher and softer and softer, and finally died away in a few last pleading notes.

The Duke had caught sight of the small swaying figure of the boy organist and told them to bring him at once before him.

Georg's father, in the meantime, pale with mortification, besought the Duke to pardon the folly of his son, but when the boy was finally before them both, the Duke turned to the worthy surgeon and said, "Thou art a good man, Herr Handel, but thy son will some day be a great one. What surgeon or lawyer could fill this chapel of God with the voices of angels as this little son of thine has done today? Never more be ashamed of this great heaven-sent gift of music that lies in the head and heart and hands of this most splendid little artist. Through him the name of Handel will be long remembered. Here is a purse of gold to train him as he should be trained, and to go on and on with his music, which is a gift from God himself."

Little Georg knew nothing of court manners, but he looked up at the Duke simply, and the Duke thought his smile one of the finest tributes ever paid to a Duke.

"And might I please buy just one new silk dress for my dear aunt, too?" he asked.

The courtiers laughed, but the Duke only placed a kind hand on his shoulder and nodded gravely.

Carolyn Sherwin Bailey

HELEN KELLER

ILLUSTRATED BY *Hilda Frommholz*

HELEN HAD felt all day that someone was expected. It seemed to the seven-year-old girl that the roses about the house in their small town of Tuscumbia in Alabama had smelled sweeter, that the kitchen quarter carried the scent of company baking. She was more restless than usual. Curls flying, eager hands feeling their way along walls or touching the hedge of fragrant box that led her through the garden, Helen tried to reach the visitor. She grasped the hand, tugged at the apron of her companion, the little Negro girl, Martha Washington, insisting that they go along the flower-bordered driveway, explore as far as the road. She had an urge to be busy always, folding and laying away clothes fresh from the laundry, hunting with Martha for guinea-hens' eggs secretly hidden in tall grass, making dough balls, helping turn the ice cream freezer and beating cakes. The milkers let Helen touch the cows. She loved to feed the horses. She and Martha had a large family of paper dolls that they had cut out and dressed on rainy days. But a day when guests came to the Keller home was an exciting one for Helen. Then she was led down to the parlor, allowed to touch a visitor's face, hold a strange hand.

A rattle of wheels and the beat of hoofs on the driveway called the household to greet a visitor late that afternoon. A trunk was unloaded from the wagon that brought this guest from the Tuscumbia station. Helen felt strange but kind arms hold her closely when she fairly tumbled down the steps of the ivy-covered porch of the Keller house. Helen had no words of greeting for Anne Sullivan who had come from the north to be her teacher and companion the rest of her life. But she touched Miss Sullivan's clothes, her face, felt the beating of her heart, knew in her alert mind that something wonderful was ahead.

Helen Keller, from the time of an illness in babyhood, had neither seen nor heard. Her world was an abyss of darkness and silence. Her hands had taught her a great deal, but the prison of the spirit in which she lived and the loving compassion of her family had made her a quick-tempered little girl. She was given to storms of rage. Now, she had one of her worst tantrums as she was not allowed to have Miss Sullivan's luggage unpacked in her room. Helen even locked her teacher in the guest room and hid the key. Her father had to climb a ladder to Miss Sullivan's window and help her down to supper. But seeing-children have had tantrums. Helen Keller's violence came from her restlessness and was due to longing to learn those everyday things that her baby sister Mildred, and her loved Martha Washington, knew without learning. The next day peace and happiness began to light her spirit.

Miss Sullivan had studied Braille—the script for the blind, a system of raised letters interpreted by one's fingers—at the Perkins Institute for the Blind in Boston. The pupils of the Perkins Institute had sent Helen Keller a stylishly dressed doll. Miss Sullivan put this doll into Helen's arms and before the happy girl could escape with it, Miss Sullivan held her hand firmly and, in Helen's sensitive palms, spelled the letters d-o-l-l. So strange and exciting an experience had never happened to Helen. Over and over Miss Sullivan spelled the word *doll* in this way. She spelled also in Helen's hand the words that were important in her days: *mug, dog, hat, milk, candy, mother, bed, knife, fork, spoon,* and many others. She helped Helen to spell these words in her teacher's own hand. Soon, since Helen had a great desire to learn, the two were talking together through this sign language.

Sometimes they had trouble. There was the word *water* that Helen could not seem to understand, so they went to a spring in the garden. Miss Sullivan held Helen's hand under the cool gushing stream and then spelled water many times in her palm. That was all Helen needed. As, from day to day she learned hundreds of words, and was able to put them together into sentences and communicate through this finger language, her ill temper faded. She could not learn enough. A new and enchanting world became hers, wider, more exciting every day. In a year she had almost the vocabulary of the seeing, the hearing child of her age. She was writing with a pencil also. She demanded that Miss Sullivan teach her every minute of the day.

Helen's active hands became trained through stringing large beads in combinations of numbers, modeling, sewing for her dolls. She had become a different person when they returned to the big house, no longer alone in her darkness and silence. She could converse with her parents. Then she began to outstrip other children, because she so wanted to learn.

Miss Sullivan took her to the circus one summer, where Helen fed the elephants, was allowed to smooth the soft coat of a young lion. She held a monkey who took off her hair ribbon. She shook hands with a bear. A keeper lifted Helen to the vast height of the giraffe who stalked around the ring with her on its back.

When Christmas came Helen made gifts for her family and hung up her stocking. That first Christmas Helen's most prized gift was a Braille slate and pencil. Miss Sullivan had begun to teach her to read by touching the raised letters of the Braille alphabet. Her guided fingers had become her eyes, her ears. Miss Sullivan read to her by means of the sign language those stories we all love. Sitting beside her, one hand laid in Miss Sullivan's lap, her teacher spelled with the rapidity the blind can follow, *The Jungle Book*, *Little Lord Fauntleroy*, *Aesop's Fables*. With the printing of more books in Braille, Helen at ten years read to herself *Little Women*, *Heidi*, *Hawthorne's Wonder Book*, *Robinson Crusoe*, *Tales from Shakespeare*, *Wild Animals I have Known*, stories of the Greek heroes, and the Bible. Her family

FROMMHOLZ

would find Helen curled in a chair in their library, her bright curls covering her closed eyes, her fingers flying across the pages of Braille, a happy child living in the world of great literature.

For many months Miss Sullivan had written reports of Helen's progress to the Perkins Institute, and the director and pupils invited her to bring Helen for a visit. She had never left home; it was thought that she would never be able to travel, but with understanding and delight she helped pack her bag and her doll's trunk. The May when she was eight years old, she said good-bye to her dog Belle and to Martha Washington. She and Miss Sullivan drove to the Tuscumbia railroad station and the great journey north began.

Helen truly *saw*, through Miss Sullivan's sign language, the sweep of the Tennessee River, the fields of cotton, the colored dress of the Negro field workers. She had come to love color, imagining that she saw it. Once she asked if her small sister's eyes were like little bits of the sky. She now *saw* the crowds at city stations, other passengers, the changes in the landscape, different architecture as they traveled north. At the Perkins Institute Helen was charmed to make friends with other blind children. They talked together, shared schoolwork, games and toys. But Helen was beyond the blind of her own age. She was always to be an example in determination, scholarship and ambition.

Boston, other visits and study that followed, gave her a chance to begin history. Helen visited and touched the earth of Bunker Hill. She went by boat to Plymouth where she stood on the rock of the Pilgrim's great adventure. She put on her first bathing suit and waded out without fear into the ocean; it was exciting and dangerous but Helen was to become a skilled swimmer.

The Horace Mann School for the Deaf in Boston was beginning to teach speech; Miss Sullivan studied the methods used there. Helen Keller's world of books, her love for her family and friends, her dogs and horses, her long country walks had filled her with knowledge and happiness that she felt an urge to voice. But at this time, when she was thirteen, she had no memory of speech. She did not know of any other way of communicating than the sign language. The sounds she made were animal-like. She crooned to her dolls, made loving sounds to her dog, stood beside the piano touching the musician's throat and hands as if she heard melody. But these sounds she made were harsh, without modulation. We speak with expression because from birth we have heard speech; Helen was without this experience. Now her training in speech began.

She put her hand on Miss Sullivan's lips as she pronounced letters distinctly. She felt her teacher's throat for modulation. She read in sign language the alphabet and the words Miss Sullivan pronounced, then spoke. Helen Keller soon had a short list of words she could speak. She could put her thoughts into sentences, read with her delicate hand the lips of others. With the years she learned a low and pleasant way of speaking. She could read aloud, but always storytelling and talking with those she loved was her more distinct and musical way of talking. She was to become a popular speaker when a woman, telling how her struggle had made her life one with the lives of her audience. She spoke foreign languages at last, and in Paris they said Helen's French was even better than her English.

The day on which Miss Sullivan came was Helen's important one for years. But each season she stepped farther into her new world, where great adventures met her. She wanted to go to

college, but how could she read the examinations? The way was made for her. The day came when she found herself in a room alone, a tutor outside the door to prevent interruptions, and her examination papers in Braille before her. She was taking the entrance examination for Radcliffe College. She was only nineteen years old. She had learned to read English and several foreign languages. She wrote many letters to her family and friends constantly. She had traveled. She was a beautiful young girl; one never noticed her closed eyes. If her hands trembled as they traced the questions, as she wrote the answers on a special typewriter for the blind, it was not due to fear; she was so eager to pass. Helen Keller passed and became one of the highest ranking students Radcliffe had ever graduated.

As she studied science, French, German, history, English composition and literature in college, her days of childhood darkness disappeared. The books Helen Keller read, the events of long-ago that she discovered in history, the skill in language that was to help her write *The Story of My Life*, had raised a curtain. The light of learning is a great light; shining brighter when it must be groped for.

Helen Keller was never, after those first years, alone. She saw Joseph Jefferson play *Rip Van Winkle* and told him backstage how much she enjoyed the theater. She went with her teacher and Alexander Graham Bell, inventor of the telephone, to the World's Fair when she was thirteen. It was, she said, like *The Arabian Nights*. The same year she visited Niagara Falls, seeing and hearing that miracle of waters. One of her best friends was Bishop Phillips Brooks who opened for her new pages in the Bible. Mark Twain told her true stories of the Mississippi River. Mary Mapes Dodge, who was editing *St. Nicholas*, gave Helen books. John Greenleaf Whittier helped her see the farm winter he wrote about in *Snowbound*.

Wonder stories are our favorites. But a true wonder story is the best of all. Such a one is the story of Helen Keller's brave, thrilling life.

VAN DYCK painted many fine religious pictures in his long career, but he is best known to us as an outstanding portrait painter who has left us a pictorial history of his colorful age. As a boy he assisted the great Rubens and held an important position in his workshop. When he was twenty-two years old, Van Dyck traveled to Italy to study Italian painting and spent seven years in Venice, Sicily, and Rome. Upon his return to Belgium, he was, for a time, official court painter of Charles I of England, and became the most outstanding portrait painter of his day, whose work influenced many great painters who came after him.

Mary Newlin Roberts

ANTONIO VAN DYCK AND HIS MASTER RUBENS

ILLUSTRATED BY *John Gee*

"HARK, all of you—the Master is away!"

"Aye, thou stupid, who does not know that? And dull enough it is without him!"

"Nay, but heed me, lads—he hath forgot to lock his own studio door."

The ten or twelve boys scattered about the great, bare studio drew closer to the speaker. They cast aside their brushes and palettes and pushed away their easels, and as they chattered and exclaimed, they glanced with curious eyes toward a small door at the far end of the room.

"Faith, I'd like to see what is going on in there!" cried one. "And wouldst not thou, Antonio?"

"If any hath the right," said another, " 'twould be thou, Antonio, for the Master thinks more of thee than all of us put together."

Antonio Van Dyck, a tall, fair youth, stood by a window where a shaft of sunlight lit up his yellow hair and brought to life the deep blue of his doublet, making him shine out a brilliant figure beside the other boys, who wore the dull green and brown smocks of the studio. He rested his hands on his hips and laughed.

"That little door hides what I want much to see," he admitted.

"Aye, aye!" shouted young Gaspard, a ringleader, a boy of the least talent in the studio save for the one matter of a vast skill in mirth and pranks. "It will be our only chance now. What a joy! What a lark, to enter that door generally so tightly locked! I dare thee, lads, to follow me. Where is thy sense of adventure? And, Antonio, if thy love of art be so great, why then, feast thine eyes on the work of the great Rubens while it is in progress!"

He was pulling them about now and urging them toward the mysterious door and Antonio, laughing and wrestling, followed with the others.

"It would seem a little sacrilege!" he cried, tugging backward.

"Nay, nay, 'tis but a game and our right."

Boys in Antwerp long ago in the seventeenth century, in spite of doublet and hose and velvet cap and smock of the studio, were much the same as boys now; and so, with laughter and carousing and tumbling about of easels and stools, they clattered and jostled down the big room and burst into the small, silent studio beyond.

In the narrow doorway Antonio alone paused, and stood leaning and gazing, his face flushed with delight and reverence.

"Ah!" he cried. "Be quiet just a space." And one by one the others stopped and stared.

On the tall easel a canvas faced them—a half-finished painting of wonderful beauty and power. The colors glowed as only the brush of Rubens could make them glow, and the figures were so full of life that it seemed hard to believe they were not actually alive. It was a sacred subject done with marvelous power, and Antonio stood rooted in the doorway, fascinated and absorbed. For a time the others were quiet and reverently admiring. But bit by bit they grew tired of this and began to look about curiously and examine the canvases. And, as they went, they pulled each other's smocks and wrestled with one another and called to Antonio to come and see this or that, and the laughter and the scuffling began again.

Then something happened. Gaspard gave a playful push to a small, slight comrade, who slipped and before he could recover his balance fell against the easel, and down went the canvas of the great Rubens—face downward on the floor.

The noise and laughter and the crash ended in a deep and frightened silence. Antonio sprang forward.

"Quick, the picture!" he cried. "Help me up with it! Oh, but this is terrible what we have done!"

Antonio had now become the leader. Gaspard had turned pale and sober and the other boys stood about, frightened and still.

"Help me raise it, lads," cried Antonio again. "No matter how terrible the damage, we must find it out."

Slowly and very carefully they lifted up the canvas and placed it on its easel, hardly daring to see how much had been ruined by their folly.

"A face and an arm," whispered Gaspard, "smirched and gone."

"There is but one thing to do," said one of the older boys. "Antonio Van Dyck will have to repaint them."

"Nay, never," cried Antonio hotly. "Without the Master's permission I would not."

"Aye, but thou must, Antonio, for listen! If we are discovered in this, the Master will keep none of us in his studio. Thou art our comrade and thou must help us. Often and often of late the Master hath given thee work on his own canvases. He hath been too busy to do all and he hath always and each time chosen thee. Thy work is as much like his as two peas."

"Nay!" cried Antonio again, his fair face suffused with color. "I am no closer to him in skill than thou art to the moon. And in any case," he added, "I paint like myself."

The boys stood in a silent, unhappy group, gazing at the damaged picture.

"But, look you, Antonio," pleaded Gaspard. "Thou wilt not desert us. What is to be done unless thou wilt paint? Our skill is not great enough, and if our Master knows of this we will all be cast out of his wonderful school."

"He would know, in any case," said Antonio, crossly, but he took the palette and brushes of the great Rubens, as he spoke. He had been studying the injured arm and face of the painting, and a queer look of absorption was creeping into his eyes. One of the boys made a motion to the others to be silent and wait, and suddenly, with no more urging, Antonio Van Dyck began to paint.

No one dared to move for a long time but while Antonio's brush, bit by bit, with exquisite success and sureness of touch, repaired the terrible damage, the anxious boys began to relax a little and sigh and shuffle with relief. "It would fool Michelangelo, himself," they whispered. "And truly, he is marvelous, our Antonio!"

"Aye," murmured the mischievous Gaspard. "He is slow sometimes at games, but with his brush he is a wizard. We are saved," he shouted, tossing his velvet cap in the air. "Oh, my Antonio, thou hast saved us a terrible humiliation!"

Slowly Antonio laid down his palette and brushes, and looked at what he had done. The color rose again in his face to see how closely he had come to the work of the great Rubens himself.

"But he will know, none the less," he said. "And I am sad, though what I have done is the best that I have ever done."

They went trooping out and closed the door.

"This afternoon," said Antonio, "he will return." And they went to their stools and easels and set to work without laughter and play.

It was a long day and yet it seemed too early when the great Rubens flung open the door and joined them, with a friendly word or two. He had had a very successful and happy journey and, being in high spirits, he warmed towards the group of talented boys, waiting for him in the old room.

"Come, lads, I'll show thee what I am doing!" he called, as he went with long strides toward the little door.

"So—I forgot to lock it. Well, come hither! 'Tis a good lesson for thee to see a work not yet completed."

The boys reluctantly came, and Antonio last of all, pale and still.

"Ah, the last touches that I made seem to me my best!" cried Rubens. "What thinkest thou, Antonio there? It seemeth to me the arm and face are not the poorest part. I will work a little, lads, that thou mayest watch, for once in a while it teacheth more than all the talk and training in the world."

The boys bowed their gratitude, and exchanged glances that told Antonio they believed that he had succeeded in saving them. But Antonio shook his head.

For some time the room was quiet while the great Master worked on his beautiful canvas, and his pupils watched breathlessly. It was a rare privilege, and a moment never to be forgotten by any of them. Then Rubens suddenly uttered an exclamation, and with a simultaneous movement Antonio sprang forward.

"Aye, Master, now thou knowest!" he said and his voice shook unhappily. "Thou seest that my brushwork is not thine, that my skill was not equal to what I tried to do. I damaged thy great work in my folly, daring to look at what was not meant for me to see, and I tried to repair the harm done, for to be turned from thy studio, as I deserved, was more than I could bear."

"Nay, 'twas I knocked the picture over," broke in the boy who had fallen. " 'Twas not thou, Antonio."

"And 'twas I knocked thee over," said the mischievous Gaspard, with tears in his eyes.

"Silence," said Rubens sternly. "Let Antonio answer my questions. Tell me," he went on, in a deep voice. "The face of the Magdalene, this arm of the Madonna—did the picture fall and they were destroyed?"

"Aye, Master."

"I imagine that, having left my door unlocked, thou camest unbidden to see my work?"

Antonio bowed his head till the yellow locks hid his face, and the other boys watched and waited in attitudes of shame and anxiety.

"And then, Antonio Van Dyck, they urged thee to cover the

damage, because thou art my first pupil and they had faith in thy power to fool Rubens himself."

Antonio could not answer.

There was a long silence, and then Rubens cast aside his palette and turned his back on his own superb masterpiece. He spread his arms wide, and the ruffles at his wrist flashed in the movement like white wings.

"Come to my arms, lad. Thy great skill and power of painting are all I care for. The folly and the lack of reverence and the fault of all of you are nothing beside it. What brooks it that boys are boys and stop at nothing, be it ever so sacred? But ah, what it means to the world and to an artist to find another artist! Leave us, lads."

They filed out slowly, with backward glances of awe at the beautiful picture glowing in the background, at the tall, noble Master Rubens, embracing the slim, blue-clad figure of their comrade.

"We shall be allowed to stay," whispered one.

"Aye," murmured Gaspard, behind his hand, "because we matter so little he hath forgotten us. I would I were Antonio Van Dyck."

MOZART was acclaimed as the "musician of musicians" after his death, but in his own lifetime he was neglected, and his life was full of privations and disappointments. A child genius, he began to play at the age of three and was composing beautiful music when only seven years old. When he grew up, Mozart lived in Vienna where he gave concerts, composed, and gave lessons to help out his low salary. Despite his financial difficulties, however, his greatest works were composed during this period. He completed his last three great symphonies in less than two months. Opera also occupied his attention, and his most famous productions were received enthusiastically—*Don Giovanni, The Marriage of Figaro,* and *The Magic Flute.* Mozart completed his most famous work, the sublime *Requiem,* just before his death at the age of thirty-five.

Mary Newlin Roberts

WOLFGANG MOZART

ILLUSTRATED BY *Clarence Biers*

IT WAS Holy Week of the year of 1769. Rome lay under the spell of the solemn festival. Throngs of people made their way to the vast temple of Saint Peter's.

In this throng moved a German boy, Wolfgang Mozart, and his father. They had been travelers now for some weeks, from their home in Salzburg. At this time a musician's education was not considered complete without a visit to Italy. Wolfgang was no ordinary young pupil of music. He was, to be sure, only thirteen years old, but he was already famous.

At Milan the chief musician had put him to severe tests that he had met with ease. In Bologna a brilliant audience had heard the extraordinary and beautiful boy play. In Florence he had played before the court of Archduke Leopold. He had worked hard and long and was working now, but he had a happy nature, and all this speed of life sat easily and well on his young shoulders.

The journey through Italy gave him great delight. He liked to watch the peasants at work in the vineyards, he liked the blue lakes and the purple mountains, the old churches and the narrow crooked streets. The fine music in the cathedrals stirred his very soul.

But there was one thing above all others that he wished to see and hear. And now as he moved with shining eyes toward the great dome of Saint Peter's, he knew that the time was close at hand.

Today in the Sistine Chapel, where Michelangelo's great paintings had transformed the walls into a thing of wonder, there was to be given the *Miserere*, by Allegri. This was a sacred and mysterious musical event, and Wolfgang's father had told him about it.

The music of this beautiful musical composition was jealously guarded. In no other chapel could it be performed, and the singers were not allowed even to take their parts out of the chapel. Wolfgang was intensely eager to hear this closely treasured music. It was not quite the hour, and his impatience grew with every moment.

They went first into Saint Peter's. The leather curtains of the wide doorways were drawn back, and after the noise outside a great stillness suddenly fell upon them.

A myriad candles burned, incense rose in clouds, but above it all the great arches and the domes formed such a height and space that the cathedral seemed a world made for giants, and not for these small human beings that moved like ants across the marble floors.

Wolfgang spoke to his father, and it was as if he were whispering, so small and tiny was his voice.

"It is marvelous, Papa," he breathed. "But when will it be the hour for the Sistine Chapel? I have waited so very long. Will the time never, never come?"

"Only a little more patience, *mein leiber,*" said the elder Mozart smiling down at this son of his who held such a great gift in his brain and hands.

Leopold Mozart was a musician himself and vice-cappelmeister in Salzburg. Music had always been honored in his home. Wolfgang's sister, Marianne, could play well on the harpsichord. Leopold took delight in his children, but this extraordinary boy was a never-ending wonder to him. His son's longing for the musical service made his own grow more intense.

They lingered in the great temple awhile and then went to the palace of the Vatican and saw its treasures. The exquisite silver and gold and bronze work of Benvenuto Cellini, the great paintings by Raphael, so different from the rugged brush or hand of Michelangelo, but great in their purity. And so the time at last came, and Wolfgang and his father moved with swifter steps towards the Sistine Chapel.

Wolfgang had never been here hitherto. He caught his breath at the sight of those perfect proportions and those glowing walls. At one end "The Last Judgment," that huge picture by Michelangelo, held his gaze. Above him the Prophets looked down, majestic and inspired figures. He stood impressed and silent, and his father had to rouse him and lead him to his seat.

There was a stillness of suspense in the chapel. Before the closely-guarded music would be sung there would first be that solemn service called *Tenebrae*, or Darkness.

On the altar at one end of the chapel six tall candles were burning. Wolfgang fixed his eyes on the beautiful flames that flickered now and burned steadily again. Slowly, solemnly the service began.

Of all that devout audience there was none more rapt and reverent than the young musician. He leaned forward with clasped hands, listening—and Wolfgang Mozart could listen well, as Rome was soon to know.

One candle was put out. The music grew deeper and more mysterious. Another candle was put out. The light in the chapel grew softer. One by one the flames were extinguished till only one was left. The older Mozart, glancing at his son, could scarcely see him. Only his shining eyes in a white small oval which was his face. The last candle, carried high by a priest in a golden robe, was removed to a space behind the altar. Wolfgang touched his father's hand.

CLARENCE BIERS

At this moment with the Sistine Chapel in almost complete darkness, the music of Allegri, that sacred, hidden music, began. A single voice was singing. It sang a short introduction which is called the Antiphon. High and clear and strange it soared, and then there was silence. It was a profound silence. Wolfgang did not dare to draw a breath. The faintest whisper would have crashed and broken such a deep and unearthly stillness.

And then came the first sad notes of the *Miserere.* It is music of supplication. A voice asking God to have mercy.

The elder Mozart forgot his son, forgot the whole world. And Wolfgang with his face buried in his hands forgot everything but the music itself, and to this his whole being was awake.

The music grew in force and intensity. The whole great building seemed to beat and tremble with the thrilling mystery. The appeal was so great and stirring that it would surely bring mercy to the whole troubled world.

It was over. The six candles blazed again upon the altar. Other lights were lit. The Prophets showed again upon the walls, and The Last Judgment again took possession with all its terrible power. The singers carried away to the chapel strongholds their secret parts of the score, and the treasured music was bolted and barred.

Wolfgang and his father did not speak. They went back to their lodgings without a word.

When bedtime came Wolfgang's father laid a hand on his son's arm.

"It was a strange and stirring experience, lad," he said. "Sleep well. Thou art tired and hast need of rest."

But the usually affectionate and light-hearted boy scarcely answered. There was a look of deep abstraction in his eyes. He murmured a low good night and slipped away to his room like a person in a dream.

Wolfgang could not sleep. He lay on his bed, but his mind was full and beating with the wonderful music.

Outside in a courtyard a fountain played a lullaby. . . . Rome was quiet, for during this week of the holy festival all the great city was solemn, and the nights were still.

But the boy from Salzburg was unable to rest. He rose and lit the lamp. From a drawer he drew out pens and paper that he always carried with him. He sat at the table in deep thought and then he began to work.

The bells of the city chimed out the hours. The long night wore on over Rome. And still Wolfgang worked. Sheet after sheet of the empty barred paper was filled with notes.

The stars grew dim in the sky. The voice of the fountain seemed to grow fainter, for other sounds were beginning to drown its airy music. Pigeons awoke and cooed under the eaves of the courtyard walls. There was a clatter of wheels over the rough Roman pavings. The first cold light of morning touched the Dome of Saint Peter's and began to pale the rays of the lamp in Wolfgang's room.

When morning came he slept, his head buried on his arms. But on the table before him there lay a pile of music.

It was the *Miserere* of Allegri, written entirely from memory. A boy of thirteen had stolen complete the guarded treasure from the Vatican.

When Rome found it out, she opened wide her doors and welcomed Wolfgang Mozart.

BEAUTY

Sir William Watson

I follow Beauty; of her train am I:
  Beauty whose voice is earth and sea
    and air;
Who serveth, and her hands for all
    things ply;
  Who reigneth, and her throne is
    everywhere.

Part II: FOR OLDER READERS

Rupert Sargent Holland

CHARLES DICKENS: THE BOY OF THE LONDON STREETS

ILLUSTRATED BY *Decie Merwin*

THE LITTLE FELLOW who worked all day long in the tumbledown old house by the river Thames pasting oil-paper covers on boxes of blacking, fell ill one afternoon. One of the workmen, a big man named Bob Fagin, made him lie down on a pile of straw in the corner and placed blacking-bottles filled with hot water beside him to keep him warm. There he lay until it was time for the men to stop work, and then his friend Fagin, looking down upon the small boy of twelve, asked if he felt able to go home. The boy got up looking so big-eyed, white-cheeked, and thin, that the man put his arm about his shoulder.

"Never mind, Bob, I think I'm all right now," said the boy. "Don't you wait for me; go on home."

"You ain't fit to go alone, Charley. I'm comin' along with you."

" 'Deed I am, Bob, I'm feelin' as spry as a cricket." The little fellow threw back his shoulders and headed for the stairs.

Fagin, however, insisted on keeping him company; and so the two, the shabbily-dressed under-sized youth and the big strapping man, came out into the murky London twilight, and took their way over the Blackfriars Bridge.

"Been spendin' your money at the pastry-shops, Charley, again? That's what was the matter with you, I take it."

The boy shook his head. "No, Bob. I'm trying to save. When I get my week's money I put it away in a bureau drawer, wrapped in six little paper packages with a day of the week on each one. Then I know just how much I've got to live on, and Sundays don't count. Sometimes I do get hungry, though; so hungry! Then I look in at the windows and play at being rich."

They crossed the bridge, the boy's big eyes seeming to take note of everything, the man, duller-witted, listening to his chatter. Several times the boy tried to say good night, but Fagin would not be shaken off. "I'm goin' to see you to your door, Charley lad," he said each time.

At last they came into a little street near the Southwark Bridge. The boy stopped by the steps of a house. "Here 't 's, Bob. Good night. It was good of you to take the trouble for me."

"Good night, Charley."

The boy ran up the steps, and, as he noticed that Fagin still stopped, he pulled the doorbell. Then the man went on down the street. When the door opened the boy asked if Mr. Fagin lived there, and being told that he did not, said he must have made a mistake in the house. Turning about he saw that his friend had disappeared around a corner. With a little smile of triumph he made off in the other direction.

The door of the Marshalsea Prison stood open like a great black mouth. The boy, tired with his long tramp, was glad to reach it and to run in. Climbing several long flights of stairs he entered a room on the top story where he found his family, his father, a tall pompous-looking man, dressed all in black, his mother, an amiable but extremely fragile woman, and a small brother and sister seated at a table, eating supper. The room was very sparsely furnished, the only bright spot in it was a small fire in a rusty grate, flanked by two bricks to prevent burning too much fuel.

There was a vacant place at the table for Charles, and he sat down upon a stool and ate as ravenously as though he had not tasted food for months. Meanwhile the tall man at the head of the table talked solemnly to his wife at the other end, using strange long words which none of the children could understand.

Supper over, Mr. and Mrs. Dickens (for that was their name) and the two younger children sat before the tiny fire, and Mr. Dickens talked of how he might raise enough money to pay his debts, leave the prison, and start fresh in some new business. Charles had heard these same plans from his father's lips a thousand times before, and so he took from the cupboard an old book which he had bought at a little second-hand shop a few days before, a small tattered copy of *Don Quixote*, and read it by the light of a tallow candle in the corner.

The lines soon blurred before the boy's tired eyes, his head nodded, and he was fast asleep. He was awakened by his father's deep voice. "Time to be leaving, Charles, my son. You have not forgotten that my pecuniary situation prevents my choosing the hour at which I shall close the door of my house. Fortunately, it is a predicament which I trust will soon be obviated to our mutual satisfaction."

The small fellow stood up, shook hands solemnly with his father, kissed his mother, and took his way out of the great prison. Open doors on various landings gave him pictures of many peculiar households; sometimes he would stop as though to consider some unusually puzzling face or figure.

Into the night again he went, and wound through a dismal labyrinth of the dark and narrow streets of old London. Sometimes a rough voice or an evil face would frighten him, and he would take to his heels and run as fast as he could. When he passed the house where he had asked for Mr. Fagin he chuckled to himself; he would not have had his friend know for worlds that his family's home was the Marshalsea Prison.

Even that room in the prison, however, was more cheerful than the small back-attic chamber where the boy fell asleep for the second time that night. He slept on a bed made up on the floor, but his slumber was no less deep on that account.

The noise of workmen in a timber-yard under his window woke Charles when it seemed much too dark to be morning. It was, however, and he was quickly dressed, and making his

breakfast from the penny cottage loaf of bread, a section of cream-cheese, and small bottle of milk, which were all he could afford to buy from the man who rented him the room. Then he took the roll of paper marked with the name of the day from the drawer of his bureau and counted out the pennies into his pocket. They were not many; he had to live on seven shillings a week, and he tucked them away very carefully in a pocket lest he lose them and have to do without his lunch.

He was not yet due at the blacking factory, but he hurried away from his room and joined the crowd of early morning people already on their way to work. He went down the embankment along the Thames until he came to a place where a bench was set in a corner of a wall. This was his favorite lounging-place; London Bridge was just beyond, the river lay in front of him, and he was far enough away from people to be secure from interruption. As he sat there watching the bridge and the Thames a small girl came to join him. She was no bigger than he, perhaps a year or two older, but her face was already shrewd enough for that of a grown-up woman. She was the maid-of-all-work at a house in the neighborhood, and she had fallen into the habit of stopping to talk for a few moments with the boy on her way to work in the morning. She liked to listen to his stories. This was his hour for inventing them. He could spin wonderful tales about London Bridge, the Tower, and the wharves along the river. Sometimes he made up stories about the people who passed in front of them, and they were such astonishing stories that the girl remembered them all day as she worked in the house. He seemed to believe them himself; his eyes would grow far away and dreamy and his words would run on and on until a neighboring clock brought him suddenly back to his own position.

"You do know a heap o' things, don't you?" said the little girl, lost in admiration. "I'd rather have a shillin', though, than all the fairy tales in the world."

"I wouldn't," said Charles, stoutly. "I'd rather read books than do anything else."

"You've got to eat, though," objected his companion, "and books won't make you food. 'Tain't common sense." She relented in an instant. "It's fun though, Charley Dickens. Good-bye till tomorrow."

Charles went on down to the old blacking factory by Hungerford Stairs, a ramshackle building almost hanging over the river, damp and overrun with rats. His place was in a recess of the counting-room on the first floor, and as he covered the bottles with the oil-paper tops and tied them on with a string, he could look from time to time through a window at the slow coal-barges swinging down the river.

There were very few boys about the place. At lunchtime he

would wander off by himself, and, selecting his meal from a careful survey of several pastry-cook's windows, invest his money for the day in fancy cakes or a tart. He missed the company of friends of his own age. Even Fanny, his oldest sister, he only saw on Sundays, when she came back to the Marshalsea from the place where she worked to spend the day with her family. It was only grown-up people that he saw most of the time, and they were too busy with their own affairs to take much interest in the small shabby boy who looked just like any one of a thousand other children of the streets. In all the men at the factory it was only the big clumsy fellow named Fagin who would stop to chat with the lad. So it was that Charles was forced to make friends with whomever he could, people of any age or condition; and was driven to spend much of his spare time roaming about the streets, lounging by the river, reading stray books by a candle in the prison or in the little attic where he slept. It was not a boyhood that seemed to promise much.

In time the boy left the factory and tried being a lawyer's clerk, then a reporter, and at last wrote a book of his own. The book was *Pickwick Papers*, and it was so original that people clamored for more. Then the young man took note of all the strange types of people among whom he had lived as a boy, and those days of poverty and drudgery were turned to wonderful account because he could write of such people and such scenes as he remembered them. The little maid-of-all-work became the "Marchioness," in the *Old Curiosity Shop*, Bob Fagin loaned his name to *Oliver Twist*, and in *David Copperfield* we read the story of the small boy who had to fight his way through London alone. Those days of his boyhood had given him a deep insight into human nature, into the humor and pathos of other people's lives; and it was that rare insight that enabled him to become in time one of the greatest of all English writers, Charles Dickens, the beloved novelist of the Anglo-Saxon people.

Kate Douglas Wiggin

A JOURNEY WITH DICKENS

ILLUSTRATED BY *Decie Merwin*

IT SEEMS to me that no child nowadays has time to love an author as the children and young people of that generation loved Dickens; nor do I think that any living author of today provokes love in exactly the same fashion. From our yellow dog, Pip, to the cat, the canary, the lamb, the cow, down to all the hens and cocks, almost every living thing was named, sooner or later, after one of Dickens's characters; while my favorite sled, painted in brown, with the title in brilliant red letters, was "The Artful Dodger." Why did we do it? We little creatures couldn't have suspected that "the democratic movement in literature had come to town," as Richard Whiteing says; nevertheless, we responded to it vigorously, ardently, and swelled the hero's public.

We never read newspapers save the weekly *Portland Transcript*, so that there was a moment of thrilling excitement when my mother, looking up from the *Portland Press*, told us that Mr. Dickens was coming to America, and that he was even then sailing from England. I remember distinctly that I prayed for him fervently several times during the next week, that the voyage might be a safe one, and that even the pangs of seasickness might be spared so precious a personage. In due time we heard that he had arrived in New York, and had begun the series of readings from his books; then he came to Boston, which was still nearer, and then—day of unspeakable excitement!—we learned that he had been prevailed upon to give one reading in Portland, which was only sixteen miles away from our village.

It chanced that my mother was taking me to Charlestown, Massachusetts, to pay a visit to an uncle on the very day after the one appointed for the great event in Portland. She, therefore, planned to take me into town the night before, and to invite the cousin, at whose house we were to sleep, to attend the reading with her. I cannot throw a more brilliant light on the discipline of that period than to say that the subject of my attending the reading was never once mentioned. The price of tickets was supposed to be almost prohibitory. I cannot remember the exact sum; I only know that it was mentioned with bated breath in the village of Hollis, and that there was a general feeling in the community that any one who paid it would have to live down a reputation for riotous extravagance forever afterward. I neither wailed nor wept, nor made any attempt to set aside the parental decrees (which were anything but severe in our family), but if any martyr in Fox's "Book" ever suffered more poignant anguish than I, I am heartily sorry for him; yet my common sense assured me that a child could hardly hope to be taken on a week's junketing to Charlestown and expect any other entertainment to be added to it for years to come. The definition of a "pleasure" in the State of Maine, county of York, village of Hollis, year of our Lord 1868, was something that could not reasonably occur too often without being cheapened.

The days, charged with suppressed excitement, flew by. I bade good-bye to my little sister, who was not to share my metropolitan experiences, and my mother and I embarked for Portland on the daily train that dashed hither and thither at the rate of about twelve miles an hour. When the august night and moment arrived, my mother and her cousin set out for the Place, and the moment they were out of sight I slipped out of the door and followed them, traversing quickly the three or four blocks that separated me from the old City Hall and the Preble House, where Dickens was stopping. I gazed at all the windows and all the entrances of both buildings without beholding any trace of my hero. I watched the throng of happy, excited, lucky people crowding the streets on their way to the hall, and went home in a chastened mood to bed—a bed which, as soon as I got into it, was crowded with Little Nell and the Marchioness, Florence Dombey, Bella Wilfer, Susan Nipper, and Little Em'ly. There were other dreams, too. Not only had my idol provided me with human friends, to love and laugh and weep over, but he had wrought his genius into *things;* so that, waking or sleeping, every bunch of holly or mistletoe, every plum pudding was alive; every crutch breathed of Tiny Tim; every cricket, and every singing, steaming kettle, had a soul.

The next morning we started on our railroad journey, which I remember as being full of excitement from the beginning, for both men and women were discussing the newspapers with extraordinary interest, the day before having been the one on which the President of the United States had been formally impeached. When the train stopped for two or three minutes at North Berwick, the people on the side of the car next the station suddenly arose and looked eagerly out at some object of apparent interest. I was not, at any age, a person to sit still in her seat when others were looking out of windows, and my small nose was quickly flattened against one of the panes. There on the platform stood the Adored One! It was unbelievable, but there he was in the flesh; standing smiling, breathing, like ordinary human beings. There was no doubt, then, that "angels and ministers of grace," called authors, had bodies and could not only write *David Copperfields*, but could be seen with the naked eye. That face, known to me from many pictures, must have looked in some mysterious way into the face of Dora, of Agnes, of Paul Dombey, of Little Dorrit! My spirit gave a leap and entered a new, an unknown world.

Dickens's hands were plunged deep in his pockets (a favorite gesture), but presently one was removed to wave away laughingly a piece of famous Berwick sponge cake, offered him by Mr. Osgood, of Boston, his traveling companion and friend. I knew him at once!—the smiling, genial, mobile face, rather highly colored, the brilliant eyes, the watch-chain, the carnation in the buttonhole, and the expressive hands, much given to gesture. It was only a momentary view, for the train started, and Dickens vanished, to resume his place in the car next to ours,

where he had been, had I known it, ever since we left Portland.

When my mother was again occupied with her book, I slipped away, and, borne along by some resistless and hitherto unrecognized force, I entered the next car; which did not seem at all to me a vehicle carrying Tom, Dick, and Harry to Boston, but a sort of traveling shrine or altar. I took a humble, unoccupied seat near the end, close by the much patronized tank of (unsterilized) drinking-water and the train-boy's basket of popcorn balls and molasses candy, and gazed steadily at the famous man, who was chatting busily with Mr. Osgood. I remembered gratefully that my mother had taken the old ribbons off my gray velvet hat and tied me down with a pretty new one under the chin, and I thought, if Dickens should happen to rest his eye upon me, that he could hardly fail to be pleased with the effect of the new ribbon that went under my collar and held a very small squirrel muff in place. Unfortunately, however, his eye did not meet mine, and my toilette made no sensation in any quarter, but some family friends espied me, and sent me back to ask my mother to come in and sit with them. I brought her back, and, fortunately, there was not room enough for me with the party, so I gladly resumed my modest seat by the popcorn boy, where I could watch Dickens, quite unnoticed.

There is an Indian myth which relates that when the gaze of the Siva rested for the first time on Tellatonea, the most beautiful of women, his desire to see her was so great that his body became all eyes. Such a transformation, I fear, was perilously near to being my fate! Half an hour passed, perhaps, and one gentleman after another came from here or there to exchange a word of greeting with the famous novelist, so that he was never for a moment alone, thereby inciting in my breast my first, and about my last, experience of the passion of jealousy. Suddenly, however, Mr. Osgood arose, and with an apology went into the smoking-car. I never knew how it happened; I had no plan, no preparation, no intention, certainly no provocation; but invisible ropes pulled me out of my seat, and speeding up the aisle, I planted myself breathlessly and timorously down, an unbidden guest, in the seat of honor. I had a moment to recover my

equanimity, for Dickens was looking out of the window, but he turned suddenly and said with justifiable surprise:

"God bless my soul, child, where did you come from?"

My heart was in my mouth, but there was still room to exercise my tongue, which was generally the case. I was frightened, but not so completely frightened as if I had been meeting a stranger. You see I knew him, even if he did not know me; so I became immediately autobiographical, although palpitating with nervousness. I had to tell him, I thought, where I came from, who I was, where I was going, or how could I account for myself and my presence beside him in Mr. Osgood's seat? So I began, stammeringly, to answer his question.

"I came from Hollis, Maine, and I'm going to Charlestown to visit my uncle. My mother and her cousin went to your reading last night, but of course three couldn't go from the same family, it was so expensive, so I stayed at home. Nora, that's my little sister, is left behind in Hollis. She's too small to go on a journey, but she wanted to go to the reading dreadfully. There was a lady there who had never heard of Betsey Trotwood and had only read two of your books!"

"Well, upon my word!" he said; "you do not mean to say that you have read them!"

"Of course!" I replied; "every one of them but the two that we are going to buy in Boston, and some of them six times."

"Bless my soul!" he ejaculated again. "Those long thick books, and you such a slip of a thing."

"Of course," I explained conscientiously, "I do skip some of the very dull parts once in a while; not the short dull parts, but the long ones."

He laughed heartily. "Now, that is something that I hear very little about," he said. "I distinctly want to learn more about those very long dull parts."

And, whether to amuse himself, or to amuse me, I do not know, he took out a notebook and pencil from his pocket and proceeded to give me an exhausting and exhaustive examination on this subject; the books in which the dull parts predominated; and the characters and subjects which principally produced them. He chuckled so constantly during this operation that I could hardly help believing myself extraordinarily agreeable, so I continued dealing these infant blows, under the delusion that I was flinging him bouquets.

It was not long before one of my hands was in his, and his arm around my waist, while we talked of many things. They say, I believe, that his hands were "undistinguished" in shape, and that he wore too many rings. Well, those criticisms must come from persons who never felt the warmth of his handclasp! For my part, I am glad that Pullman chair cars had not come into fashion, else I should never have experienced the delicious joy of snuggling up to Genius, and of being distinctly encouraged in the attitude.

I wish I could recall still more of his conversation, but I was too happy, too exhilarated, and too inexperienced to take conscious notes of the interview. I remember feeling that I had never known anybody so well and so intimately, and that I talked with him as one talks under cover of darkness or before the flickering light of a fire. It seems to me, as I look back now, and remember how the little soul of me came out and sat in the sunshine of his presence, that I must have had some premonition that the child, who would come to be one of the least of writers, was then talking with one of the greatest;—talking, too, as it were, of the author's profession and high calling, for were we not discussing books? All the little details of the meeting stand out as clearly as though it had happened yesterday. I can see every article of his clothing and of my own; the other passengers in the car; the landscape through the window; and above all the face of Dickens, deeply lined, with sparkling eyes and an amused, waggish smile that curled the corners of his mouth under his grizzled mustache. A part of our conversation was given to a Boston newspaper next day, by the author himself, or by Mr. Osgood, and was long preserved in our family archives, while a little more was added a few years after by an old lady who sat in the next seat to us. (The pronoun "us" seems ridiculously intimate, but I have no doubt I used it, quite unabashed, at that date.)

"What book of mine do you like best?" Dickens asked, I remember; and I answered with the definite assurance of childhood, "Oh, I like *David Copperfield* much the best. That is the one I have read six times."

"Six times—good, good!" he replied; "I am glad that you like Davy, so do I;—I like it best, too!" clapping his hands; and that was the only remark he made which attracted the attention of the other passengers, who glanced in our direction now and then, I have been told, smiling at the interview, but preserving its privacy with the utmost friendliness. I had never looked behind to see how my mother was faring. There are great crises in life when even mothers must retire to the background. For the moment I had no mother, family, friends, or acquaintances, no home, no personality; I was a sort of atom floating in space, half conscious that I could not float forever, but must come to earth again.

"I almost said *Great Expectations*," I added presently, "because that comes next in our family. We named our little yellow dog 'Mr. Pip' out of your book. They told Father when they gave him to us that he was part rat terrier, and we were all pleased, because, if he was, he wasn't all mongrel. (That means mixed-up.) Then one day Father showed him a trap with a mouse in it. The mouse wiggled its tail just a little, and Pip was so frightened that he ran under the barn and stayed the rest of the day. That showed that there wasn't enough rat terrier in him to be right, and the neighbors made fun of him and used to call 'Rats!' when he went down the street. We loved him just the same and he had as hard a time as Pip in *Great Expectations.*"

Here again my new friend's mirth was delightful to behold, so much so that my embarrassed mother, who had been watching me for half an hour, almost made up her mind to drag me away before the very eyes of our fellow passengers. I had never been thought an amusing child in the family circle; what, then, could I be saying to the most distinguished and popular author in the universe?

Dickens here told me little stories about English dogs, but I remember them too vaguely to repeat them or give them their inimitable mingling of fact and nonsense. "Have you only one dog?" he asked.

"We had another," I answered, "a big curly one called John Brent, out of a novel, but he died, and we take all our names from your books now. We know a dog who stays with us most of the time. He doesn't belong to anybody and he likes to visit Pip, so we named him Mr. Pocket after Mr. Pip's friend. The real Mr. Pip and Mr. Pocket met first in Miss Havisham's garden and they had such a funny fight it always makes Father laugh till he can't read properly! Then they became great friends. Perhaps you remember Mr. Pip and Mr. Pocket?" And Dickens thought he did, which, perhaps, is not strange, considering that he was the author of their respective beings.

Mr. Harry Furniss declares that *Great Expectations* was Dickens's favorite novel, but I can only say that to me he avowed his special fondness for *David Copperfield.* I can never forget that and never be mistaken in my remembrance of it.

"Did you want to go to my reading very much, child?" was another question. Here was a subject that had never once been touched upon in all the past days—a topic that stirred the very depths of my disappointment and sorrow, fairly choking me, and making my lip tremble by its unexpectedness, as I faltered, "Yes, I did, more than tongue can tell! I know how I feel when I read one of the books, but I wanted to hear how it sounded."

I looked up a second later, when I was sure that the tears in my eyes were not going to fall, and to my astonishment saw that Dickens's eyes were in precisely the same state of moisture. That was a never-to-be-forgotten moment, although I was too young to appreciate the full significance of it.

"Do you cry when you read out loud, too?" I asked curiously. "We all do in our family. And we never read about Tiny Tim, or about Steerforth when his body is washed up on the beach, on Saturday nights, for fear our eyes will be too swollen to go to Sunday School."

"Yes, I cry when I read about Steerforth," he answered quietly, and I felt no astonishment. "I cried when I wrote it, too! That is still more foolish!"

"Where do you cry the worst?" I asked. "Our time is when it says, '*All the men who carried him had known him and gone sailing with him and seen him merry and bold*' "; and here I grew tearful and reminiscent.

We were now fast approaching our destination—the station in Boston—and the passengers began to collect their wraps and bundles. Mr. Osgood had two or three times made his appearance, but had been waved away with a smile by Dickens—a smile that seemed to say, "You will excuse me, I know, but this child has the right of way."

"You are not traveling alone?" he asked, as he arose to put on his overcoat.

"Oh! my goodness!" I said, coming down to earth for the first time since I had taken my seat beside him—"certainly not; I had a mother, but I forgot all about her." Whereupon he said, "You are past-mistress of the art of flattery!"

But this remark was told me years afterwards by the old lady who was sitting in the next seat, and who overheard as much of the conversation as she possibly could, so she informed me. Her penciled notes, read to me when we met by chance in South Reading, Massachusetts, have helped me greatly in the minor details of the interview and my own phraseology, which amused her because of its chatterbox fluency and the amazing response it elicited from so great a man.

Dickens took me back to the forgotten mother, and introduced himself, and I, still clinging to his hand, left the car and walked with him down the platform until he disappeared in the carriage with Mr. Osgood, leaving me with the feeling that I must continue my existence somehow in a dull and dreary world.

That was my last glimpse of him, but pictures made in childhood are painted in bright hues, and this one has never faded. The child of today would hardly be able to establish so instantaneous a friendship. She would have heard of celebrity hunters and autograph collectors and be self-conscious, while I followed the dictates of my countrified little heart, and scraped acquaintance confidently with the magician who had glorified my childhood by his art.

Henry Thomas
and Dana Lee Thomas

THOMAS ALVA EDISON

ILLUSTRATED BY *Hardie Gramatky*

GENIUS is the ability to do the hardest things the easiest way. One day, when Edison was working on a practical lamp for his newly discovered electric light, he found it necessary to get the cubical content of an irregular glass bulb. Too busy himself to attend to the job, he called in his most brilliant mathematician to help him. Arming himself with many sheets of foolscap, the great savant sat down to work. A week later Edison asked him how he was getting along.

"Very nicely, Mr. Edison, but I am not finished yet."

Edison looked at the formidable array of charts and figures submitted by the mathematician. "How much longer will it take you to solve the problem?"

"Oh, another week, I expect."

"Let me show you how to do it in a minute," said Edison.

He filled the bulb with water.

"Now measure the water, and you've got the answer."

Edison possessed not only a knack for hitting upon the obvious, but an infinite capacity for taking pains. In his effort to perfect the storage battery, he had made ten thousand unsuccessful tests on various chemical combinations. "Isn't it a shame," said a friend, "that with all this tremendous labor you haven't been able to get any results?"

"Why, man," said Edison, "I've got lots of results. I've discovered several thousand things that won't work."

Edison came by his energy from a stock of sturdy pioneers who were forever seeking for the things that worked through the discarding of things that wouldn't work. His great-grandfather, John Edison, fled from Staten Island to Nova Scotia in order to escape hanging as a Tory in the Revolutionary War.

His grandfather, Samuel Edison, migrated from Nova Scotia in search of a better home and found it on the banks of the Otter River, in Upper Canada. His father, Samuel Edison—"a giant of a man"—became involved in a plot to overthrow the Tory regime in Canada and to replace it with a representative government like that of the United States. The plot was discovered, and "Sammy" Edison made his escape across trackless forests and icebound rivers—"it was my long legs that saved me"—until he found safety in the village of Milan, Ohio. Here he set up a mill and sent for his family through the kindly offices of a barge captain by the name of Alva Bradley. And here, in the midst of a blizzard on the morning of February 11, 1847, he greeted the arrival of his seventh child, a son. They christened the baby Thomas Alva—the second name in honor of Mr. Bradley.

From his very infancy Alva was preoccupied, ingenious, and ready to "learn something about everything." At six he set his father's barn on fire "just to see what it would do." It burned down to the ground, and almost burned Alva along with it. For this, the first of his experiments, his father punished him with a public spanking in the village square.

On another occasion he tried sitting on a nest of goose eggs to see if he could hatch them. All that he hatched was an omelet on the seat of his pants. Another spanking, another discovery of the things that wouldn't work.

His entire childhood was a succession of experiments. When he was seven years old his parents moved to Port Huron, Michigan. The new Edison home had a lofty tower overlooking Lake Huron and the St. Clair River. Young Alva—Al for short—spent a great part of his time scanning the horizon through an old telescope perched on top of the tower, watching the heavens above, and studying the elements below. In the cellar of his house he had set up a chemical laboratory with "Poison Don't Touch" labels on all the bottles, in order to keep them away from inquisitive fingers.

"An addled youngster," said the neighbors. One day he fed an enormous quantity of seidlitz powders to his little Dutch playmate, Michael Oates. "Why did you do it, son?" asked his father. "Well, Pop," said Alva, "I wanted to see if the seidlitz would form enough gas in his stomach to make him fly."

The children left him alone to his "crazy" games. The elders shook their heads. Even his father thought there was something queer about him. The only one who believed in him was his mother. She encouraged him in his experiments, and on his ninth birthday she bought him a copy of Parker's *School of Natural Philosophy.* "The greatest present I ever received," said Edison of this book many years later.

He used this book not only as a basis for his experiments but as a stimulant to his imagination. And he fed his healthy imagination on many another volume. By his tenth birthday he had familiarized himself with such works as Hume's *History of England*, Sears' *History of the World*, Burton's *Anatomy of Melancholy*, Gibbon's *Decline and Fall of the Roman Empire*, and the *Dictionary of Sciences.*

Yet Al Edison was no bookworm. On the contrary, he was a very practical youngster. When the railroad was built between Port Huron and Detroit, he applied for a job as "news-butcher" on the train. A "merchant on his own" at twelve, he wasn't content with only one occupation. In his spare moments, when he had finished peddling his newspapers, he busied himself in the baggage car, writing and printing a newspaper of his own, or in a chemical laboratory which he had set up in another car. This laboratory, incidentally, cost him his job on the train and thus indirectly led to his study of telegraphy and to his first invention. One day, as the train was bumping over a rough road, a stick of phosphorus from Edison's pile of chemicals fell to the floor and set fire to the baggage car. The conductor extinguished the flames and kicked Edison out of his railroad laboratory into the bigger laboratory of the world.

Al Edison—at that time he pronounced his name *Eadison*—was not sorry to lose his job as a news peddler. In his daily trips from city to city he had become acquainted with the telegraph operators at the railroad stations. Their work fascinated him. He decided to become one of them. Devoting as many as eighteen hours a day to practice, he soon mastered the job, stretched

a wire between the drugstore and the depot at Port Huron, and set himself up as a "private merchant of local messages." But the businessmen of the town preferred to receive and to deliver their local messages in person. His earnings averaged less than fifty cents a month.

Yet his knowledge of telegraphy, combined with his mental resourcefulness, enabled him to come to the rescue of his townsmen on one occasion when an ice jam had severed the wires between Port Huron and Canada. Due to the floating ice, it was impossible to make the repairs. But this did not phase Tom —he had now changed from his second to his first name. He promised to deliver the messages across the lake to Canada if they would supply him with a locomotive and an engineer. Smiling skeptically, the railroad authorities granted his request. But their skepticism changed to admiration when they saw the simplicity of his plan. All he did was to toot out a telegraph message on the engine in whistles of dots and dashes. At first there was no answer; but when Edison had repeated the message several times, a Canadian operator caught on and tooted back a message in reply. It was perhaps the first instance of "wireless telegraphy" on record.

A remarkably clever young fellow. And remarkably untidy. He spent his money on books and left practically nothing for his clothes. One winter he went without an overcoat and nearly froze to death. An experimenting vagabond. From city to city he drifted, and from job to job. Easily hired, easily fired. His ideas were too "crazy" for his superiors. Talked about sending two messages over a wire. "Why, any old fool knows that a wire can't be worked both ways at the same time." This "lunatic" was a bad influence upon the other fellows. "Out you go!"

And out he kept going, until finally he found his way to Boston. It was on a midwinter day in 1868 when he walked into the Boston office of the Western Union and asked for a job as a telegraph operator. The superintendent, George F. Milliken, looked up from his desk. What a disreputable-looking hobo! Pants too short and too tight and all but waterproof with smudge. Shoes torn and twisted out of shape. Hat so ragged that one of his ears protruded through a hole. Shirt a patchwork of tatters that hadn't been washed for weeks. And hair a matted jumble that seemingly had never known the touch of a comb.

Tom Edison had written from Canada to a Boston friend about this job, and the friend had shown the letter to Milliken. "If he can take it off the wire in such a script," said Milliken as he looked at the printlike handwriting of the letter, "tell him he can have the job."

But when Milliken looked at Edison, with his unkempt hair and his unwashed shirt and his rickety shoes, he was not quite so sure of the young fellow's ability. "Come back at five-thirty," he said reluctantly, "and perhaps I'll give you a trial."

Edison came back at the appointed hour and found the clerks grinning at their desks. They had prepared a practical joke against their country bumpkin who dared to ask for a job as a city telegrapher. They had wired to one of the fastest New York operators to send a special news report of eight hundred words, and now they sat back to see the fun.

Picking up a bundle of blanks, Edison placed himself at the table assigned to him. "Ready!" he signaled, and the message began to pour in. Faster and faster came the words, but Edison was equal to the job. As his fingers flew over the sheets, he glanced up; and then for the first time he understood the grin on the other fellows' faces. So they wanted to show him up, did they? Very well, he would teach them a lesson! Opening the key of his instrument, he tapped to the galloping operator at the other end: "Come on, boy, don't go to sleep. Shake yourself and get busy with the other foot."

The New York operator surrendered, and the clerks in the Boston office rushed up to Edison and showered him with their congratulations. Right then and there they acknowledged him as the fastest telegraph operator in the Western Union.

"Any old fool knows that a wire can't be worked both ways." Again and again the skeptics kept reminding Edison of this natural "fact." But Edison persisted in his experiments and proved the "fact" to be a fiction. In the May issue of 1868 the *Journal of The Telegraph* made the announcement that Edison has "achieved the impossible." A few months later the following note appeared in the same journal:

"T. A. Edison has resigned his situation in the Western Union office, Boston, and will devote his time to his inventions."

A daring step for a penniless young man. It meant foodless days and sleepless nights. Offers to sell his inventions, delays, refusals, disappointments, but never despair. "You wait, they will come to me yet."

And they came to him sooner even than he had dreamed. A shrewd businessman for whom Edison had once worked, General Marshal Lefferts, was watching his inventions. He saw their financial possibilities. One day he summoned the hungry wizard to his office. "What will you take for all your contraptions?"

Edison thought quickly. Should he ask for three thousand? He could manage with that sum for the present. Five thousand? Oh no, that was preposterous! Lefferts would most likely kick him out of the office if he dared to mention that sum.

"Make me an offer, General."

"Very well, would you accept forty thousand?"

Until he received his check, Edison wasn't sure whether Lefferts had said *four* thousand or *forty* thousand. When he looked at the check he almost fainted. What would he do with all this fabulous amount of money?

Yet the fabulous amount melted away in a fabulously short time. His experiments always ran ahead of his cash. Opening a workshop in Newark, he paid the highest possible wages for the best possible workmen. "I have one shop which employs eighteen men," he wrote to his parents, "and I am fitting up another shop which will employ one hundred and fifty men." He had no accountant and kept no books. On one hook he hung all the bills he owed; on another, all the bills owed him. "This is the simplest sort of bookkeeping. Why ball myself up with all kinds of complicated figures?"

And thus, pouring his money and his mind into the secret crucibles of nature, he went on with his experiments. Multiple telegraphy—two, four, eight messages over a single wire at the same time. An electric stock-ticker instrument. An instrument that reproduced the human voice—"I'll bet you a barrel of apples against three dollars," he challenged the skeptics, "that this instrument will talk." An Aladdin's lamp that would light up the world with a new electric force. Crude discoveries thus far, mere foreshadowings of the miracles that he was to perform in these fields later on.

All work and work, save for a brief vacation to the "Wild West"—and time off to get married. Hardly a prepossessing bridegroom. Refused to wear white gloves at his wedding. "I've married a bear of a man," said his wife—the former Mary Stillwell—"But what an adorable bear!" Though gruff and absent-minded toward the rest of the world, he was all tenderness toward Mary.

And, later on, toward the children—Marion and Tommy. He nicknamed them *Dot* and *Dash*. It was his greatest pleasure to play the clown for them in his spare moments. "He would don Mary's dresses"—we are quoting his sister-in-law Alice, who lived with the Edisons—"and romp and play around the house with the youngsters. They had a stereopticon and he would sometimes go behind the screen and stand on his head, and go through various antics to amuse them."

And there were times when to amuse his children meant the greatest physical torture. "He was a great sufferer from earache"—again we are quoting Alice—"and I have seen him sit on the edge of a bed and fairly grind holes in the carpet with the heels of his shoes, he would be suffering such pain."

A little play, much work, incessant pain, and an infinite patience—these were the ingredients which, combined with a flaming imagination, enabled Edison to transmute matter into motion and light. But most important of all, perhaps, was his extraordinary memory for details—his ability to co-ordinate apparently isolated facts into a coherent unit. Edison's memory was the amazement of psychologists. It was almost photographic in its scope. One day, as he was working over the plans for a new mechanical device in a cement plant, he examined the old machine, went home without having jotted down a single note, and compiled a list of six hundred items in the old machine that required modification or improvement. Hardly a bolt or a screw had failed to impress itself upon the retina of his mental eye.

His retentive memory was like a well-stocked and well-organized mechanic's toolbox. Everything was in its logical place; and whenever he wanted to put several facts together, he could get at them without any waste of time or unnecessary fumbling. As a result of this faculty of orderly analysis, he was able to do more constructive thinking in a day than the average man is able to do in a lifetime.

But his inclusive memory and his ability to mold individual facts into related units would never have got him very far were it not for his endurance. As a general rule, he slept only four hours a day. "Life," he said, "is too important to waste in excessive snoring. There are too many things to be done. There are so many experiments waiting, and it takes so long to bring even a single experiment to a definite conclusion." It took him many years to perfect some of his inventions—years of incessant toil, sixteen hours, seventeen hours, sometimes even eighteen hours a day. "I have no time for loafing as yet," he said on his sixty-seventh birthday. "I shall begin to loaf when I am eighty."

A sublime endurance, an equally sublime courage. In 1915 his laboratory at West Orange, consisting of six buildings, burned down to the ground. The buildings were not insured, and the loss amounted to five million dollars. "That's all right," he said, "I'll make a fresh start tomorrow morning. No one's ever too old to make a fresh start."

While he was in the midst of his experiments with the electric bulb there was a sudden blackout in his own household. His wife Mary died of a heart attack. Eighteen months of mourning, and then he married again. In his personal habits he was still very much of a baby and needed someone to mother him. And fortunately his second wife, Mina Miller, proved, like his first wife, to be a good mother and congenial companion. It takes great patience to live with a genius. But it gives great satisfaction. Mina was able not only to appreciate his inventions but to share his thoughts. He often discussed his philosophy with her at the dinner table. He was profoundly interested in the mystery of life. He believed that every atom within the body, like the entire body itself, possesses an individual intelligence. "Look at the thousand ways in which atoms of hydrogen combine with other atoms to form the most diverse substances. Do you mean to tell me that they do this without intelligence?"

And then he went on to clarify this thought. "Atoms in harmonious and useful combinations assume beautiful shapes and colors, or give forth a pleasant perfume. In sickness, death, decomposition, or filth, the disagreement of the component atoms immediately makes itself felt by bad odors."

And the upshot of it all? The final union of the most intelligent atoms into the most intelligent substance. "Gathered together in certain forms, the atoms constitute animals of the lower orders. At last they combine in man, who represents the total intelligence of all the atoms."

"But where," asked Mina, "does all this come from?"

"From some power greater than ourselves."

"Then you believe in an intelligent Creator?"

"I certainly do. The existence of a personal God can, to my mind, almost be demonstrated by chemistry."

Edison was not only a great inventor but a constructive idealist. He was interested primarily in the things that further the plans of God. In his own experiments he aimed at the inventions that serve life, and not at those that produce death. "Making things which kill men," he once said, "is against my fiber. I would rather make people laugh."

This was the principal objective of his life—to bring laughter into the hearts of the people. More laughter and greater light. "The world has been steeped in darkness long enough."

The invention of the electric light was the direct outgrowth of Edison's philosophy. And it was as simple in its conception as it was eventful in its result. It was one of those surprising discoveries of the obvious. If electricity can produce power and heat, argued Edison, there is no reason why it shouldn't produce light—provided we can find something that will burn properly under the stimulus of heat and power. And so he began to seek a substance, which, like the bush of Moses, would burn without being consumed. In this quest Edison was not alone. Many others, on both sides of the Atlantic, had thought of electric lighting. An American inventor, J. W. Starr, had worked on incandescent lamps even before Edison was born. Another American, Moses G. Farmer, had provided his sitting room with a number of crude electric lamps twenty years before Edison's

HARDIE GRAMATKY

invention of incandescent light. In England, in France, and in Russia a number of scientists were producing equally crude lamps that would flare up for a short time and then flicker out. But Edison's chief rival in the search for the secret of practical and permanent electrical illumination was W. E. Sawyer. This American inventor had much of the brilliance, but little of the patience, of Edison. It was Edison who sat tirelessly in his laboratory, trying out one filament after another in his vacuum bulbs, ransacking every nook and cranny of the earth for the fiber that would give a brilliant and steady and, so far as possible, indestructible glow. And it was Edison who, refusing to admit defeat in the face of financial failure and the jeers of the scientific and journalistic world, finally discovered the magic fiber—a carbon filament which, heated in a vacuum bulb, radiated light. On New Year's Eve, 1879, a throng of people from the surrounding cities had come to Edison's laboratory at Menlo Park, New Jersey. The ground of the little village was covered with snow. Suddenly, the switch of a button, and the darkness bloomed into a silver radiance under the flood of a dozen street lamps. On that New Year's Eve the genius of Edison had, for the first time in history, transformed night into day.

Just before the miracle had happened, a leading New York editor had exclaimed: "It has been absolutely proved that this sort of light is impossible—it is against the laws of Nature!"

Edison has been accused of being a second-rate inventor and a first-rate businessman. He capitalized, it has been said, on the inventions of others. This accusation is, we believe, unfounded. It is true that others worked simultaneously with Edison on many of the inventions for which he is credited. But Edison worked harder and faster than the rest of them. And he worked under the handicap of his chronic earaches and his deafness. Indeed, he turned his handicap into an advantage. "It takes a deaf man to hear music," he remarked when he was experimenting on the phonograph. And when he was asked to explain this paradox, he said: "Most people hear only through their ears. I hear through my teeth and through my skull. Ordinarily I place my head against the phonograph. If there is some faint sound that I don't quite catch this way, I bite into the wood and I get it good and strong."

It was this faculty of hearing through his teeth and skull that enabled him to improve upon Alexander Graham Bell's invention of the telephone. Bell's instrument had been quite definitely a primitive mechanism, owing to the fact that it had been designed to serve both as a transmitter and a receiver. But Edison transformed it into an object of practical utility by giving it a separate mouthpiece and earpiece, instead of allowing the same tube to be used clumsily for both purposes. It sounds simple today. But it took Edison to think of it.

And many of the "simple" things that today make life worth living have had their origin in the magical laboratory of Edison's thought. Almost to the last day of his eighty-four years he worked on his experiments—an inspired, whimsical, untidy, modest, gentle, shrewd, and indefatigable Merlin. Out of his sorcerer's brain came an endless stream of electrical and mechanical servants to bring new amusements and new comforts to the human race. His inventions of the phonograph, the electric light, the motion picture, and the first crude "talkie" are merely the most popular of his hundreds of vital contributions to the applied science of the present day. His was perhaps the most universal mind in America during the nineteenth century. Once, when he visited Luther Burbank in his garden at Santa Rosa, the "plant wizard" asked him to register in his guest book. The pages of the guest book were divided into four columns:

Name *Address* *Occupation* *Interested In*

Under the caption *Interested In*, Edison wrote: "Everything."

. . . In his endless quest for the practical, he was never satisfied with his past achievement. Always he looked toward the future. His prophetic vision saw many years ahead of the contemporary needs of his country. It is interesting to note that one of his very last experiments when death overtook him (1931) was concerned with the production of synthetic rubber.

And death itself, he was convinced, is but the transition into a new laboratory for greater experiments.

LOUISA MAY ALCOTT, author of *Little Women,* the story of her own early struggles, was one of the first great writers for boys and girls. Louisa obtained her education from her father Bronson Alcott, the philosopher friend of Emerson and Thoreau. She sold her first story at sixteen, but her first successful book was *Hospital Sketches,* her experience as an army nurse in the War between the States. *Little Men, Eight Cousins,* and *Under the Lilacs* were other famous books by this great American writer, books that continue through the years to be read and re-read by young and old. Here are some of her earlier experiences.

Cornelia Meigs

EARLY DAYS WITH INVINCIBLE LOUISA

ILLUSTRATED BY *James Ponter*

THE ALCOTT FAMILY was moving. It was not the first time, as we well know, nor yet the last; for, in the first twenty-eight years of Louisa's life, this household was to achieve the record of twenty-nine moves. Scars on the mahogany and walnut dressers bore witness, now, of perhaps a dozen upheavals through which they and the Alcotts had gone together. Louisa, standing on the threshold and watching the low-posted beds and the horsehair sofas come staggering in, was now thirteen years old.

Moving had never ceased to be an adventure with the casual Alcotts, and, with the exception of that single, heavy-hearted departure from Fruitlands,* was invariably a gay occasion. The rambling brown house, which was now to be their domicile, re-

*Fruitlands was a farm run by the Alcotts and other impractical idealists who believed in the philosophy called Transcendentalism. After a hard struggle the experiment failed.

sounded with cheery voices all along its dark passages. The corridors offered steps up and steps down, to betray unwary feet not yet used to the small individualities which every one expected in houses of the Revolutionary period. No one, however, cared about such small inconveniences. Louisa's spirit thrilled to the adventure of taking up life in a new place, in a storybook old dwelling with a pine-covered hill behind it, and with a gate opening upon the Concord-to-Lexington highroad. Down that road Paul Revere had galloped; over the pine-covered hill had marched a company of redcoats to take part in the first battle of the Revolution. The family was glad to come back to Concord, the peaceful, pleasant town with its square white houses and with its neighbors who were all friends.

Since leaving Fruitlands two years before, they had dwelt, first for eight months in Still River, later for a short time in Concord, taken into the house of a good friend who was glad to help them in their extremity. Finally they moved to Boston, where Abba as well as Bronson looked for work for the support of the family. Now, however, under the suggestion of that unfailing friend, Mr. Emerson, and with his help, they were returning to Concord, this time to reside in a house that actually belonged to them. It seemed as though at last they might be settling upon some permanent plan of living. They decided to name the house Hillside; it is now known as Wayside.

The big, wooden dwelling had been surrounded, at first, with various buildings, sheds, a wheelwright's shop, and a barn across the way. Mrs. Alcott, with vigorous enterprise, had the barn moved to their side of the road, had the shop cut in two and each half attached to an end of the house. In one of these two small wings was a little room which was to be Louisa's very own, where she could keep all her treasures, write and read, and do whatsoever she liked. It had a door into the garden, so that she could run outside, under the trees, whenever the fancy seized her. How long she had desired just this, a place of her very own!

The house had eight outside doors, so that, as they were settling to the table, or to read about the lamp in the low-ceilinged sitting room, a rap somewhere would send every member of the family flying, each one to a separate door, to admit the arriving friend. It was there, with a great deal of flurry and fluttering, that the household sat down at last, that evening of the moving-in. Anna had been busy in the kitchen; Louisa had kindled crackling fires in the numerous fireplaces. The smaller children were washed, and Bronson came out from the congenial task of unpacking his books. Around the table there began a hilarious account of the adventures of the day, each person having her own joke to tell of the absurd mishaps which go with moving, of the things which were lost and broken, of the lack of things which could not be had in a household where money was still as scarce as good spirits were abundant.

In Louisa's eyes, the two great assets of the new abode were the little room in the wing, and the barn. The Alcotts never kept a horse, although the girls often dreamed of galloping down the shady Concord roads, as did the more fortunate members of their acquaintance. There are, however, a hundred good uses for a roomy barn, other than those intended by the original builder. As every one knows, barns are particularly well suited for dramatic purposes. The drama, at that time, was Louisa's ruling passion. It is probable that before she slept that night, she was already busy outlining plots wherein beautiful heroines were rescued from dungeons, and princesses, disguised as slaves, won the hearts of disillusioned kings. As soon as the little room was in order, very bare and neat, with the scent of dried herbs in the closet, Louisa sat herself down to the table and fell to creating. Thus were born not only Duke Roderigo, but Duke Roderigo's boots.

Some little time later the Alcotts' Concord friends were invited to witness the first, and possibly the only performance, of a drama in three acts by Louisa Alcott, enacted, from the hero and the villain down to the page boy who brings in the cup of poison, by the four Alcott girls: stage manager and mistress of costumes, Louisa Alcott. She was good at creative dressmaking and knew just what her characters should wear. The hero was of the extravagantly noble kind, full of splendid motives and

manly virtues. It was absolutely impossible to portray him without a slashed doublet, a sash, and tall, romantic boots. Louisa, with her vigorous mixture of fanciful and practical energy, made not only the hero, but the boots as well.

Somewhere she laid hands upon some skins of tanned leather and cut out crude profiles of what she imagined a nobleman's boots to be. These she sewed together, over and over, as a less enterprising young person sews patchwork. The result was truly magnificent. To walk any distance in the boots would have been quite impossible; but noblemen of Louisa's kind did not walk, fortunately; they strode a few paces to the rescue of captive maidens. Louisa trod the boards of the barn theater through her first play, in a blaze of glory. The curtain went down to applause which shook the old barn rafters. Some of the acclaim was for Anna, who was a really gifted actress, some of it was for Louisa; and a great deal of it was, deservedly, for the boots.

Excited and delighted by her first success, Louisa worked away in the little room, writing more and more dramas of the same sort. So many plots came crowding to her brain that from plays she overflowed into stories of the same grandiloquent sort. They were cut out, as the boots had been, by the pattern of what she imagined the life of the high nobility to be, and they were put together with the same industrious ingenuity.

Between the stories and plays she dreamed long dreams of the great things she hoped to do. "Am I going to be an actress," she wondered, "or a playwright, or a story writer?" She had no idea which it was to be.

Whatever it was, she was going to be it with all her might. Yet underneath her soaring fancies there lay a firm foundation of practical resolution. She saw plainly that her father, though recovered now, had very little real knowledge of the jostling world about him, that her mother was worn and worried over the problems of living. She could see that her sister Anna was as ambitious as herself, that Elizabeth was not strong, and that little May was growing up with a beauty-loving nature of passionate intensity. No children ever loved one another and their parents more than did the Alcotts. The way in which Louisa adored them all, as the years passed, could never be put into words,—the way she loved and intended to take care of them.

There in the little room she made what she called the plan of her life and vowed to herself that she would give these beloved ones what each one needed. There was to be security for her father, peace and comfort and "a sunny room" for her mother, opportunity for Anna, care for Beth, education for May. One of the most interesting tales in the world is the record of how resolutely Louisa kept that promise and how, no matter what things went against her, she always refused to be beaten.

She was not, however, taken up continually with thoughts of the drama and of the future. She still ran in the fields and climbed the hills; she loved to sit under the pine trees on the ridge behind the house and think long, intense thoughts. Through all that first summer at Hillside she was free and happy. She would write busily in the little room, undisturbed, and would often work late into the evening. When she was tired at last, she would put down her pen and run out into the garden.

Louisa was as busy in her little room as her heroine Jo was in her garret

The grass would be dewy and soft under her feet, the tall fruit trees would be dark against the stars. She loved to climb up into the crooked, comfortable branches and sit there, dreaming, until her thoughts had traveled far away from ordinary things. She would look back, within her memory, upon Fruitlands and all that incomprehensible incident which still cast a dark memory over their lives. She would wonder whether it was over and whether they were going to follow an ordinary existence now, to the end of their days. She hoped that they would not.

It is not certain whether she ever knew of the very last act in that curious drama of Fruitlands. Abba Alcott, whose struggle for the safety of her family had been so silent and so desperate, Abba whose will had stood against Charles Lane's and had finally won the day, seems in the end to have regretted her victory. Bronson's illness and despondency lasted so long, his heartfelt sorrow over the failure of the experiment was so great, that at last even his wife's brave determination faltered. She sat down and wrote a letter, such a letter as once she never would have dreamed that she could indite. She wrote to Charles Lane and asked him to come back, asked him to take up work once more with Bronson, so that he might be happy again. She knew what such a thing meant. But she asked Charles Lane to come.

With what agony of anxiety she must have waited for his answer. As has been said, she was a woman of most intense feeling. We know she was, for otherwise she could not have humbled her pride and put by her greatest desire for the sake of her affection for Bronson Alcott. Perhaps not even he knew of her offer; it seems scarcely possible that she told the girls of it. The reply came at last. Charles Lane had not continued with the Shakers, whom he had joined on leaving Fruitlands. Somehow that connection also had been unhappy. He was going back to England. With his departure, the shadow of his presence vanished from their lives forever. The Alcotts never saw him again.

One former member of the Fruitlands establishment, Joseph Palmer, came back to buy the abandoned land and to keep up a strange sort of idealized existence on the old place. He vowed that no traveler should ever go away hungry from his door. On one side of the farmhouse hearth stood a great iron pot of beans, on the other a similar one full of potatoes. Any one was welcome to come in and help himself. Destitute people took refuge there, sometimes staying for months or years. Joseph Palmer and his wife, Nancy, made no profession of being Transcendental philosophers; their only system of thought was a complete overflowing of human kindness. Yet there was nothing weak and vacillating about the character of old Joseph. A farmer near him, Silas Dudley by name, disputed with Palmer the right of way across Dudley's land from the Fruitlands farm down to the high road.

Mr. Emerson recounted to the Alcotts how, when a deep snow fell, Joseph Palmer undertook to clear the drifts away from the path across the disputed land, while Silas, the owner, sallying out with his shovel, fell grimly to work to shovel it on again. Regardless of the pleas of their alarmed households, they worked against each other all day long, two old men in the bitter cold. Finally a compromise was suggested. If Mr. Emerson were called upon to decide which was right, would both agree? They said they would; Emerson's was a name to conjure with, such was every one's confidence in his justice and his impartial friendship. The dispute was decided and the tale carried home to the Alcotts. Louisa and her sisters could laugh over it, in spite of the dark memories of Fruitlands. But it is not certain whether Abba could join in their laughter.

What a friend Mr. Emerson was! Always, when things seemed difficult, when troubles were on the point of overwhelming this happy-go-lucky family, he was at hand to offer aid. Advice, belief, more substantial things, he was ready to give them all. His big, square white house was not far away, a refuge and meeting place for all of his legion of friends. Here in the parlor, sitting before the broad, white-paneled fireplace, Bronson Alcott could talk and talk of the things deepest in his heart and know that he spoke to one who would truly understand. Those red velvet, cushioned chairs, the long sofa against the wall, the crackling flames shining on Emerson's unclouded face, what a scene of peace it was for a storm-tossed philosopher! Sometimes there sat with them a very shy young man, who did not say much, but whose ideas were like clear flame when once he gave voice to them. Henry Thoreau, so diffident that very few people ever could say they really knew him, was a warm and close friend of the Alcott and Emerson families. What talk it was, there by the fire, of the threat of war still a great way off, of the new ideas, of Transcendentalism, of regrets and wondering over Fruitlands. Fiery talk, quieted by Emerson, gloomy talk cheered by him! Wonderful talk that will not easily be matched in our hurried time!

For Abba Alcott, Mr. Emerson had practical, steadying counsel, shrewd advice concerning those money matters which perplexed her so sorely. To Louisa he gave the freedom of his library and all that went with such a privilege. She was at liberty to choose anything from those tall mahogany shelves which reached to the ceiling, to curl herself in a corner of the comfortable sofa and read to her heart's content. Her curiously varied education, got partly through her father, and a great deal of it through reading by herself, received a strong impetus here where such a wealth of wise, friendly books was ready to her hand. She could read anything she wished; but she got advice now and then, suggestions dropped gently by the owner of that hospitable library. She would slip in, see Mr. Emerson sitting at work, writing busily on a board upon his knee, for he never even owned a desk. She would take down a volume, get a quick smile from that strong, sensible, infinitely friendly face, and slip quietly out again. She would stop in one or another of the other rooms, the broad, sunny dining room, or the shabby, beloved parlor where the chairs and the carpet were so worn by the coming and going of philosophic feet. She might perhaps peep into the guest chamber, the room of honor opening from the dining room, which the Emersons, also fond of "Pilgrim's Progress," called "The Room Looking to the East." Its windows opened upon fields and stone walls, upon rows of apple trees along the road which wound up the hill and disappeared. Matthew Arnold slept there and many another distinguished guest who came from afar to seek out Ralph Waldo Emerson.

It was no wonder that Louisa, just growing into the romantic age, acting extravagant dramas and composing them, reading the great tales of romance, should have plunged, herself, into the very depths of fathomless sentiment. She found, in Mr. Emerson's library, a book which told of a little girl's adoring admiration for the great poet, Goethe. She made up her mind, at once, that she would be like Bettine, and that Mr. Emerson would be just the proper subject for such hero-worship. Little by little, she built up a dream of romantic feeling about this dear friend of them all. When she had been writing late, in the little room, she would, as has been said, slip out into the darkness of the garden, climb into the friendly arms of one of the big, hospitable cherry trees and sit there watching the moon come up over the dark hills, thinking deeply romantic thoughts. Louisa was growing up. That she was not quite grown and still a little girl, we know from the fact that the owls, swooping silently through the still night, would frighten her so much that she would run headlong into the house to bed.

She left flowers very shyly on the doorstep of her adored Mr. Emerson. She sang a serenade under his window, sang it in German and in such a small voice that nobody heard her. The object of her devotion was utterly unconscious of what was going on in her youthful heart. Years later, when Louisa was so well grown up that all this seemed like a past existence, she told their friend of the period of sentimentality concerning him, and the two laughed together over the intensity of her young feelings. She had written him letters which she never delivered. He asked for them, when he heard of them so long afterward; but he was not allowed to see them. It was probably Louisa's first act when she came to years of discretion to destroy those missives; for when Mr. Emerson finally heard of them, they had long since been burned.

In the barn were held meetings of an important organization, the Pickwick Club. Only the Alcott girls were members; but they published a paper just the same, with laboriously written numbers full of stories by all of them, sentimental tales of Anna's, dashing poems by Louisa. The sisters also maintained a post office on the hill behind the house, where a girl friend of theirs would leave her letters, flowers and books, and where the Alcotts would post their replies. The post office was a well-loved institution which lasted as long as they lived at Hillside.

Thus passed the first summer. There was a day in the autumn when Louisa had gone out for an early run and stood at the summit of a wooded ridge, to watch the day break above the river. The maples were scarlet and the birch trees gold, all about her; the morning was absolutely still, there was a thin mist over the low meadows beyond which the sun was coming up. It was a moment of such complete and unbelievable beauty that it made her suddenly feel that she was transformed into a different person. She said afterward that she never understood God so fully as she did at that second, and that she understood Him forever after, from having realized, all at once, the beauty of the world which He had given her to dwell in. She went home with something new in her heart which she was never to lose.

From the spring that she was thirteen until the autumn of the year that she was sixteen years old, she lived at Hillside. Not much seemed to happen to her; and yet, those years were extraordinarily important in what she learned, in what she discovered, and in what friends she made. There is no doubt that they were the happiest years of her life.

For the first time she went to school, the winter that she turned fourteen. Louisa and Anna had much ado to persuade her father and mother to let them go; for it had been Bronson's pride that, although he had no other pupils now, he could at least undertake the education of his daughters. He and Abba were wise enough to see, nevertheless, that the girls needed companions of their own age and should not always study alone. Anna found the new life interesting and easy to get used to; but it was not so simple for Louisa. She was very shy and was now so tall as to be conspicuous amongst girls of her own age. She was awkwardly conscious of being oversized and always felt large and clumsy and unduly burdened with hands and feet. She was so gay and so full of good spirits, however, that she

was immediately welcomed by her new comrades. As they all grew better acquainted, some of them were surprised and startled by the sudden changes of mood which so often came over her, when, instead of being the most lively company in the world, she was, all at once, silent and unresponsive, wrapped in thoughts whose strange gloom she could not explain. Then the cloud would pass, leaving Louisa as cheerful and as much in demand as before. The Alcott girls made a great addition to Mr. John Hosmer's district school. Louisa could run faster and jump higher than any other girl there, and vault over fences with long-legged ease. She was always lamenting the fact that she was not born a boy.

The girls did not go to school a second year, but had lessons with their father and Mr. Henry Thoreau. Louisa seemed so much occupied with all the delights of a girl growing up, that it hardly seemed evident to any one how deeply she had resolved to set her shoulder to the wheel of the family fortunes. When she reached sixteen, she decided it was time to begin.

The barn, scene of her first dramatic triumph, was also the setting for her first venture in the greater enterprise of helping to take care of her dear family. She organized a little school there, probably at the suggestion of Mr. Emerson; for it was his children who made up the greater number of the pupils. In spite of his great love for Bronson Alcott and his belief in his friend's ideas, Emerson chose Louisa, rather than her father, to teach his own children. Bronson had really great views upon education; but it fell to Louisa to translate those views into something which the young persons about her could truly absorb and understand.

What she had learned from her father made her a good teacher; but it could not make her love the task of instruction. Besides knowledge, she brought to the task energy and an enthusiasm for succeeding, along with that boundless friendliness which is the heart of a real teacher's success. The little girls got much from her; she in turn got much from them. There is no better way to learn how to understand the minds of children than to teach them. Louisa gave generously and taught well;

but she could not learn to like her work. She was too restless and impetuous; she was too prone to find the long hours of sitting still as trying as did even the smallest of her pupils.

Determination, however, can take the place of patience, if earnestly applied. As Louisa sat at her desk, presiding over the small flock, her own thoughts, still busy with romance, flitted far above their labors, just as the steel-blue swallows were flitting high above, amongst the rafters, or skimming out through the open door into the sunshine. Little Ellen Emerson loved Louisa and was often at Hillside, in just the same way that Louisa ran in and out of the big, white Emerson house. For her, Louisa began to write some stories, very different from those of her usual melodramatic style. They were about flowers and birds and fields, little fables which were the natural flowering, in her own mind, of what she had learned while teaching the school. After reading them to Ellen, she tossed them aside amongst the plays and the tales of counts and nobles, which she so loved to compose. As yet few eyes besides her own had seen any of the scribbled manuscripts.

It may be guessed that the proceeds from this scholastic undertaking were not very great and were of far less value than the experience which came out of the summer's work. In the autumn certain questions became acute in the Alcott family. They had a roof over their heads, it was true. But with so little income, it was impossible for Abba Alcott to see that the six members of the household were properly clothed and fed. Bronson Alcott must not be misjudged. He was untiringly industrious, and anxious, above everything in the world, to do what he could for his family. Yet it was impossible for him to find employment of any sort which would support them. He could not, by the labor of his hands, do enough work to supply all their wants. He knew much of farming, but it had been proved at Fruitlands that his ideals and theories interfered with success, even in that form of occupation. For commercial work he had no talent at all and could not be of any practical use in a counting house or in any pursuit of buying and selling. He was beloved by all who knew him and looked up to with admiration by every one who understood what he had to offer. He gave lectures on Transcendental philosophy and on many others of the deep subjects being studied in that day. He was an excellent speaker, an exceedingly indifferent writer, a profound thinker and a devoted friend. As a practical support for his family, he was always striving, but in the eyes of the world, never successful. He was to come into his own, at last, but it was not now.

As they had done at Fruitlands, the family held council over ways and means, an unhappy depressed council, for it was evident that the pleasant life they were leading at Hillside must come to an end. Mrs. Alcott had been offered employment in Boston, as an official visitor to the poor, and a brother had offered the family his house in which to live. It seemed that the necessities of food and raiment came before the affection they all had for friendly, happy Concord and the nearness of their guide, philosopher and friend. The decision was made; they moved to town and once more entered upon a new era.

Louisa's experience with teaching gave her enough confidence to start bravely with the same sort of work in Boston. For two years she taught here and there, helped her mother, took care of small children as a nursery-governess, sewed, did anything to which she could turn her hand. The family fortunes did not prosper very greatly, so that there were often difficult times in those various dwellings in which they lived, one after another. There was never depression or discouragement, however, for something ridiculous was always to be seen in every misadventure, something to call forth mirth and become the basis for a treasured family joke. Every evening they would gather about the lamp on the table and each one tell of the occurrences of the day, always making a good story of it, to the great entertainment of the rest. Anna was teaching, Louisa was doing a dozen things, May was going to school. When the record of their doings was complete, Mrs. Alcott would read to them or tell them ever-new tales of her own childhood and girlhood. One of her audience, at least, never forgot any of those stories.

One day there came to the house a gentleman in clerical

garb who wished to consult Mrs. Alcott about finding a companion for his invalid sister. He wanted some "lady-like young woman, who would read to her, perform a few light household duties and be treated exactly like a member of the family." People often came to Abba Alcott on such errands; for part of her work was the keeping of an intelligence office to find places for the needy women in whom she was interested. There was nothing unusual in the errand of this stranger, except that the position he described seemed so marvelously easy and pleasant. Whoever came to them, so it seemed, would have all the comforts and the consideration of a very good home.

Louisa overheard him and was fired with enthusiasm. She would love to take the place herself. She was eighteen; she had done no work so far except amongst friends and acquaintances; but this was too great an opportunity to miss. She pictured easily the interesting, suffering sister, the great comfortable house, the figure of herself, flitting about, distributing comfort and cheerfulness and being loved and appreciated in return. When her mother asked her if she had any person to suggest she responded instantly, "Only myself."

After the man was gone, Abba Alcott reasoned with her daughter a little, since it was a most impulsive decision. But with Louisa, all conclusions came rapidly, and to this rosy plan she clung with persistence. The man had been asked about wages, but his reply had been slightly vague. There would be no occasion to use such a vulgar term as wages, he asserted; the young companion was to be so much a part of the family that wages was not the word. Certainly she would be well compensated, but payment would be offered under some more suitable name. Louisa's sisters laughed at her and her mother still offered protest; but the girl was firm. They were in such need that it was not wise to let any proper opening escape her. She did not stop to think that she was taking up employment with total strangers, without any definite agreement as to the matter of salary, and without real understanding of what her duties were to be. On the appointed day she betook herself to the address which had been given her, and was duly introduced to

Miss Eliza, the ailing sister, who was a "martyr to neuralgia." Louisa had agreed to a trial on both sides for a month.

What a wretched awakening followed! In that cold, dismal house, a feeble old father dozed all day; the invalid sister sat about, helpless and unhappy; a very ancient serving woman trudged back and forth in the kitchen, unable to compass more than the meager cooking which the household afforded. Reading aloud? Such a thing was never thought of. Light duties? They consisted of bringing in coal from the shed and water from the well, carrying the heavy burdens up long, steep stairs, sifting ashes, shoveling snow from the walks, cleaning and scrubbing when nothing else was insistently necessary. Inwardly Louisa raged, stormed to herself, but admitted, with sturdy honesty, that she had brought the whole of the misery upon her own head.

She had promised to stay a month and stay she did, carrying ashes, splitting wood, making fires and waiting upon the plaintive invalid. In all this time nothing was said about paying her. The brother, who had employed her, treated her with lofty disdain and one day took her to task for not performing the whole of her duties. He observed coldly that she had not cleaned his boots and directed that she should do so.

No, she would not. She made no attempt to gild the refusal; she was sorry for Miss Eliza and the doddering old father, but she had small respect for the man whose misrepresentations had brought her to this pass. He attempted to show injured dignity and to insist; but he got nowhere. Louisa decidedly would not black his boots.

Late that evening she heard a small noise in the dim corridor and, peeping out of her door, caught sight of the dignified gentleman sorrowfully collecting brushes and rags and boots and attacking the hated task himself. Louisa enjoyed the prospect for a long time, shivering in the cold, delighted to have found one thing at last in this wretched house over which she could laugh, even though all alone. When the unhappy month was nearly over, she announced in no uncertain terms that she would not stay longer. Poor Miss Eliza wept so pitifully that

Louisa, too impulsive again, agreed to remain until some one else could be found. Two others came in turn, looked about them, briefly called Louisa a fool and went away.

Three weeks passed while she still toiled on. When the third victim arrived, she gave her no time to consider. Her small effects were packed and the moment the substitute came in at the door, Louisa betook herself to the sitting room and bade the household farewell. The gentleman who had hired her had disappeared from sight. The old father spoke shakily of his sorrow over her going and the unfortunate Miss Eliza wept anew. She put a small pocketbook into Louisa's hand, the payment for her seven weeks of hard labor. As Louisa went downstairs, the old servant emerged from the kitchen to look strangely at the little purse in the girl's red, chapped hand and to make the ominous remark:

"Don't blame us for anything; some folks is liberal and some ain't."

"Don't blame us!" Queer devotion which identified itself with this ungenerous family and made the toiling old woman the one memorable and admirable figure in that sordid place. As she walked away from the house, Louisa was exultant over one thing. Her own family needed money sorely and she had earned it for them! Stopping in the chilly, windswept street, she opened the pocketbook. Within was four dollars, the sum total of her wages! Four dollars for seven weeks of cruelly unhappy toil! Louisa was not prone to be bitter, but bitter anger swept through her then; she had hoped so much, had given so much, and this was what they thought was the appropriate return. It was not love of money, not even the need of it, which made that moment so hard. It was the disillusionment, the knowledge that any one could treat her so, could take her trusting, eager service and dismiss her with such a pitiful reward as this.

She laughed over most of her impetuous mistakes, but there is no record that either she or her sisters ever made sport of this sorry experience. When she showed the money at home, it was characteristic of the Alcotts that the immediate step taken was to return it. Bronson, moved to rare anger, wanted to lay violent hands upon the man in the garb of a minister who had come to his house and made such misstatements to warm-hearted, credulous Louisa. In the effort to calm him, the rest of the family forgot a little of their righteous wrath. Louisa scarcely ever mentioned that incident in her life, in all the years following. Truly it attacked her very faith in the goodness of mankind. It was an experience of some value, but of miserable memory.

Thus material matters continued to go badly with the Alcotts. Plainness of living they did not mind. Had they not learned that every sort of plainness can accompany the real treasure of spiritual life? But, even amid their cheerfulness and good spirits, there were moments of such hardship that the present seemed bad and the future desperately insecure. One plan was always at the back of Louisa's mind. She had very beautiful and very long, dark hair, "not just the fashionable color," as we are told, but of wonderful luxuriance. An exuberance of hair was as fashionable then as it is unfashionable today; chignons, waterfalls and cascades of curls were a necessity, whether they flourished naturally or not. Louisa's hair, which almost touched the ground when let out of its net, was the envy of all her feminine friends. It was, in her mind, her reserve capital. When affairs were at a desperate pass with the Alcott fortunes, she went one day to a barber, let down the cloud of dark hair and asked him what he would give for it.

The sum he named seemed vast wealth to her, but she could not make up her mind to the sacrifice at once. Unless matters mended within seven days, she told herself sternly, her hair should go. It was like laying her neck upon the block, for cropped heads looked ugly then, and Louisa's, with her tall figure, would seem more awkward than another's. The week passed and Providence, in the guise of a generous friend, saved Louisa's hair. Substantial help came suddenly from a hand accustomed to offering assistance. There is reason to believe that it was Mr. Emerson's.

In the summer of that same year, the family all fell ill with smallpox, caught from some destitute emigrants who had come, begging, to the gate, and whom Mrs. Alcott had brought into the garden and fed. Abba Alcott and Bronson were very ill; the girls only slightly so. Anna and Louisa nursed their parents through those desperate days, with no help from outside. Not a neighbor came near them, nor a doctor. An unquenchable family, they survived the ordeal without despair or bitterness and girded themselves to face the world again.

Life in a city was not really the proper one for these four growing girls, especially a restricted, grubbing life such as they were forced to lead. After the smallpox experience, the Alcotts left their uncle's house and took a place in High Street. Abba went to her work every day, May to school, Bronson to his lectures, Anna and Louisa taught, while Elizabeth, now seventeen, did the housekeeping. "Our angel in a cellar kitchen," Louisa

speaks of her thus, with resentment and rebellion. They moved, finally, to Pinckney Street, where Mrs. Alcott kept boarders so that she might be at home with her children. Bronson had gone on a journey into the West to lecture. Boarders do not pay much at best and are apt to play upon the feelings of a kind-hearted landlady. Finances were still very low and great hopes were built upon what was to come out of the lecturing. It is a famous incident, that night in a cold February, when Bronson returned home late, chilled and tired from his long travel. Every one rushed down to hug and to embrace him, to ply him with comforts, and to rejoice over his return. After the first flurry was over there was, suddenly, a little silence, of waiting, of wondering. It was enterprising May who broke it.

"Well, did they pay you?"

Very slowly, Bronson drew out his pocketbook and displayed its contents. He had come home from far journeys before, after those excursions into Virginia, having gathered the riches of learning new things on the way and having left the riches of his glowing thoughts wherever he passed. Fortunes had always been varying; he had returned from the South sometimes prosperous, sometimes bankrupt. It mattered little to him then; it mattered little now, as he drew forth the fruit of his enterprise, —a single dollar.

"Another year, I shall do better," he observed cheerfully.

There was a minute of choking silence.

"I call that doing *very well,*" said Abba Alcott suddenly, as she threw her arms about his neck.

Louisa, watching in the lamplight, saw all at once what real love can do, what heights it can reach. She knew very clearly how her mother had hoped, what were the things she might have said; she knew what courage was behind those words of approval and affection.

A great event had occurred during this period and had been brought about through Bronson's means. He found one of Louisa's little flower fables written for Ellen Emerson in Concord; he showed it to a publishing friend and it had been approved, actually accepted, bought and printed! A very small

incident, apparently, scarcely making a ripple on the surface of literary affairs. In spite of her inward excitement, Louisa called it a little matter also and cheerily pronounced the story "great rubbish." The tales of wild adventure were still far more to her taste. She was writing them busily, whenever her varied wage earning gave her a moment to attend to them. Her brain was teeming with plots and excitements every hour, as she went about sewing and teaching and watching over children. She said very little to any one of all that was going on within herself.

The little story was liked and the rest of the stories written for Ellen Emerson were gathered together and published in a small book, "Flower Fables." Louisa could actually be spoken of as an author, although she made great game of herself in the light of such a rôle.

The following summer she was invited by good Cousin Lizzie Wells to spend some time in Walpole, New Hampshire. It was pleasant to be in the green hills again, to take long walks through the fields and feel the fresh wind blowing about her. She wrote more flower stories here, and began to think more seriously of what she might be able to do with her pen, of what she could accomplish for her family. Her mother decided, finally, that the life in the city was assuredly not the thing for her children, where they had barely enough to keep their heads above water, in spite of their cheerful struggle and their continual insistence that all was well. She moved to Walpole with the rest, and settled down to spend the winter. It was then that Louisa came to a great resolve.

She had never been any distance from her mother before, had never taken any momentous step without the support of her family behind her. But she found that she could earn nothing in Walpole and that, as the weeks passed, she was too restless even to write. She would set out alone, she concluded, and, if she could do no more, could earn her own living and be less of a care to her family. It was not an easy decision for a shy, untrained girl to make, in a time when work for young women, especially young women of the class called ladies, was extraordinarily difficult to find.

It was November; it was chilly and raining that day she set her face, alone, to the great world. She had very little money, a small trunk, a package of manuscripts and an enormous fund of hope and determination. The rumbling stage carried her out of sight of the little house amongst the New Hampshire hills. It bore her down the roads lined with leafless maples, between the gray stone walls and the tangles of frost-bitten blackberry bushes. Courage, terror, dismay and relentless determination were all in her heart as she heard the hollow rumble of the wheels on the covered wooden bridge and knew that she was actually launched upon the first enterprise of seeking her fortunes single-handed.

ONE OF Alexander MacKenzie's first exploring trips, which were later to make him famous, was in the region of the Great Slave Lake. The river he discovered there, with the Arctic Circle as its source, was named after him and it is Canada's longest waterway. A few years later he became the first white man to reach the Pacific Ocean by crossing the Rocky Mountains. In later life he settled down to being a successful fur trader.

Maxine Shore
and M. M. Oblinger

ALEXANDER MACKENZIE: HERO OF CANADA

ILLUSTRATED BY *Henry C. Pitz*

STARS were paling in the sky and the dawn wind had freshened when young Alexander Mackenzie leaned from his saddle to bid his two aunts good-bye. Then, before he could half taste the painful excitement of parting, he was off with the other fleeing Loyalists in the thinning dark.

The journey to Canada was made by way of Lake Champlain. But first came the long overland trail, northeast from old Johnstown, through forests frequented by Indians and occasional bands of white travelers like themselves. . . .

Astride a small roan mare, Alex was remembering former journeys which had changed his life, as this one would surely do. The first when, at ten, he had left Stornoway, his birthplace on the Isle of Lewis in the Hebrides, to sail across the Atlantic to the thriving New World settlement of New York. The second, a year later, when rebellion against the King had broken out in the colonies and his father and his Uncle John Maciver had joined the British Army, while he and his aunts had been sent inland to Scotch Bush for greater safety. Safety they had not found. So, once again, he was going on a trip—this time to Montreal—and alone. . . .

Montreal! Was there ever a fairer town? Alex found it hard to sit still that evening in the boat that carried him toward the picturesque settlement. Around it he saw the old stone wall the French had built and, reaching skyward behind, a mountain thick with forest and tarnished with the last rays of the sun. The harbor ahead was prickly with lofty masts and clotted with bobbing birch canoes. He let his hand over the side of the boat to trail in the cool water. The mighty St. Lawrence! Up this great river from the ocean came sailing ships, full-skirted and haughty, bringing English governors and other official dignitaries. From inland came the fur brigades, bearing their wealth of pelts jauntily. . . .

Disembarking, Alex's group hired a guide to show them along the narrow unfamiliar streets, between the rows of quaint wooden houses. Alex had the queer feeling that Montreal welcomed him, that somehow he belonged here. It was as if the town had been waiting for him and was pleased that at last he had come. . . .

Alex explored his romantic new surroundings eagerly, whenever he could. Having been born on an island, he felt very much at home on this one. . . .

It was at Montreal that the furs were stored and packed for shipment to England, there to be sold. Beaver, mink, marten, fox, raccoon and muskrat were highly valued—especially beaver, which had come to be a medium of exchange. Always observant, Alex learned to recognize the most prominent fur lords. Among these were the brothers, Benjamin and Joseph Frobisher, and the imposing Scot, Simon McTavish. . . .

So absorbed was Alex one morning that he was unaware when someone came behind him. Stepping back out of the way of a busy worker, he trampled the toes of the fur lord, Simon McTavish.

Mr. McTavish brought his cane down on the boy's shoulders.

"Learn some manners, young scoundrel!"

Alex's eyes smarted from the stinging blow.

"I'm no scoundrel, sir. If I stepped on you, I'm sorry. But it was an accident. Surely—"

"Surely—" Again the cane rapped him smartly—"surely I'll not be talked back to."

Flaming with indignation, Alex threw back his curly head. Mr. McTavish's lips were set in a thin tight line. He was a tall man, haughty-eyed and arrogant. His manner had earned him the nicknames of "Le Marquis" and "Le Premier" among the *voyageurs,* who did not dare speak thus to his face, however. Without doubt, here was a man to fear and obey. But Alex had not the inclination to do either.

"Surely," he said, "I will not be caned after proper apology." His brilliant wide-set eyes met those of the older man defiantly.

Simon McTavish's brows drew together over his nose in a black frown.

"Will you not, young rascal? Indeed, 'tis time you were taught respect for your betters."

Simon McTavish, paling with anger, raised his stick again purposefully. But before it could descend, Alex caught it and wrenched it away. He flung it to the ground.

With an outraged roar, McTavish reached for him. Alex turned and ran, ducking through the crowd of Indians and *voyageurs.* He plunged into a dim street. Behind him he could hear running feet.

A *habitant's* cart blocked his way. Desperately, he darted into the dark doorway of a shop. He would hide here until his pursuer went by.

But the man who followed had seen where Alex went. He hurried toward him.

"Young man, are you Alexander Mackenzie?"

"Y-yes, sir." No use to flee now. They knew his name. They could track him down wherever he was, and mete out fitting punishment. A boy who had been impudent to the great Simon McTavish.

"I'm John Gregory, lad."

The man was smiling—actually he was holding out his hand!

"Good day to you, sir," faltered Alex.

The name of John Gregory he recognized instantly, a noted one in the fur business. He was a partner of the firm of Gregory and McLeod.

Mr. Gregory was considering him earnestly. Alex shifted uneasily. The scrutiny embarrassed him. Finally, John Gregory nodded, as if satisfied.

"Young man," he said, "you're the first, boy or man, who ever stood up to Simon McTavish."

"Oh, sir, it was all an accident. I never meant—"

"You mean you're sorry?"

"Oh, yes, sir. That is, I'm sorry it happened."

"And you'll never do it again?"

Alex took a long uneven breath. "I cannot promise," he said. "After I've made proper apology for a mistake, I don't mean to be caned by anyone."

The Englishman's eyes, oddly enough, were twinkling. He reached a hand to Alex's shoulder.

"Lad, I could use a clerk like you in my business."

Alex could not speak. It was as if Mr. Gregory had dug into his very mind and brought forth his greatest desire. He was fifteen now, ready and willing to earn his own livelihood and to take care of his aunts, too, if necessary. Until now, they had lived on the money his wealthy uncle, "Ready Money" John Maciver, had smuggled out of New York, when they had moved to Scotch Bush. But even before he had gone to Montreal that had dwindled fast. Alex suspected that Aunt Sybilla had paid out most of what remained to Mrs. McDonell for his own maintenance. If his aunts were anything like the other Loyalists pouring into Canada, they would probably be almost destitute when they arrived, and might have to look to charity for aid. It was high time, Alex resolved, to prove himself a man.

"Oh, sir," he cried eagerly, "I'd like nothing better than to go into the fur business. I'll work hard, I promise. You'll never be sorry for giving me this chance."

John Gregory smiled. "I'm sure of that, lad. You're a likely young man. 'Tis my opinion you'll go far."

Promising to report early the following morning, Alex parted from Mr. Gregory.

Unaware of where he went, or why, he walked down the street, his thoughts dancing with excitement. The day's misfortune had been transformed miraculously into fortune. Opportunity had knocked, and his future stretched ahead invitingly.

THOUGH Orville Wright was four years younger than his brother Wilbur, the two had worked as a team since they were boys. From childhood they liked to make things for themselves, and while in high school, Orville built a printing press and started a weekly newspaper. Wilbur joined him in this and thereafter the two were inseparable. After high school they opened a bicycle shop in Dayton, Ohio which they operated until they became interested in flying. First they experimented with gliders, but in 1903 they built a biplane with a four-cylinder gasoline motor and a propeller. They named it *Kitty Hawk* and succeeded in flying in it for twelve seconds—the first men to fly in a motor-driven, heavier-than-air plane. Shy, retiring men, the Wrights lived a secluded life after their historic flight. Wilbur died of typhoid fever in 1912. Orville continued to experiment in his laboratory until his death at seventy-six.

Joseph Cottler
and Haym Jaffe

THE WRIGHT BROTHERS

ILLUSTRATED BY *Alexander Key*

THE STORY is told that in very ancient Greece lived Daedalus, a famous mechanic, and his son Icarus. Once, when the two were far from home visiting Crete, King Minos there clapped them in prison. Seeking a means of escape over the vast sea, Daedalus fashioned wax wings for himself and Icarus, and away they flew to Sicily. Daedalus fared safely, but unhappily Icarus soared too near the sun. The wax melted and down he plunged into the sea.

Every age has told a story like this, because there have always been those who are wistful to fly. "If a bird can master the air, why can't we?" But the daring ones who tried were usually killed and pointed out as warnings to other rash souls.

To Otto Lilienthal in Pomerania, Germany, the fate of other men was not a warning. "No wonder we failed," he said. "We know too little about the laws of flying. First we must watch the birds."

For a long time he watched these creatures who glide about in the air so easily. "How does the wind lift a bird's wings?" was the question he studied. And then in 1891, the world was aghast at the sight of Lilienthal gliding through the air on tremendous wings. He looked like a gigantic bat hovering aloft. The legend of Daedalus had come true.

"Man can fly. All he needs is practice," said Lilienthal as he would thrust his arms through padded tubes and hold fast to a crossbar. Now he would be ready to leap from a hill into the air, the gliding machine firmly attached.

He could glide as much as a hundred yards and learned to soar as well. To steer himself, he tried moving his body about —forwards, backwards, or from side to side. "I need more practice," he thought.

"When I can balance myself as a cyclist who controls his wheel, I'll have won out."

And after a fashion, he did win out. For he learned to turn a complete circle and to stay poised in the air like a gull.

But one day in 1896, a sudden gust of wind capsized the bird-man, and, like Icarus, Lilienthal fell.

The newsboy had left a paper, as usual, at the Wright Cycle Company, in Dayton, Ohio.

Wilbur Wright, a large man with gray eyes and a long aquiline nose, glanced through the paper. "What's this!" he exclaimed, as he turned to his brother, Orville. "The flying man killed!"

Orville looked up from his work. Wilbur continued, "Berlin, August 12. Herr Otto Lilienthal, an engineer, who for many years was experimenting in the building of flying machines, met with an accident that resulted in his death."

As he continued reading about Lilienthal, both brothers became greatly interested. Deeply impressed by Lilienthal's work, they sent to Berlin for a copy of his book.

The book came. "It's in German," they said disappointedly. They could only look at the pictures. But within a short time they had learned enough German to know the book thoroughly.

They liked the way Lilienthal emphasized the idea of constant practice. "Every bird is an acrobat," he wrote. "Whoever would master the air must learn to imitate the birds. We must fly and fall, and fall and fly, until we can fly without falling."

From the time of Lilienthal's fall, Orville and Wilbur were thinking less and less of their bicycle business. The lure of flying had seized them. They read all they could about flying, and they began to watch the birds on wing. If, when they were in their shop, one of the brothers spied a flock of birds winging by, "Birds!" he would shout. Both would drop their work and rush to the window, gazing until the birds were out of sight.

And for the rest of the day, during their spare time, they would argue on what they saw—on how the bird soars, on how its wings are shaped when outstretched, on how it balances. For days on end they would talk about these matters.

"I'm right," Orville would say. "It's like this—"

"No, I'm right," Wilbur would insist. "It's like that—"

"Well," Orville would scratch his head. "I guess you are right."

Wilbur would be silent for some moments. "No, Orville. I see that you have the better idea," he would finally admit. And they would laugh and go on happily.

They could hardly wait till Sunday afternoon. Then, for hours and hours, they would lie on their backs on a hill outside of Dayton, watching the buzzards soar on the rising currents of air.

For five years, they studied and argued about flying. They made tiny machines which they flew in the air like kites.

"I've figured it out," reflected one of the brothers. "Lilienthal, in five years, spent about five hours of actual gliding in the air."

"The wonder is not," returned his brother, "that he accomplished so little, but that he accomplished so much."

"Imagine a bicycle rider attempting to ride through a crowded city street after five hours' practice, spread out in bits of ten seconds each over five years! Yet even with this brief practice, wasn't Lilienthal remarkably successful in overcoming the eddies in the gusts of wind? If we could only find some way by which we could practice by the hour instead of by the second, we could solve the problem."

And to this most dangerous of hobbies, they began to devote all their time and energy. For Wilbur and Orville Wright were thorough in all they undertook.

When Orville was fifteen years old, he and a friend decided to publish a newspaper. It was to consist of four pages. They called it "The Midget," but the first issue was even smaller than its name. For, alas, they ran short of news. They solved the difficulty in a very novel way: they left page three blank!

Orville's father, Bishop Wright, was given a copy of "The Midget." "It is imperfect work," he commented, and he suppressed the entire edition.

Three years later, not at all abashed in the failure of "The Midget," both brothers again decided to publish a paper. But not having enough money to buy a press, they made one themselves. And one Saturday night "The West Side News" was delivered to as many as four hundred subscribers.

From printing, however, they soon turned to the craze of the day—bicycles. They set up a little shop for repairing and making wheels. They made their own tools, even complicated ones like lathes.

Before long, people began to know and like these quiet, pleasant brothers. Not only were their wheels well made, but on them they installed a splendid safety-brake they invented.

One day they thought of having a bit of fun. They rode all over town on a huge tandem bicycle they built. It was made of two old high wheels, connected by a long pipe. "It's a better sight than seeing a circus!" was the town's comment.

And then came the death of Lilienthal. The torch his helpless fingers let go the brothers grasped, to blaze the way to higher glories.

"Lilienthal was not on the right track when he shifted his body at every gust of wind to balance himself. It's both too difficult and too exhausting," said one brother.

"Yes, the wind often veers several times a second, much quicker than you can think," agreed the other.

"But how can we get control? If I let a piece of paper fall, it doesn't swoop down straight. It turns over. The air resists it. How can we ride a steed like this and keep our balance?"

After much study, they concluded that if you could lie flat in the airplane instead of standing upright, as in Lilienthal's machine, the wind resistance could be reduced. And instead of the rider shifting about in the machine when he wanted to balance and steer about, they decided that the machine should do this work. They put a rudder in front, and soon were able to control the airplane.

One day an elderly man appeared on the field. He watched them leap and soar, grasshopper fashion, from spot to spot on their wings of wood and canvas.

"Do you young men know," he finally said, "that you have come nearer to the art of flying than any other man who ever lived?"

It was Octave Chanute speaking, the greatest authority in America on the history of the flying machine. He, too, had been experimenting with flying machines. Chanute was encouraging, and the brothers worked harder than ever.

On December 17, 1903, they were ready. A general invitation was sent to the people of Kill Devil Hill, North Carolina, to come and watch the fliers. But only five people were willing to face the cold wind to see a flying machine that wouldn't fly, as they thought.

The machine was got in readiness. The engine which the brothers had to build themselves (for no company would undertake to construct one) was started. Orville got in.

And then, a miracle! For the airplane rose and stayed in the air twelve seconds! For the first time in history did a machine carrying a man raise itself into the air by its own power and land without being wrecked.

Twelve seconds! From such beginnings, we have witnessed the ocean crossed and the earth circumnavigated. At last man has nothing to envy the birds for. He now can fly faster than any bird.

BENJAMIN FRANKLIN became one of our greatest Americans. He was not only a printer and an author. We all know his famous *Autobiography* and his *Poor Richard's Almanac.* He invented other things besides lightning rods. There were bifocal glasses, the Franklin stove, and dozens of other articles. He was an editor, too. His *Pennsylvania Gazette* later became *The Saturday Evening Post.* He was a public-spirited citizen who helped found the first hospital in America, the first circulating library, the first fire department in Philadelphia, and the academy that later became the University of Pennsylvania. Franklin was a great statesman, too, whose wisdom and common sense helped shape our *Declaration of Independence,* the *Constitution,* and other important documents that helped build America into a great nation. Benjamin Franklin, "patron saint of common sense," had some interesting early adventures.

André Maurois

BEN FRANKLIN'S FIRST ADVENTURES

ILLUSTRATED BY *DeWitt Whistler Jayne*

IT IS A GREAT ADVENTURE for a seventeen-year-old boy to start off alone, without even telling his family, for a city where he knows no one, with only a few cents in his pocket. But Benjamin Franklin was not a timid soul and he felt very sure of himself, for he possessed two assets more precious than wealth: a strong character and a trade. He had a strong character because he had adopted a certain number of rules for himself which he observed as best as he could (not without breaking them from time to time): not to eat meat, to drink only water, not to lie, not to speak ill of others, to do whatever he did to the best of his ability and to take advantage of his leisure moments to improve his mind. As to his trade, which was printing, he knew it perfectly, being able not only to compose a text, but also to repair the machines, and even to build new ones.

His plan was to find work with the town printer as soon as he reached New York. But when he presented himself to William Bradford, who was then an old man, the latter said to him:

"Young man, I like you; I should like to hire you. But New York until very recently was a Dutch town, and there is little demand for an English printer. Besides, I have no need of a workman. You will have a much better chance to succeed if you go to Philadelphia. There my son Andrew Bradford, who is a printer like myself, will be able to give you work."

Benjamin realized that the old man was right. But he did not have enough money left to pay his boat passage to Philadelphia. He decided to walk a good part of the way. This meant that he could not take with him the little trunk which contained his clothes and his books. He stuffed his pockets with shirts and handkerchiefs, shipped his trunk by boat and started off.

He planned to go as far as Amboy by sea, from Amboy to Burlington on foot (a three days' walk), and again by boat from Burlington to Philadelphia, down the Delaware River. The journey by foot went off very well. In those days a well-read young man was a rarity, and Benjamin's conversation was so interesting that it won him friends wherever he went. But by the time he reached Burlington the boat he was hoping to catch had already left. Happily, he met a kind old woman who gave him board and invited him to lodge with her, but would take no money from him in return. However, that evening, while walking along the bank of the Delaware, he saw a boat which was going to Philadelphia, signalled to it, and was taken aboard. He did not have to go for his baggage since he was carrying it all in his pockets. His only regret was to go off without bidding good-bye to the good mistress of the inn, who must have been completely mystified by his disappearance.

The trip was long, and the passengers took turns at the oars. Franklin was never afraid of work, and he was such a good oarsman that upon their arrival in Philadelphia the captain did not want to take money for his passage. But Benjamin insisted upon paying the usual fare. This was another of his rules. He would not accept favors, and never got into debt.

When he stepped ashore at the Market Street wharf, he was very hungry. He went into a bakery.

"Give me a biscuit," he said, for in Boston people ate biscuits. But in Philadelphia the baker did not seem to understand what Benjamin wanted.

"Then give me a three-penny loaf."

"We have no loaves costing three pennies."

"Well, then, give me three pennies' worth of bread—whatever you have."

To his great surprise, he was handed three enormous round loaves. Bread was apparently cheaper in Philadelphia than in Boston. As he walked down the street he began to munch at one of the loaves. With the other two loaves under his arm, his pockets stuffed with linen and his mouth full, he must have been an amusing sight. A pretty young girl, standing in front of her parents' home, burst out laughing as she watched him pass. Her name was Deborah Read. We shall hear of her again.

Benjamin was enchanted with the streets of Philadelphia. The city was well laid out, in the English style, with pretty gardens around the red-brick houses. It had been founded by the Quakers, or the Society of Friends, a religious sect which attempted to establish brotherly love among men, and it was true that both tolerance and kindness were to be found in Philadelphia. The Quakers and their wives dressed austerely, in dark, drab colors. Many among them were wealthy, which was apparent from the beauty of their homes and the richness of their shops, but not from their dress, for they disapproved of personal adornment. They thee-and-thoued one another, which at first surprised Benjamin, for he had never heard anything like this in Boston.

He went down to the wharves where he breathed the good river smell, heavy with the scent of hemp and of tar, gave his two extra loaves to a mother and her child, and began to look for a shelter. He was utterly exhausted from the long journey. He went to an inn to which a young Quaker had kindly directed

A pretty girl burst out laughing as she watched him

him, and slept for twenty-four hours. The next day he went to see the printer, Andrew Bradford. To his great surprise he found there his old friend, William Bradford of New York, who had arrived some time before on horseback, and had already spoken to his son, in the highest terms, of the young Franklin. But Andrew did not need a helper at this moment, and he took Benjamin to another printer, named Keimer, who hired Benjamin and found him lodging with the Reads, the parents of the pretty young girl who had laughed on seeing Franklin pass by with his three loaves of bread. Soon Franklin and Deborah became fast friends.

Keimer was not at all intelligent, but he was quickly forced to recognize that his new worker was far superior to all those he had known. Before long many people in Philadelphia were talking of this young man who was so upright, so hard-working and at the same time so entertaining, who wrote so well and had read so much. One day Keimer was quite overcome to see Sir William Keith, the governor of Pennsylvania, step into his shop in his beautiful embroidered suit. Keimer, all eagerness, bowed low, thinking fortune was about to smile on him. But not at all. The governor asked for young Benjamin Franklin and invited him to the tavern for a glass of Madeira. Keimer was furious.

"I know," the governor said to Benjamin, "that you are a talented boy. How would you like to become a master printer yourself? Bradford and Keimer are both incompetent. Set yourself up on your own. I will give you all the government orders."

"But I have no money to buy the presses and the type," said Benjamin.

"Your father will advance you what you need. I am told he is a man of some means. I am going to give you a letter for him; I will tell him my high opinion of you, and you must leave immediately for Boston. I am sure you will come back with the necessary money."

Benjamin was not sorry to return to Boston in triumph, after having left his native town as a fugitive. When he ran away from Boston he had been nothing but an apprentice living in his father's home, working for his brother without pay. In Philadelphia he had become a free man, earning his own living, putting a little money aside, highly esteemed by everyone and dining with the governor, who treated him as a friend. It would not be unpleasant to relate his success to his brother and former master, James Franklin.

So in 1724 he took the boat for Boston. This time the fare was no problem. Benjamin, well dressed, had his pockets filled with money and owned a superb watch of which he was particularly proud. Though they were surprised to see him, all his family welcomed him with open arms—all of them except James, whom he went to see at the printing shop and who, when he saw Benjamin, turned on his heel and went back to work. This did not keep Benjamin from giving his brother's workmen an enthusiastic account of the life he was leading in Philadelphia, showing them his handsome watch, clinking his money and tossing them a coin with which to drink his health. James was furious and told their father that Benjamin had insulted him before his employees. This was not true. Benjamin's only insult had been his success.

Benjamin's father read the letter from the governor of Pennsylvania with surprise. For several days he made no mention of it to Benjamin. Finally he told him that it was a strange idea to want to put a boy at the head of a business three years before he was of age, that he was flattered by the fine opinion Sir William Keith had of his son, but that he would not give him a penny. Like all parents, he would have liked to reconcile his two sons. When he realized that this was impossible, he said that the best solution was for Benjamin to return to Philadelphia where he had been so successful, and to continue working for a master until he became of age.

When Benjamin came back and told Sir William Keith that his father would not give him the money, the governor said,

"In that case I will give it to you myself. Make me a list of everything you need and I will have it sent from England. You will reimburse me when you can. I want a good printer here and I am sure you will be a success."

Franklin, who did not yet know the governor very well, believed everything was settled and shortly after brought him the list, which he had prepared very carefully.

"That's fine," said Sir William. "But now I want you to go to England to buy all this yourself. You will make a better selection than anyone I could commission. Besides, you will make acquaintances there who will later be valuable to you. I will give you letters of recommendation to my friends, and a letter of credit for the money you will need. Get ready to leave."

Young Franklin was thrilled at the prospect of going to England. He looked upon it as his motherland—the source of all the ideas and of all the books he so loved. What he did not yet know was that the word is not always father to the deed, and that Sir William Keith was as generous with his promises as he was miserly with his deeds. He wanted to please everyone, which often leads to making trouble for everyone. When Franklin was ready to leave for England and asked for his letters, the governor said to him,

"Don't worry, they are all written. You will find them when you get on board."

Franklin got aboard; the ship sailed, and when Benjamin asked the captain for the letters he was told the governor had sent no letters for him. Such are the mighty of this earth, and it is not without value to know it. Once again Benjamin found himself launched upon a great adventure, in a strange land, without money, without friends, without plans. But he had already been able to take care of himself in a similar situation in Philadelphia and he bravely decided that he would manage just as well in London.

For a young man like Benjamin Franklin, who loved books and was passionately interested in what was going on in the world, to arrive in London was a marvelous experience. He had come from two small colonial towns; he was entering the great English-speaking capital, the city which was the home of all the men he admired. Unfortunately he was entering it without quite knowing how he would manage to live. But Franklin was lucky, as upright, prudent and hard-working men almost always are. For what we call *luck* is in fact a reward which life bestows on certain virtues.

On the boat Benjamin had met a very fine man, a Quaker merchant from Philadelphia, named Denham. He helped the young man get a job with an English printer who, though at first suspicious, quickly came to admire this young American who was not only able to print a book but also to write one, and who showed so much good sense. Benjamin's new fellow workers asked him to come and drink with them. They were all great beer drinkers.

"I only drink water," he told them. "It is cheaper, my mind is clearer, and I am able to buy books with the money I save."

At first they made fun of him, then a few of them tried imitating him and discovered he was right. Franklin enjoyed another triumph in London the day the English saw him swim. They admired his technique and asked him to give their children lessons. Before long he succeeded, here, as everywhere, in obtaining friends and recognition. He might also have undertaken a trip to the continent if it had not been for Denham.

"Thy place is not here," the good Quaker told him. "Thee belongs to Philadelphia. Return with me. I will take thee into my business."

Benjamin agreed. Uppermost in his mind, perhaps, was the thought of Deborah Read, to whom he had believed himself engaged at the time he left. But when he returned he discovered that she had married someone else. That is the danger of traveling.

He had another misfortune: the good man Denham, his new employer, died almost immediately.

But Benjamin always landed on his feet. Did he not possess an excellent trade, that of printer, as a last resource? Once more he asked for a job with Keimer, who was only too happy to employ him.

At Keimer's he met a young man named Meredith whose father had money. Meredith, who wanted to go into the printing business on his own, was not much of a worker and knew little about the trade.

"Would you like to go into partnership with me?" he asked Franklin. "I will contribute the presses, the fonts, and the building which my father will give me. You will contribute your labor and your brains and we will divide the profits equally."

Franklin agreed. Later he was able to buy Meredith's share and became the sole owner of the printing shop. It immediately prospered. The whole town was glad to give work to a man who did it so well. Franklin, who was shrewd and knew that a master printer as young as he would have some trouble inspiring confidence, once more imposed severe rules upon himself. He dressed simply, stayed away from taverns, and to prove that becoming his own boss had not made him proud, he himself would sometimes push a wheelbarrow loaded with papers through the streets. Such exemplary conduct won him an excellent reputation.

And so when Deborah Read became a widow and Franklin offered to marry her, her parents were happy to give their consent. Deborah was much less intelligent than Franklin; she did not share his love of books and ideas, but she was a pretty young woman who knew how to keep house and care for the children. They were very happy together and had a son, William, and a daughter, Sarah, whom they called Sally.

Franklin was now in a position to undertake greater things. Soon he owned his own newspaper, the *Pennsylvania Gazette.* Then each year he printed an almanac, *Poor Richard,* which quickly found its way into many homes. In those days every farmer wanted an almanac containing weather forecasts, current events, anecdotes, thoughts and proverbs. Franklin's became famous. He sold up to ten thousand copies a year, an enormous number for a country which at that time was not highly populated, and he made quite a lot of money.

Poor Richard was not limited to weather forecasts. Richard, an imaginary character, would tell the story of his life; he would write about his wife, about his children, and he wrote very well. Many of his sayings are still famous: "There is no little enemy." "The rotten apple spoils his companions." "The cat in gloves catches no mice." "An egg today is better than a hen tomorrow." Franklin had not invented all these sayings. Some were proverbs, some were from the works of other authors, but he had made them more brilliant, more lively, and above all it was he who had chosen them. The wholesome wisdom which had stood him in such good stead in life now appeared in the pages of *Poor Richard,* and it pleased its readers.

The success of Benjamin Franklin, the printer, was but one part of his life. Franklin was not only a good husband and a good businessman; he wanted to be a good citizen and take part in town affairs. This was not easy in Philadelphia, where the Quakers at that time controlled the assembly. Franklin began by forming, with a few friends, a small group of twelve members which he called the *Junto.*

The *Junto* met once a week, on Fridays. Its members agreed to help one another on all occasions. For example, they would bring customers to Franklin's printing shop, and he, in return, would favor them in their trades or professions. But in their meetings each member had the right to ask all sorts of questions which the others would answer if they could. The idea was so successful that the *Junto* soon had to refuse new members and several other *Juntos* were founded.

At this time there were a great many fires in Philadelphia. The blame lay with the inhabitants, who took no precautions, and also with the municipality, which had no firemen. Franklin suggested forming a company of volunteers, who, at the first notice of a fire, would arrive with leather buckets and large sacks in which to rescue objects. The results were remarkable. Soon Philadelphia had better fire-protection than almost any city in the world. Once more Franklin's activity had brought useful results.

"What about books?" he said one day to his friends of the *Junto*. "Don't you think Philadelphia lacks reading facilities? Why couldn't we bring our books together and lend them to one another? We can do something even better. Let us each give a specified sum annually, have books sent from London, and lend them to all who may wish to subscribe."

Today this idea seems quite simple. At that time it was astonishing and original. Thus it was Franklin who created the first circulating library in the United States. It is not surprising that the governor appointed him postmaster of Philadelphia, for he was becoming one of its most public-minded citizens.

Printer, postmaster, fireman, librarian. . . . This was already a good deal, but it was not enough for Franklin's tireless zeal. He wanted to become a scientist besides. Everyone was talking of a new force, electricity, about which little was known. Franklin wished to study it and made some amazing experiments in his home.

"I have built a number of small machines," he would say. He had in fact constructed what was later to be known as a condenser, and he offered his friends turkeys killed by electric current. This was a game not without hazard, and one day, having carelessly given himself a shock, he fell unconscious to the floor.

He was one of the first to notice that metal points attract electricity.

"If lightning," he thought, "were simply electricity, would it not be possible to protect our homes and our churches against its bolts by surmounting them with metal rods, or clusters of rods, connected with the ground by metal wires?"

This did not seem absurd, but first it would be necessary to prove that lightning was electricity. How was he to catch the current from the storm-laden clouds? Suddenly he remembered the kite which had once carried him across the pond. Why not send up a silk kite into a cloud, and conduct the electricity, if there were any in the cloud, to a key he would hold in his hand? If the storm were electric, sparks would fly from the key.

"Come along, William," he said to his son, "we are going to make an experiment."

He needed an assistant and he chose Billy in preference to another as he was afraid a stranger might go around saying that the famous Mr. Franklin had taken to playing with a kite. The contraption rose up to the clouds. Franklin saw the strands of hemp straighten as they did when he held them close to the electric machine; then, as soon as the cord became wet, the key gave off sparks. He had his proof.

Soon Franklin published his discovery in *Poor Richard's Almanac* and at the same time explained the principle of the lightning conductor. All the rods we see today on our steeples and our roof tops are the result of the experiment made that day when William and his father launched a kite from the Philadelphia countryside.

Margaret Thompsen Raymond

A GREAT SOLDIER: ROBERT E. LEE

ILLUSTRATED BY *Rafaello Busoni*

THE TALL BOY of seven, with blonde hair and flashing dark eyes, stood with clenched, angry fists behind the picket fence around his mother's yard. The rumble of cannon was in his ears. He could hear the broadsides from the British squadron at the mouth of the Potomac, as they fired on the forts. He could hear the deeper, heavier shots of the fortress guns. "That's it! That'll show them," he said under his breath.

"Don't go outside the gate, Robert," called his mother, Mrs. Lee.

"I'm not afraid of the British," replied the boy, tossing his head scornfully.

"Neither am I," replied his mother, with a small smile. After all, she had been through the Revolutionary War; she was the wife of Light Horse Harry Lee, who had been one of George Washington's most famous generals.

For a long time Robert and his brother and two older sisters stood by the fence watching the hurry and scurry of the traffic in the street. Great family carriages with coachmen on the high drivers' seats rumbled by. Hooves clattered over the cobblestones as the horses trotted past. Mostly women, hurrying from town, were mounted on the horses. Some had babies in their arms, or small children on the saddle before them, or larger children seated behind them, clinging to their waists.

Soon the rumble of cannon lessened and ceased, and word flew about that the squadron had demanded the surrender of Alexandria. In no time at all, the streets were filled with British redcoats.

Robert and the other three children ran indoors.

"Now what do you think has happened?" demanded Robert. "The mayor has surrendered! My father would never have given up without a fight!"

Mrs. Lee was feeding the baby, Milly, who was sitting on her lap. "A wise soldier," she said quietly, "surrenders when he knows that to fight would mean hopeless defeat and useless death for others. Alexandria has no troops or ships; it is undefended. It would have been foolish to fight."

"Where are our ships? Where are the troops?" asked Smith Lee, the older brother.

"Where's Admiral Perry?" asked Robert. He remembered that they had celebrated Admiral Perry's victory over the British Fleet on Lake Erie the year before with fireworks and gun salutes.

"The ships and troops are gathering to defend Washington and Baltimore. They are much more important towns than Alexandria," their mother told them.

The next weeks were hard ones for Robert E. Lee. The British burned the Capitol, and the boy watched the smoke and flames from the other side of the river.

At Baltimore, though, the Americans stood firm, while Francis Scott Key, prisoner on a British man-of-war, wrote the brave and stirring words of "The Star Spangled Banner." Soon the War of 1812 was over; the United States had proved once more to the British that she was independent and meant to remain so!

One day after the war had ended, Mrs. Lee called Robert to her. "I have taught you your letters and numbers, but now you need proper schooling. Your Aunt Elizabeth Carter Randolph has a school for the Carter first-cousins at Eastern View. You're to go there. Your sister Ann is going to the school for girl cousins at Shirley, where I was born and raised and went to school."

There were literally hundreds of Carter first cousins, although only a few dozen were of the right age to go to school.

At first Robert and his aunt did not get along too well. "Robert," she wrote to his mother, "is very headstrong. You should do as I do with my boys, whip and pray, and pray and whip!"

His mother, though, had other methods. She and Robert always understood each other, and his father, who was away in the West Indies during most of Robert's childhood, said, "Robert was always good and will be confirmed in his happy turn of mind by his ever-watchful and affectionate mother."

When Robert was eleven, his father died. At thirteen the boy, who was always a good student, was old enough to go to Alexandria Academy. There he studied Greek, Latin, English literature, and American history. But he was especially interested in mathematics, most of all in algebra and geometry.

He talked with his mother of his longings. "Do you suppose," he said, "I could go to West Point? I'd like to be a soldier, as my father was; and I'd like to be an engineer, too. I can be both if I go to West Point."

"We'll consult the family," said his mother. And so the older brothers and cousins and uncles came together, or wrote letters to one another. Plenty of Lees and Carters, Randolphs and Fitzhughs were in this large family. One or another knew most of the great men of the day. That is how it came about that the boy, Robert E. Lee, stood in the office of the Secretary of War, John C. Calhoun.

Secretary Calhoun questioned him closely. He saw that the boy's knowledge of mathematics was indeed outstanding.

He said, "I have long been an admirer of your father, Henry Lee. He was a great soldier, and one of Washington's greatest generals."

"Thank you," said the boy.

"Many boys from the South are applying for appointments to the United States Military Academy at West Point. I will have to consult President Monroe about you. And I'll try to tell him what all your brothers and cousins have to say about you," Mr. Calhoun said, smiling. "I even have a letter about you signed by eight United States senators!"

"If I get the appointment," said Lee modestly, "I'll try to be worthy of it—and of my father's memory, too."

At home Robert's mother said, "Now we've done all we can. You must wait in patience."

Within three months, however, the appointment came. "I must answer immediately," the boy said eagerly. "And you have to give your consent, too."

"We'll write it together," Mrs. Lee answered. With her hands crippled by arthritis, she wrote the consent at the top of a large, plain sheet of paper. Below it the boy wrote slowly and carefully, in a hand so precise that the letters looked almost as though they were engraved, and accepted the appointment. Boylike, though, he misspelled one word, for he wrote "honnoured" for "honoured."

One disappointment came with the letter of appointment. So many boys had been selected, that Robert must wait more than a year—until July, 1825—before he could become a cadet.

Meanwhile, there was plenty of excitement. Lafayette, his father's old friend of Revolutionary days, was coming from France for a visit to America. He was going to visit at Mount Vernon, and his road led through Alexandria.

On that October day when he arrived, the streets of the town were gay with flags and bunting, and a triple arch was spread over the main street. In huge lettering were the words:

WELCOME LAFAYETTE
A NATION'S GRATITUDE THY DUE

An American eagle had been chained to the largest arch. "Did you notice how it appropriately spread its wings just as Lafayette passed under it?" Robert asked his mother and sister.

They were still talking of the parade when a knock came at the door. The servant opened it and found Lafayette standing on the doorstep. What a wonderful time Mrs. Lee had talking with Lafayette of her husband and other great men, and how eagerly Robert listened to it all!

In June, 1825, Robert E. Lee arrived at West Point. He rode up the Hudson River in one of the early steamboats and was landed from boat to dock in a tiny, rocking skiff. He reported to Sylvanus Thayer, Superintendent of the Academy, who sent him to the adjutant. The adjutant assigned Lee to a tent in the summer encampment, Camp Adams, where Robert was to sleep and put his clothing temporarily.

For a day or two, until more applicants arrived, Robert had little to do but watch the cadets of the years before drilling on the parade ground and to look about at the splendid scenery. No other spot in America is lovelier than this little plateau on the cliffs above the rolling Hudson River, surrounded by the low, wooded mountains of New York State.

In a few days Robert appeared before the board of examiners and found the oral examinations much easier than he had expected. He had been well prepared indeed.

At last came the day when at roll call the names of the successful candidates were read. Robert was much dismayed to see how many men were skipped as the roll was called. Would they skip him, too? At last came several H's, a few J's, two K's, then—

"Robert E. Lee!"

The boy stepped forward four paces as he had been ordered to do. He was now Cadet Lee.

He shopped with other successful cadets for equipment: basin, pitcher, pail, broom, and scrubbing brush. He was proud of his dress uniform with its gray jacket and white drill trousers, his blue fatigue uniform, and the silk stocks that wound about the neck and held the head proud and high. But he thought that finest of all was the shining black leather cadet cap, with its eight-inch black plume dangling above it and the brass eagle on the chin strap to lift the chin in air!

Two days later these new cadets were ordered out in review in their shining uniforms for no one else but—of all people—the Frenchman, Lafayette! Robert had no chance to speak with him this time.

Robert found that life at West Point was not soft and easy. During the summer, while the upper classmen were on vacation, the drill master worked hard with the new cadets. He drilled them endlessly on the parade ground. He also informed the young men of some of the things they were forbidden to do: smoking, playing cards, and drinking. They could not read romances or novels, and there were to be no visitors during study or drill hours.

In late August the upper classmen returned, and the cadets moved into the barracks from the tents. Robert lived in a room with three other young cadets, and once every four weeks it was his turn to scrub and clean this room and get it ready for inspection.

When reveille sounded, the cadets answered roll call. After roll call Robert put his equipment into shape, polishing buttons, buckles, shoes, sword handles, or cleaning guns and rubbing them to a gleam. From sunrise gun to seven o'clock in the morning he studied mathematics, then marched with his squad to Commons for mess. Robert did not think much of the food. It was, he said, terrible!

Except in severe weather, not unusual on the windy parade ground, the men drilled outdoors. Sylvanus Thayer was a strict superintendent, and he did not consider many days bad enough for the cadets to drill indoors, in the hall of the barracks. The boys marched to the schoolrooms and studied there for nine hours a day. They had only a short recreation period at noon. They drilled again from four o'clock until sunset gun, when they assembled for dress parade and roll call.

After supper Robert studied in his quarters until nine-thirty, when the bugle sounded, and the boys reported once more for roll call. After that came inspection and lights out. With such a daily routine only boys with rugged bodies and fine minds could last the four difficult years. Often in winter the boys had to break the ice in their pitchers to shave and wash. Often their hands grew numb as they wrote out their problems in the cold barracks under the whale-oil lamps.

Robert graduated second in his class. As second lieutenant he was assigned to the Engineering Corps of the United States Army. He began his work as an Army Engineer on fortifications in the harbor at Savannah, Georgia.

In 1831, two years after his graduation, he married Mary Anne Custis, the great-granddaughter of Washington's wife. The young people could scarcely be said to "settle down" anywhere. At first Mary Anne lived at the various army engineering posts. Then the babies came, one after another until there were six of them, four girls and two boys. Mary Anne went to her father's mansion, Arlington, across the river from Washington, near Alexandria, Lee's boyhood home, to raise their family.

It was at this time that Lieutenant Lee was given a big job to do, one of the biggest jobs any man could be assigned. He was sent to put the great Mississippi River, the Father of Waters, back into its proper course along the docks of St. Louis!

Lieutenant Lee decided that he could make the Mississippi do some of his work for him. The trouble lay in two sandy islands that blocked the entrance to the docks. He figured that by building a dike from the top end of one of the islands to the Illinois shore, and another dike at the lower end, he could pour all the force of the Mississippi against the lower island and wash it away. And that is exactly how it worked out.

For his work on the Mississippi he was promoted to captain and was put in charge of building forts in the harbor at New York. While there he rescued a little dog from "the Narrows,"

a channel between the upper and lower bays. The dog, Spec, became a great favorite in the Lee family and insisted on attending church with them. One Sunday Captain Lee decided Spec must be taught to stay at home. He locked the dog in a second floor bedroom. As the family entered the church door, Spec trotted in with them. He had jumped out of an upper window! After that he was allowed to lie quietly in the family pew under Captain Lee's feet.

The United States declared war on Mexico in 1846. Although Lee's work on the forts was important, he hoped to be sent to join the forces on the border. He saw boatload after boatload of men sail away, and still he received no orders from Washington. Then, joyfully, he received his orders to join General Wool in Texas. It was the first time since Lee had taken up soldiering, twenty-one years before, that he would see war firsthand.

Building military roads and bridges to the Rio Grande River was his first assignment. Since a dispute over the boundary formed by the Rio Grande was the cause of the war, this was an important task. Lee accomplished his mission very quickly.

General Winfield Scott was now put in command of an army that was to try to take the Mexican ports and then move inland to capture the capital of Mexico City. He asked that Lee be permitted to join his command.

Several ports were soon taken. The Americans planned carefully before attacking. They sailed into the harbor of Vera Cruz, but no shots came from the cannon. The Americans were able to land and set up batteries. Robert's brother, Smith, of the Navy, was in command of the battery which had been built with the help of some of the sailors. The sailors objected to throwing up earthworks, saying it was a "dirty business," and not for seamen. The next day, though, during the battle for Vera Cruz, as the Mexicans opened fire, the sailors were glad of the earthworks that protected them.

After several days of fierce fighting Vera Cruz was taken. The next step was to march into the interior. No one knew anything about the country. Scott ordered Lee to see if he could locate Santa Anna and his army and also find a way to get around them into Mexico City.

Lee traveled north alone, stepping quietly through the underbrush. He heard voices once, speaking Spanish. He dropped behind a log, close to a stream, and in the steaming tropical weather the ants, flies, and mosquitoes crawled over him. He lay quietly and listened and saw a group of Mexican soldiers sauntering toward him. They sat on the log, and one even jumped over it, but none of them saw Lee, he lay so still. All afternoon Mexicans moved in and out of the thicket, but as darkness came, they started fires some distance away. Lee sat up, rubbed his aching limbs and bitten hands and face. He slipped away, back to his own troops.

The next day, with a group of trained men, Lee cut a trail north of Santa Anna's troops, and then he led a small company of men through the trail so quietly that the enemy did not hear them until eleven o'clock that night. Lee ordered his men to get some rest while he, despite several days of scouting, cutting roads, and marching, saw that the heavy guns were put in position for the battle the next day. He fought, too, in that battle, and for his bravery in this victory at Cerro Gordo he was made Major Lee.

Lee continued to build roads, cut trails, and find a path across an almost impassable field of lava rock. At last the American troops stormed the castle of Chapultepec and took Mexico City. After the treaty of peace was signed, General Scott said, "My success through the war was largely due to the skill, valor, and undaunted courage of Robert E. Lee."

Lee was now a colonel. When he returned to Arlington, he took with him a big, raw-boned Mexican horse for himself, and a small white pony for his namesake, Robert. In order to care for his horses, he came a long way around and missed the carriage that had been sent out to meet him. Only his little dog, Spec, recognized him and flew barking to greet him and to tell the rest of the family the master was home.

For a short time Lee was superintendent of West Point. He was a good superintendent. His oldest son Custis was graduated from West Point while Lee was there. That must have been a proud day for both father and son.

Lee preferred a life of action, and so he accepted a transfer to the Southwest, in the Comanche and Apache country. This region had only recently been annexed to the United States by the treaty with Mexico.

The country was troubled by the problem of slavery. When Lee was home on vacation, a raid broke out not far away at Harper's Ferry. John Brown, a Kansas preacher, and his sons, felt that they were called to lead the slaves of the South to revolt against their masters. They tried to raid the United States Arsenal to get arms for the slaves.

Lee was ordered to suppress the raid and arrest the men, which he did, turning the Browns over to the authorities. He said, however, that John Brown was a sincere man who believed in what he had done.

The situation became more and more serious, and two years later, in 1861, after the election of Lincoln, the South decided to secede from the Union and form a Confederacy where slavery could be legally continued or abolished state by state. Lincoln, although he saw that the nation could not remain "half slave and half free," believed that the Union must be preserved, even if it meant war; then the question of slavery could be taken up and settled by legal means.

When South Carolina withdrew from the Union, however, she demanded that the United States Government remove its troops from Fort Sumter in Charleston harbor. The officer in charge, Major Anderson, had no instructions from Washington and he refused to give it up. The South Carolina batteries fired, and to save his men, Major Anderson surrendered; no one was killed on either side. President Lincoln, however, called immediately for seventy-five thousand volunteers to restore order.

Everyone who had been with Lee in Mexico and knew what a capable soldier he was, advised Lincoln to make him the commander of the United States Army. Lee was now fifty-four, seasoned by many years of training and leading men. Lincoln asked another man to approach Lee and find out how he felt. Virginia had not yet seceded from the Union, and Lee was torn between his affection for the South, especially for Virginia, and his love for the Union and the flag under which he had fought and served.

When Virginia finally joined the Confederacy, Lee resigned from the Army and wrote, at the same time, to his old friend General Scott. In this letter he spoke of his sorrow over the approaching war and his inability to accept the command that had been offered him.

At first he was made military adviser to the new President of the Confederacy, Jefferson Davis, who had been at West Point with Lee and also had served with him in Mexico. It was Lee's plans that helped win the earliest battles of the war. Lee was put in charge of the Army of Northern Virginia, and though it failed to carry out his plans, Lee was sent to a more important command in Charleston. There he strengthened the forts.

His tremendous ability as a general and leader was slowly recognized, and at last he was put in command of the whole Confederate Army. He fought battle after battle, defeating four Northern generals. In 1863 Lee invaded Pennsylvania, but he was turned back at the battle of Gettysburg. Although the war continued for two or more sad, weary years, it ended at last when Lee surrendered at Appomattox Courthouse in 1865.

No commander that ever lived was more loved by his men. During the early days of war, Lee gave up all privileges of rank in so far as he could. He wore the same plain gray uniform and fatigue cap as the men in the ranks. He mingled with them and tried to comfort both his officers and his men as defeat drew near.

When he returned to them after the surrender, he said, "Soldiers, we have fought through the war together. I have done the best for you I could." With tears in their eyes his men stepped forward to take his hand or to touch the flanks of his gray horse, Traveler, on which he had ridden through four years of war.

Lee wrote afterwards to an artist who wanted to paint him on horseback, telling of Traveler's "deep chest, broad forehead, delicate ears, quick eye, small feet, and black mane and tail." He said, "A poet could then depict his worth and describe his endurance of toil, hunger, thirst, heat and cold, and the dangers and sufferings through which he passed. . . . He might even imagine his thoughts through the long night-marches and days of battle through which he has passed." In speaking of his horse, General Lee also told much of his own endurance and worth.

The last years of his life Lee spent as president of Washington College, afterwards called Washington and Lee University in his honor. Lee devoted himself to teaching young men. He made every effort to heal the wounds left by the war. To one southern woman he said, "Don't bring up your sons to hate the United States Government"; and to another, "Remember that we form one country now."

He died on October 12, 1870, mourned and loved greatly in the North as well as in the South.

GUGLIELMO MARCONI, the son of an Italian father and an Irish mother, grew up a delicate and studious child, and as a boy read widely from his father's scientific library. His father wanted him to be a musician, but Marconi had become interested in electrical science and he continued to study in this field. His greatest success came when he found a way to send messages without the aid of wires. The important part which wireless telegraphy has played in rescue work on land and especially at sea has made the inventor's name known throughout the world and won for him the 1909 Nobel prize in physics. Other scientists added their improvements to Marconi's discoveries, and by 1921 "wireless" had become "radio." The next step in this scientific progress was the development of television. Marconi continued his experimental work until his death at sixty-three.

Joseph Cottler
and Haym Jaffe

GUGLIELMO MARCONI

ILLUSTRATED BY *Alexander Key*

HIS SCIENCE PROFESSOR had shown him some wonderful and inspiring adventures, while he could only gaze and murmur in his shy, soft way, "What heroes these men are!"

To young Marconi there were no greater heroes than the men of science; no adventure more thrilling than theirs. He would try to fill his own life with such adventures, he determined. The trouble was, he felt, all the great things had been done already. Nothing was left. Or if there was something to invent or discover, some great man would do it soon. But no!

"There will always be inventions or discoveries to make," Professor Righi had told him. "Who ever dreamed a hundred years ago that a conversation would pass between people miles away? Who ever imagined a voice or a message carried on a wire? Some day, perhaps, we will send messages without the help of wires!"

Without wires! How could that be possible ever? Here was the inspiring sight that the professor had shown him. First, he had buried the two ends of an electric wire in the earth and turned on the current.

"Now put your ear to this telephone receiver," Professor Righi instructed. The telephone was about one hundred feet away. He took it up. To his ear came a faint growling and crackling.

"What is that?" the wide-eyed lad asked.

"The sound of the electric current."

"But you sent the current only through this wire!" exclaimed Marconi.

"Don't be surprised. Notice, I buried the ends of the wire in the earth. The voice of the electricity spreads through the earth. Have you ever cast a stone in a pond? It is like that; the waves spread in a circle, growing fainter and fainter until they strike the shore. The waves of sound sent out by the electric current have struck the wire of the telephone which carried them to your ear. So you see we don't need wires to carry sound. The earth can do it."

But the most marvelous thing that Professor Righi had shown him happened with two coils of wire. They were put some distance apart. One of them had a gap of several inches. Professor Righi sent a current of electricity through this one.

With a piercing flash and a crackle, the current jumped the gap. And here is the wonder; the second coil of wire, lying apart, received a shock of current sent out by the flash!

"Soon we may not need Morse's telegraph or Bell's telephone, which depend on wires, to carry our messages." Young Marconi had felt that soon one of the heroes of science would invent a wireless telegraph. Every day he read the newspapers, expecting it to happen: "Great Scientist Invents Wireless." Day after day he was disappointed. Such beautiful dreams shattered—dreams of making more neighborly all the peoples of the earth, of connecting city with city, nation with nation, ship with ship and shore—by the wireless message!

One day it flashed into his mind that if no one else would invent a wireless telegraph, he himself might try. True, he was so young—only nineteen; but he was also ambitious. He began to study all about these wonderful electric waves. He devoured every scientific book that fell into his hands.

His father encouraged him, gave him the garden to experiment in and funds to buy his wires, poles, string, tin, and whatever else he needed. The poles he planted at opposite sides of the garden. One of them had the wire with the spark gap. A Morse telegraph-key caused the spark. When Marconi pressed the key, the spark crackled in the air. If he held down the key for several seconds—there was a dash of the spark. If he just clicked—there was a dot. These dots and dashes sounded in the wire on the opposite pole and could be heard through a telephone receiver. Young Marconi, helped in this way by Bell and Morse, was able to send messages across the garden—without wires.

"But suppose there's a hill or a wall between my poles. What will happen then?" he thought anxiously. He tried the experiment. He set his poles up in the fields, with a hill between, and several walls. The electric wave went right through the hill and the walls.

But he was not yet satisfied with his invention. "The signals I receive must be clear," he determined. "I need a special instrument for catching these faint electrical waves." More experiments followed, therefore, until at last he had his instrument and had learned to "tune in" the wireless waves.

Soon he could signal eight miles away!

He announced his invention to the world. The world greeted him as it had greeted Bell and Morse before him. It laughed and scoffed. "You are exaggerating slightly," it said with sarcasm. "Do you mean these waves go through rocks? At the most you've only got a toy. It can never be of any real use."

"Toy!" said Marconi. "This invention will connect continent with continent. It will save lives."

He did not boast. He made wireless do both.

"Your system works well for short distances," he was told. "But it can never do for great lengths. The earth curves. Somehow that will stop you."

Marconi planned a great test. For distance he would use the Atlantic Ocean, on one shore a pole with a wire sending out electric waves; on the opposite shore, beyond 3,000 miles of curving ocean, a kite struggling in the air would catch the electricity.

Someone would tap the telegraph-key in the Old World, and through the kite in the New World, the click would be heard!

The dream was too daring to publish. Marconi knew what it might mean to the world if he made it come true—nations brought closer to one another, perhaps acting more kindly as close friends do. But suppose he told his great hope—and failed!

Very quietly, therefore, he sailed for America and landed at St. John's, Newfoundland, on December 6, 1901. Before he left England, he had instructed his assistants there at Poldhu, the southwestern tip of England, to signal at a certain hour each day the letter "s," three dots in the Morse code.

The first day for the signal was December 12th; it was a raw, bleak day. The wind was high and so wild that Marconi had difficulty raising his kite which, like Franklin's, was to catch the electric signal—three dots in current. A telephone receiver, attached to the wire of the kite, was to transmit the sound to Marconi.

At length, by noon, the nine-foot kite was lost in the sky, held by 400 feet of swaying wire. Eagerly Marconi sat at his window in a house on the cliff, below which thundered a cold sea. The receiver was at his ear.

Three thousand miles away at Poldhu, England, a group of men had crowded about the "sending set."

"Is it time?" asked the operator anxiously.

"Right."

The operator pressed a key. A spark, a foot long and as thick

as a man's wrist, sprang across the gap in the gigantic coils of wire. Heaven's lightning had found a rival. The very ground quivered and crackled.

Three times the operator pressed and released the key.

That same moment, three thousand miles away in St. John's, Newfoundland, Marconi heard, through the receiver at his ear, three little clicks. "S," it said. It meant: "Another wonder of the world has come. Marconi," it bade, "prepare for glory."

Yet it was not to come so soon. The world heard and doubted. It trusted Marconi no more than it had trusted Morse and Bell. But it was soon convinced, and when it wasn't pressing its honors upon him, it set Marconi busy building wireless stations the earth over. Of course he did not need to use a kite any more. A regular "aerial" is used which works just as the kite does.

The great man now turned his attention to the preservation of human life. "If ships had wireless sets, they could signal for help in distress."

On board the good ship *Philadelphia* he fitted out a new kind of wireless—one that printed on a tape the message it received. He tried it out one day for the first time in the captain's cabin. The chief officer happened to step into the room. He saw with his own eyes a message from Poldhu being written out. Excitedly he rushed from the room and about the ship, telling all about the marvel.

Everyone laughed. "Do you want us to believe that?" they asked.

"Go and see for yourselves!" said the officer. They crowded into the cabin. "Tap, tap, tap," sounded the ticker as it clicked its message on the tape. Marconi smiled as he noticed the amazed stares.

If Guglielmo Marconi had saved a human life from drowning, he would have been given a medal for heroism. How much more is he a hero that by his invention he has saved scores of human beings from drowning!

The first boatload of people to owe their lives to him were the passengers and crew of the liner *Republic*. One dark night, in 1903, off the port of New York, this ship suddenly collided with another. In a few moments the water was rushing through a hole in her side. The ship was sinking. Had the accident happened three years before, nothing could have saved the lives of those on board. But now it was a simple matter of a moment to send a wireless C. Q. D., the call which was later changed to SOS. The electric messengers brought aid, and the passengers and the crew were saved.

Although Marconi's work on the wireless is not finished, we owe much more to him than that magnificent invention. The radio, for one thing, is a direct descendant of the wireless, even if Marconi did not build it.

On July 2, 1924, Marconi astounded the world with a new wonder. We know that wireless waves travel in all directions. They are like waves in a pool of water, when a stone is thrown in. Now Marconi's new invention directs his wireless waves in a straight line, like the beams of a searchlight.

That does not seem like a great improvement. Yet we are beginning to realize how important it is; a wireless wave can be caught by anybody who cares to tune in. For waves go in all directions. But now that the Marconi signal speeds in a straight line, we can send private messages as we do over the telephone.

But it is only a key that Marconi found, a key that will unlock the vast treasure-house of radio waves. What new treasures the future has in store for us we can scarcely picture.

From MIRACLES

Walt Whitman

Why, who makes much of a miracle?
As to me I know of nothing else but miracles,
Whether I walk the streets of Manhattan,
Or dart my sight over the roofs of houses toward the sky,
Or wade with naked feet along the beach just in the edge of
the water,
Or stand under trees in the woods. . . .

Or watch honey-bees busy around the hive of a summer forenoon,
Or animals feeding in the fields,
Or birds, or the wonderfulness of insects in the air,
Or the wonderfulness of the sundown, or of the stars shining
so quiet and bright,
Or the exquisite delicate thin curve
of the new moon in spring . . .

OUR FIRST PRESIDENT is truly one of the great men in history. Before distinguishing himself in the French and Indian War he was a noted surveyor. In 1774 he began his national career as a statesman when he was a delegate to the Continental Congress. His military ability was again recognized in the war against England a year later. Following the war's conclusion, he, more than anyone, firmly established the struggling new government. Mount Vernon, his home and burial place, is still visited by thousands each year to pay tribute to him.

Eva March Tappan

TWO SCENES FROM THE LIFE OF GEORGE WASHINGTON

ILLUSTRATED BY *John Dukes McKee*

IT WOULD seem as if a few groups of colonists might live in peace together when they had a whole continent on which to choose places for their homes; but during the half century following the settlement of Philadelphia there was a great deal of fighting in America. Much of it was caused by the fact that whenever England, France, and Spain were at war, their colonies also fought. After awhile, however, the colonists of England and France had a quarrel of their own. Its occasion was the land along the Ohio River. This message came to the French: "Those Englishmen are planning to send out settlers to the Ohio."

"That will not do," declared the French. "We want to be able to float down the Ohio into the Mississippi, and so on to the

Gulf of Mexico. La Salle explored the Ohio. Moreover, we discovered the Mississippi, and the Ohio flows into it; therefore the Ohio is ours."

The English laughed at this. "The French claim all the rivers that flow into the Mississippi!" they cried. "They might as well claim all the countries that drink French brandy."

Both nations knew that a strong fort built at the point where the Allegheny joins the Monongahela would hold the river, for no enemies could sail by such a fortification. Governor Duquesne of Canada began quietly to build forts, each one a little nearer this spot. Governor Dinwiddie of Virginia was wide awake and keeping a close watch on the doings of the French. When he heard that a third fort had been begun, he said to himself, "That has gone far enough. I will send some one to warn them that this land belongs to us."

It was not easy to choose a messenger. The governor thought it over. "It is a hard journey," he said to himself. "There will be ice and snow and Indians and all sorts of dangers. We must have a man who knows how to make his way through the forest and will not be afraid of difficulties. That young surveyor who has done so much work for Lord Fairfax is a good woodsman. He is cool and sensible, and whatever he undertakes he does well. He is not the man to be imposed upon, either; and even if those smooth Frenchmen treat him as if he were the king of France, he will not forget what he was sent for." There was something else to be careful about. "It won't do to send any rude, blunt messenger," thought the governor. "Such a fellow would get us into a fight in three days. This young Washington knows how to behave in a parlor as well as in the forest. The youngster is only twenty-one, but I believe he is the man to go."

Then the governor sent for the young man and told him what was needed. He set out with a little company of white men and Indians. The mountains were covered with snow, and the cold November rains were falling. Drip, drip, came the water from the branches as the men pushed on in Indian file through the wilderness. For two weeks it either rained or snowed, and it was always cold and wet. The wind blew upon them in tempests whenever they left the shelter of the forest. The heavy rains had swollen the brooks to creeks, and the creeks to rivers; but, large or small, they must all be crossed.

At last Washington saw through the trees the gleam of the French flag and smoke rising from a chimney. This was the nearest of the three forts, though it was hardly a fort as yet. The French were most polite to their English visitors; but they were exceedingly careful not to say a word that would show what their plans were. "The commander is at Fort Le Bœuf," they said, "and the reply must come from him. It is time for supper now; come and eat with us." At supper they drank a good deal of wine, and then they forgot their caution. "We are going to have the Ohio," they declared; and went on good-naturedly, "Of course you can raise two men to our one, but you English are slow folk. We can build our forts and take the whole country while you are getting ready." Washington did not boast about what the English could do, but he wrote all this carefully in his journal to show to Governor Dinwiddie.

The next day he went on to Fort Le Bœuf. He presented the governor's letter, which reminded the French that they were on land belonging to the English. The commander replied, "I will send the letter to Governor Duquesne; but this is where he has placed me, and here I must stay until he sends me somewhere else."

Washington took his leave. The horses went so slowly through the snow that, to save time, he returned on foot with only one man. The coming had been hard enough, but the return was much worse. The cold had become more intense; the rivers were full of floating ice. Washington was knocked off the raft into ten feet of bitterly cold water, and had to spend that night on a little island without fire or shelter. There was danger from the Indians, and more than once he was fired upon by them; but he came out safely from all dangers and gave Governor Dinwiddie the French commander's reply.

"We must get ahead of them," declared the governor. "We will build a fort just where the Allegheny joins the Monongahela, and we will hold the Ohio." So he sent men there to build

In the early gray of the morning they entered the town

the fort; but the French drove them away, and in high glee built a fortification of their own, which they named for the governor, Fort Duquesne. Governor Dinwiddie had sent another band of men to help the first, with Washington at its head. He heard that the French had driven the first colonists away and were coming to attack his company. With his few men he could not meet them, so he went back a little way to wait for more troops.

It was not long before a few militiamen and fifty regular soldiers came. Their captain put on a great many airs because his regulars were paid by the king. "We belong to the king's army," he declared, "and the king's soldiers do not take orders from a young fellow in the colonial militia." His men followed their captain's lead and refused to help make a road or drag the cannon. They were soon frightened into helping, however, for the scouts told them that the French were coming upon them. Then they forgot that they were taking orders from a colonial major and worked as hard as they could to help make an intrenchment, dig a ditch, and cut down trees for breastworks. The French came upon them, twice as many as the colonists. The fight lasted for nine hours. The powder gave out and the provisions gave out. There was nothing to be gained by lying down behind the logs and starving; so Washington surrendered. The French were jubilant. They had driven off the English and they held the Ohio.

But somehow the English would not stay driven off. At length the king of England began to find out that the French were trying to crowd his colonies into a little strip of land near the coast, and that if he expected to have any more than that he must fight. Then he sent General Braddock to Virginia with one thousand men.

Long before the vessel came to the wharf, the colonists could see the red coats of the soldiers. The regulars were with them, and they were delighted. Braddock made Washington one of his officers, but he had no idea of listening to his advice. Washington was much troubled. "The general knows how to fight the French," he thought, "but he seems to think that the Indians

mister mckee

will march out in line like white men." So he told him respectfully how the Indians behaved in a fight. "They hide behind rocks and trees," he said, "and there will be a storm of bullets when no one is in sight."

"Regulars know how to return bullets," replied Braddock. "It would be a strange thing if British troops could not meet a handful of naked Indians."

The line of redcoats and of colonial soldiers set out on the long hard march through the forest. They crossed the Monongahela. They were climbing a hill when suddenly shots began to come from all directions and the forest echoed with the yells of the Indians. The French were in front, the Indians were on both sides, but hidden behind trees. The regulars were so dazed at this new kind of fighting that they ran like sheep. The colonists had learned how to meet Indians, and so they hid behind trees and returned the fire. Even then Braddock could not see that there was any other way to fight than the one he had learned, and he shouted to his men to come out and form in line. Of course the only end to such a battle was the wild retreat of the English. Cannon, provisions, food, arms, clothes, horses, and money were forgotten in the mad rush for safety. Braddock was mortally wounded and soon died. When the fugitives dared to stop, he was buried in the forest, and wagons were rolled over his grave lest the Indians should find it.

It was owing chiefly to Washington's skill and coolness that any of the men escaped. Four bullets were shot through his coat, but he was not hurt. Afterwards an Indian chief said, "He will never die in battle. I told all my braves to aim at him, but they could not hit him." If the Indian had known what severe fighting lay before the young officer, he might not have been so sure that Washington would never die in battle.

WASHINGTON SURPRISES THE HESSIANS

It was Christmas night in 1776, the second year of the Revolutionary War, and the Hessian soldiers were making merry at Trenton. They were Germans who had been hired by the king of England to help him conquer the American rebels. Just then there was no fighting on hand. They had good warm quarters, plenty to eat, and plenty to drink. They feasted and they drank, they sang songs and they told stories. They were in the best of spirits, for Washington, the commander-in-chief of the Americans, was retreating. "There won't be much more trouble from him," declared one soldier. "He had to leave the Hudson, and we have chased him out of New Jersey and into Pennsylvania."

"We'll soon be in Pennsylvania ourselves, in Philadelphia," said another, "and that will be the end of the war. They say Washington's troops are deserting by the hundred."

The carousing went on until late in the night, and then the men went to their warm beds and to heavy sleep.

About the time that their feasting began, Washington marched his men down to the opposite bank of the Delaware. The ground was covered with snow. It was bitterly cold. The sleet was driving furiously. The river was full of masses of floating ice, pitching, tumbling, and plunging in the strong current; but boats were waiting at the shore. They were rowed by fishermen from Marblehead, who knew how to meet storms. The soldiers got into the boats. The fishermen rowed and paddled, and pushed away the cakes of ice with long poles. The wind blew more furiously, the sleet was more biting; but at last the boats came to the New Jersey side of the river. The men leaped or tumbled ashore as well as they could in the storm and darkness. Then they swung their arms, they stamped their feet, they marched back and forth, they jumped, and they ran—anything to keep from freezing. The storm was growing worse; there was no shelter; and on the river bank they must wait till the boats had been back and forth many times and had brought the whole force across. Ten hours they waited, all through that terrible night of tempest.

Trenton was nine miles away, but Washington had given the word to march on. One man was frozen to death, and a little later a second was overcome by the cold. "The muskets are wet and cannot be fired," an officer reported.

"Use the bayonets, then," replied Washington; "the town must

mister
mckee

be taken." And he pushed on toward Trenton. He divided his men into two parties, and in the early gray of the morning they entered the town by two different roads.

Washington planted his cannon so as to sweep the streets. The Hessians rushed out, almost dazed by the sudden attack. They ran in one direction, and a volley of musket balls met them; they ran in another, and the cannon mowed them down; in another, and a bayonet charge drove them back. The commander ran out half-dressed and tried to form his lines, but he was shot down. In one hour Washington was master of the place. He had lost two men, and he had taken nearly one thousand prisoners.

The British general, Cornwallis, was in New York, getting ready to return to England; for he thought the rebellion of the colonies was so nearly over that he need not stay in America any longer. The news from Trenton was an unpleasant surprise, but he started out promptly to crush that troublesome Washington, who never seemed to understand that he was beaten and who would not stay beaten.

Cornwallis had more men than the Americans, and Washington did not want to fight a battle with him. "Cornwallis will come upon us, but keep him away as long as you can," was Washington's orders to part of his troops; and therefore the British had a hard time in their march across New Jersey to Trenton. A storm of bullets would come suddenly from some little thicket on one side of the road; and by the time the trees had been well peppered with British shot, another leaden storm would come from some thicket on the other side. A few hundred men with two cannon were continually attacking him in front. He could make them retreat, but he could not make them hurry; and it was late in the afternoon when he came to Trenton. Washington was not in the town, but just across a stream that flows into the Delaware. The troops that had been such a torment to Cornwallis retreated across the bridge and joined their comrades.

The British officers said, "Let us attack him at once." But Cornwallis replied, "No, our men are tired out, and it will soon be dark. He is safe enough. In the morning we shall have two thousand more troops, and we can shut him in between the stream and the Delaware. He will have to surrender, and then the rebellion will be over." He wrote a letter home which said, "We have run down the old fox, and we will bag him in the morning."

There seemed nothing that Washington could do but prepare to fight. All night long his camp-fires burned along the south side of the stream. The British sentinels on the north side could see the men piling on wood, they could hear the noise of spades and pickaxes, they could even hear the soldiers talking together. But when it began to grow light, the British found that Washington and his army had slipped away quietly in the middle of the night. A few men had remained behind to keep the fires burning and make as much noise as possible with their spades and pickaxes; but they, too, were gone. They had run through the woods and joined their commander. The British were welcome to the gravel that had been shoveled up and to the ashes of the camp-fires, but nothing else was left for them. While Cornwallis stood on the bank of the stream gazing across at the deserted camp, he heard the booming of cannon ten miles away. "That was from Princeton," he thought. "The old fox is there already, and he will try to destroy our stores at Brunswick."

This was exactly what Washington had planned to do. At Princeton he met the British forces just starting to go and help Cornwallis conquer him. There was a sharp fight, and the Americans won the day. Cornwallis was in pursuit, of course, but there were several streams between the armies. They were badly swollen by a sudden thaw, and Washington had unkindly burned the bridges. The British marched with dripping uniforms into the streets of Princeton, but Washington was not there. He had hoped to go on to Brunswick, but his men were too tired and too nearly barefooted for a march of eighteen miles. So he made his way to the heights of Morristown, and there he was safe for the winter.

Walter Ransom Barrows

ROBERT LOUIS STEVENSON

ILLUSTRATED BY *Lynd Ward*

THIS IS the story of Robert Louis Stevenson, a man who wrote stirring tales of adventure and romance as well as poems of great beauty, a man who wrote them while bravely fighting a constant battle against ill health.

Stevenson was born in Edinburgh, Scotland. He was the only son of an engineer who specialized in building lighthouses and breakwaters. Because of his ill health, Louis, as a boy, spent much time in bed and his schooling was irregular. He could not take part in sports with other boys but he was able to amuse himself. He had a vivid imagination and his counterpane was the scene of battles while his bed was frequently a boat in which he could voyage to far-off places. When he was strong enough to go out into the garden of his beautiful country home, he would often compose gay, imaginative rhymes, some of which he used later in his book *A Child's Garden of Verses.* He wrote poems such as this:

When at home alone I sit
And am very tired of it,
I have just to shut my eyes
To go sailing through the skies—
To go sailing far away
To the pleasant Land of Play;
To the fairy land afar
Where the Little People are;
Where the clover tops are trees,
And the rain pools are the seas
And the leaves, like little ships,
Sail about on tiny trips.

At the age of sixteen Louis was well enough to enter the University of Edinburgh as a student in engineering. In the summer time he was even able to go with his father on tours of inspection of various lighthouses and harbors. Here he was thrilled by lonely moors, wild coastlines and seagirt isles. Here he learned how to make maps and he made use of map-making later in *Treasure Island.*

But Louis's heart was not in the study of engineering nor in the study of law which he tried next. The frail young man had to abandon everything for awhile, going to Switzerland, France and Germany for a rest.

At this time Stevenson began to write graceful and beautiful prose. He wrote *An Inland Voyage*, a delightful story about European canal boats, and he wrote *Travels with a Donkey*, his famous account of a walking trip through France.

It was in France that he fell in love with Mrs. Osbourne who, later in California, he married. Now he began writing his zestful tales for which he is so well-known. He wrote *Treasure Island*, the first book which brought him fame, and he sold it to a magazine called *Young Folks*. This colorful story about pirates and hidden treasure has long delighted both young and old.

Three years later Stevenson wrote the book he considered his best, *Kidnapped.* This is a tale of David Balfour, a young Scottish boy, and his exciting adventures when his uncle placed him on a sailing ship going to America where the boy was to be sold into service.

Finally, when Stevenson was thirty-nine, he sailed to the beautiful island of Samoa in the South Seas. Here he spent the last five years of his life. The Samoans grew to love this kindly, unselfish friend who helped them in so many ways and when he died they sadly carried his body up to the top of Mount Vaea. On his tombstone is an epitaph written by Stevenson himself:

> Under the wide and starry sky
> Dig the grave and let me die.
> Glad did I live and gladly die,
> And I laid me down with a will.

This be the verse you grave for me—
Here he lies where he longed to be;
Home is the sailor, home from the sea,
And the hunter home from the hill.

What Stevenson did for others during his last years in Samoa is recounted in this tribute written after his death:

THE ROAD OF THE LOVING HEART

"Remembering the great love of his highness, Tusitala, and his loving care when we were in prison and sore distressed, we have prepared him an enduring present, this road which we have dug for ever."

In a far-off island, thousands of miles from the mainland, and unconnected with the world by cable, stands this inscription. It was set up at the corner of a new road, cut through a tropical jungle, and bears at its head the title of this article, signed by the names of ten prominent chiefs. This is the story of the road, and why it was built:

A number of years ago a Scot, broken in health and expecting an early death, sought out this lonely spot, because here the climate was favorable to the disease from which he suffered. He settled here for what remained to him of life.

He bought an estate of several hundred acres, and threw himself earnestly into the life of the natives of the island. There was great division among the many chiefs, and prolonged warfare. Very soon the chiefs found that this alien from a strange land was their best friend. They began coming to him for counsel, and invited him to their most important conferences.

Though he did not bear that name, he became a missionary to them. He was their hero, and they loved and trusted him because he tried to lead them aright. They had never had such a friend. And so it came about that when the wars ceased, the chiefs of both sides called him by a name of their own, and made him one of their own number, thus conferring upon him the highest honor within their power.

But many of the chiefs were still in prison, because of their political views or deeds, and in constant danger of being put to death. Their sole friend was the Scot, whom they called Tusitala. He visited them, comforted them, repeated passages from the history of Christ to them, and busied himself incessantly to effect their release.

At length he obtained their freedom, and then, glowing with gratitude, in despite of age, decrepitude, and loss of strength, they started directly for the estate of their benefactor, and there, in the terrible heat, they laboured for weeks in building him a road which they knew he had long

desired. Love conquered weakness, and they did not cease their toil until their handiwork, which they called "The Road of the Loving Heart," was finished.

Not long after this the white chief suddenly died. At the news the native chiefs flocked from all parts of the island to the house, and took charge of the body. They kissed his hand as they came in, and all night sat in silence about him. One of them, a feeble old man, threw himself on his knees beside the body of his benefactor, and cried out between his sobs:

"I am only a poor black man, and ignorant. Yet I am not afraid to come and take the last look of my dead friend's face. Behold, Tusitala is dead. We were in prison and he cared for us. The day was no longer than his kindness. Who is there so great as Tusitala? Who is there more loving-compassionate? What is your love to his love?"

So the chiefs took their friend to the top of a steep mountain which he had loved and there buried him. It was a mighty task.

The civilized world mourns the great author. The name of Robert Louis Stevenson is lastingly inwrought into English literature. But the Samoans mourn in his loss a brother, who outdid all others in loving-kindness, and so long as the far-off island in the Pacific exists, Tusitala will be gratefully remembered, not because he was so greatly gifted, but simply because he was a good man.

THE CELESTIAL SURGEON

Robert Louis Stevenson

If I have faltered more or less
In my great task of happiness;
If I have moved among my race
And shown no glorious morning face;
If beams from happy human eyes
Have moved me not; if morning skies,
Books and my food, and summer rain
Knocked on my sullen heart in vain:—
Lord, Thy most pointed pleasure take
And stab my spirit broad awake!

IN THE following selection taken from his autobiography, Booker T. Washington tells the story of his education with such skill and power that the reader can actually see and feel the hardships and privations which he endured in order to secure his education.

After graduation from Hampton Institute, Washington taught school in West Virginia until 1881, when he accepted a call to organize and become the principal of a normal school at Tuskegee, Alabama. He opened his school in an old church and a dilapidated shanty with an attendance of only thirty students. Washington devoted his life to the educational and social advancement of his race.

Booker T. Washington

MY STRUGGLE FOR AN EDUCATION

ILLUSTRATED BY *Matilda Breuer*

ONE DAY, while at work in the coal mine, I happened to overhear two miners talking about a great school for colored people somewhere in Virginia. This was the first time that I had ever heard anything about any kind of school or college that was more pretentious than the little colored school in our town.

In the darkness of the mine I noiselessly crept as close as I could to the two men who were talking. I heard one tell the other that not only was the school established for the members of my race, but that opportunities were provided by which poor, but worthy, students could work out all or a part of the cost of board, and at the same time be taught some trade or industry.

As they went on describing the school, it seemed to me that it must be the greatest place on earth, and not even Heaven presented more attractions for me at that time than did the Hampton Normal and Agricultural Institute in Virginia, about which these men were talking. I resolved at once to go to that school, although I had no idea where it was, or how many miles away, or how I was going to reach it; I remembered only that I was on fire constantly with one ambition, and that was to go to Hampton. This thought was with me day and night.

After hearing of the Hampton Institute, I continued to work for a few months longer in the coal mine. While out at work there, I heard of a vacant position in the household of General Lewis Ruffner, the owner of the salt furnace and coal mine. Mrs. Ruffner had a reputation all through the vicinity for being very strict with her servants, and especially with the boys who tried to serve her.

From fearing Mrs. Ruffner I soon learned to look upon her as one of my best friends. When she found that she could trust me she did so implicitly. During the one or two winters that I was with her she gave me an opportunity to go to school for an hour in the day during a portion of the winter months, but most of my studying was done at night, sometimes alone, sometimes under some one whom I could hire to teach me. Mrs. Ruffner always encouraged and sympathized with me in all my efforts to get an education. It was while living with her that I began to get together my first library. I secured a dry-goods box, knocked out one side of it, put some shelves in it, and began putting into it every kind of book that I could get my hands upon, and called it my "library."

Notwithstanding my success at Mrs. Ruffner's I did not give up the idea of going to the Hampton Institute. In the fall of 1872 I determined to make an effort to get there, although, as I have stated, I had no definite idea of the direction in which Hampton was, or of what it would cost to go there. I do not think that any one thoroughly sympathized with me in my ambition to go to Hampton unless it was my mother, and she was troubled with a grave fear that I was starting out on a "wild-goose chase." At any rate, I got only a half-hearted consent from her that I might start. The small amount of money that I had earned had been consumed by my stepfather and the remainder of the family, with the exception of a very few dollars, and so I had very little with which to buy clothes and pay my travelling expenses. My brother John helped me all that he could, but of course that was not a great deal, for his work was in the coal mine, where he did not earn much, and most of what he did earn went in the direction of paying the household expenses.

Perhaps the thing that touched and pleased me most in connection with my starting for Hampton was the interest that many of the older colored people took in the matter. They had spent the best days of their lives in slavery, and hardly expected to live to see the time when they would see a member of their race leave home to attend a boarding school. Some of these older people would give me a nickel, others a quarter, or a handkerchief.

Finally the great day came, and I started for Hampton. I had only a small, cheap satchel that contained what few articles of clothing I could get. My mother at the time was rather weak and broken in health. I hardly expected to see her again, and thus our parting was all the more sad. She, however, was very brave through it all. At that time there were no through trains connecting that part of West Virginia with eastern Virginia. Trains ran only a portion of the way, and the remainder of the distance was travelled by stagecoaches.

The distance from Malden to Hampton is about five hundred miles. I had not been away from home many hours before it began to grow painfully evident that I did not have enough money to pay my fare to Hampton. One experience I shall long remember. I had been travelling over the mountains most of the afternoon in an old-fashioned stagecoach when, late in the evening, the coach stopped for the night at a common, unpainted house called a hotel. All the other passengers except myself were whites. In my ignorance I supposed that the little hotel existed for the purpose of accommodating the passengers who travelled on the stagecoach. The difference that the color of one's skin would make I had not thought anything about. After all the other passengers had been shown rooms and were getting ready for supper, I shyly presented myself before the man at the desk. It is true I had practically no money in my pocket with which to pay for bed or food, but I had hoped in some way to beg my way into the good graces of the landlord, for at that season in the mountains of Virginia the weather was cold, and I wanted to get indoors for the night. Without asking as to whether I had any money, the man at the desk firmly refused to even consider the matter of providing me with food or lodging. This was my first experience in finding out what the color of my skin meant. In some way I managed to keep warm by walking about, and so got through the night. My whole soul was so bent upon reaching Hampton that I did not have time to cherish any bitterness toward the hotel keeper.

By walking, begging rides both in wagons and in the cars, in some way, after a number of days, I reached the city of Richmond, Virginia, about eighty-two miles from Hampton. When I reached there tired, hungry, and dirty, it was late in the night. I had never been in a large city, and this rather added to my misery. When I reached Richmond, I was completely out of money. I had not a single acquaintance in the place and, being unused to city ways, I did not know where to go. I applied at several places for lodging, but they all wanted money, and that was what I did not have. Knowing nothing else better to do, I walked the streets. In doing this I passed by many food stands where fried chicken and half-moon apple pies were piled high and made to present a most tempting appearance. At that time it seemed to me that I would have promised all that I expected to possess in the future to have gotten hold of one of those chicken legs, or one of those pies. But I could not get either of these, nor anything else to eat.

I must have walked the streets till after midnight. At last I became so exhausted that I could walk no longer. I was tired, I was hungry, I was everything but discouraged. Just about the time when I reached extreme physical exhaustion, I came upon a portion of a street where the board sidewalk was considerably elevated. I waited for a few minutes, till I was sure that no passers-by could see me, and then crept under the sidewalk and lay for the night upon the ground, with my satchel of clothing for a pillow. Nearly all night I could hear the tramp of feet over my head. The next morning I found myself somewhat refreshed, but I was extremely hungry, because it had been a long time since I had had sufficient food. As soon as it became light enough for me to see my surroundings I noticed that I was near a large ship, and that this ship seemed to be unloading a cargo of pig iron. I went at once to the vessel and asked the captain to permit me to help unload the vessel in order to get money for food. The captain, a white man, who seemed to be kindhearted, consented. I worked long enough to earn money for my breakfast and, it seems to me, as I remember it now, to have been about the best breakfast that I have ever eaten.

My work pleased the captain so well that he told me if I desired I could continue working for a small amount per day. This I was very glad to do. I continued working on this vessel for a number of days. After buying food with the small wages I received there was not much left to add to the amount I must get to pay my way to Hampton. In order to economize in every way possible, so as to be sure to reach Hampton in a reasonable time, I continued to sleep under the same sidewalk that gave me shelter the first night I was in Richmond. Many years after that the colored citizens of Richmond very kindly tendered me a reception at which there must have been two thousand people present. This reception was held not far from the spot where I slept the first night I spent in that city, and I must confess that my mind was more upon the sidewalk that first gave me shelter than upon the reception, agreeable and cordial as it was.

When I had saved what I considered enough money with which to reach Hampton, I thanked the captain of the vessel for his kindness, and started again. Without any unusual occurrence I reached Hampton, with a surplus of exactly fifty cents with which to begin my education. To me it had been a long, eventful journey; but the first sight of the large, three-story, brick building seemed to have rewarded me for all that I had undergone in order to reach the place. If the people who gave the money to provide that building could appreciate the influence the sight of it had upon me, as well as upon thousands of other youths, they would feel all the more encouraged to make such gifts. It seemed to me to be the largest and most beautiful building I had ever seen. The sight of it seemed to give me new life. I felt that a new kind of existence had now begun—that life would now have a new meaning. I felt that I had reached the promised land, and I resolved to let no obstacle prevent me from putting forth the highest effort to fit myself to accomplish the most good in the world.

As soon as possible, after reaching the grounds of the Hampton Institute, I presented myself before the head teacher for assignment to a class. Having been so long without proper food, a bath and change of clothing, I did not, of course, make a very favorable impression upon her, and I could see at once that there were doubts in her mind about the wisdom of admitting me as a student. I felt that I could hardly blame her if she got the idea that I was a worthless loafer or tramp. For some time she did not refuse to admit me, neither did she decide in my favor, and I continued to linger about her, and to impress her in all the ways I could with my worthiness. In the meantime I saw her admitting other students, and that added greatly to my discomfort, for I felt deep down in my heart, that I could do as well as they, if I could only get a chance to show what was in me.

After some hours had passed, the head teacher said to me:

"The adjoining recitation room needs sweeping. Take the broom and sweep it."

It occurred to me at once that here was my chance. Never did I receive an order with more delight. I knew that I could sweep, for Mrs. Ruffner had thoroughly taught me how to do that when I lived with her.

I swept the recitation room three times. Then I got a dusting cloth and I dusted it four times. All the woodwork around the walls, every bench, table and desk, I went over four times with my dusting cloth. Besides, every piece of furniture had been moved and every closet and corner in the room had been thoroughly cleaned. I had the feeling that in a large measure my future depended upon the impression I made upon the teacher in the cleaning of that room. When I was through, I reported to the head teacher. She was a "Yankee" woman who knew just where to look for dirt. She went into the room and inspected the floor and closets; then she took her handkerchief and rubbed it on the woodwork about the walls, and over the table and benches. When she was unable to find one bit of dirt on the floor, or a particle of dust on any of the furniture, she quietly remarked, "I guess you will do to enter this institution."

I was one of the happiest souls on earth. The sweeping of that room was my college examination, and never did any youth pass an examination for entrance into Harvard or Yale that gave him more genuine satisfaction. I have passed several examinations since then, but I have always felt that this was the best one I ever passed.

I have spoken of my own experience in entering the Hampton Institute. Perhaps few, if any, had anything like the same experience that I had, but about that same period there were hundreds who found their way to Hampton and other institutions after experiencing something of the same difficulties that I went through. The young men and women were determined to secure an education at any cost.

The sweeping of the recitation room in the manner that I did it seems to have paved the way for me to get through Hampton. Miss Mary F. Mackie, the head teacher, offered me a position as janitor. This, of course, I gladly accepted, because it was a place where I could work out nearly all the cost of my board. The work was hard and taxing, but I stuck to it. I had a large number of rooms to care for, and had to work late into the night, while at the same time I had to rise by four o'clock in the morning, in order to build the fires and have a little time in which to prepare my lessons. In all my career at Hampton, and ever since I have been out in the world, Miss Mary F. Mackie, the head teacher to whom I have referred, proved one of my strongest and most helpful friends. Her advice and encouragement were always helpful and strengthening to me in the darkest hour.

I have spoken of the impression that was made upon me by the buildings and general appearance of the Hampton Institute, but I have not spoken of that which made the greatest and most lasting impression upon me, and that was a great man—the noblest, rarest human being that it has ever been my privilege to meet. I refer to the late General Samuel C. Armstrong.

It has been my fortune to meet personally many of what are called great characters, both in Europe and America, but I do not hesitate to say that I never met any man who, in my estimation, was the equal of General Armstrong. Fresh from the degrading influences of the slave plantation and the coal mines, it was a rare privilege for me to be permitted to come into direct contact with such a character as General Armstrong. I shall always remember that the first time I went into his presence he made the impression upon me of being a perfect man: I was made to feel that there was something about him that was superhuman. It was my privilege to know the General personally from the time I entered Hampton till he died, and the more I saw of him the greater he grew in my estimation. One might have removed from Hampton all the buildings, classrooms, teachers and industries, and given the men and women there the opportunity of coming into daily contact with General Armstrong, and that alone would have been a liberal education. The older I grow, the more I am convinced that there is no education which one can get from books and costly apparatus, that is equal to that which can be gotten from contact with great men and

women. Instead of studying books so constantly, how I wish that our schools and colleges might learn to study men and things!

For some time, while a student at Hampton, I possessed but a single pair of socks, but when I had worn these till they became soiled, I would wash them at night and hang them by the fire to dry, so that I might wear them again the next morning.

The charge for my board at Hampton was ten dollars per month. I was expected to pay a part of this in cash and to work out the remainder. To meet this cash payment, as I have stated,

I had just fifty cents when I reached the institution. Aside from a very few dollars that my brother John was able to send me once in awhile, I had no money with which to pay my board. I was determined from the first to make my work as janitor so valuable that my services would be indispensable. This I succeeded in doing to such an extent that I was soon informed that I would be allowed the full cost of my board in return for my work. The cost of tuition was seventy dollars a year. This, of course, was wholly beyond my ability to provide. If I had been compelled to pay the seventy dollars for tuition, in addition to providing for my board, I would have been compelled to leave the Hampton school. General Armstrong, however, very kindly got Mr. S. Griffitts Morgan, of New Bedford, Mass., to defray the cost of my tuition during the whole time that I was at Hampton. After I finished the course at Hampton, and had entered upon my lifework at Tuskegee, I had the pleasure of visiting Mr. Morgan several times.

After having been for awhile at Hampton, I found myself in difficulty because I did not have books and clothing. Usually, however, I got around the trouble about books by borrowing from those who were more fortunate than myself. As to clothes, when I reached Hampton I had practically nothing. Everything that I possessed was in a small hand satchel. My anxiety about clothing was increased because of the fact that General Armstrong made a personal inspection of the young men in ranks, to see that their clothes were clean. Shoes had to be polished, there must be no buttons off the clothing, and no grease spots. To wear one suit of clothes continually while at work and in the schoolroom, and at the same time keep it clean, was rather a hard problem for me to solve. In some way I managed to get on till the teachers learned that I was in earnest and meant to succeed, and then some of them were kind enough to see that I was partly supplied with second-hand clothing that had been sent in barrels from the North. These barrels proved a blessing to hundreds of poor, but deserving students. Without them I question whether I should ever have gotten through Hampton.

When I first went to Hampton I do not recall that I had ever slept in a bed that had two sheets on it. In those days there were not many buildings there, and room was very precious. There were seven other boys in the same room with me; most of them students who had been there for some time. The sheets were quite a puzzle to me. The first night I slept under both of them, and the second night I slept on top of both of them; but by watching the other boys I learned my lesson in this, and have been trying to follow it ever since and to teach it to others.

I was among the youngest of the students who were in Hampton at that time. Most of the students were men and women—some as old as forty years of age. As I now recall the scene of my first year, I do not believe that one often has the opportunity of coming into contact with three or four hundred men and women who were so tremendously in earnest as these men and women were. Every hour was occupied in study or work. Nearly all had had enough actual contact with the world to teach them the need of education. Many of the older ones were, of course, too old to master the textbooks very thoroughly, and it was often sad to watch their struggles; but they made up in earnestness much of what they lacked in books. Many of them were as poor as I was and, besides having to wrestle with their books, they had to struggle with a poverty which prevented their having the necessities of life. Many of them had aged parents who were dependent upon them, and some of them were men who had wives whose support in some way they had to provide for.

The great and prevailing idea that seemed to take possession of every one was to prepare himself to lift up the people at his home. No one seemed to think of himself. And the officers and teachers, what a rare set of human beings they were! They worked for the students night and day, in season and out of season. They seemed happy only when they were helping the students in some manner. Whenever it is written—and I hope it will be—the part that the Yankee teachers played in the education of the Negroes immediately after the war will make one of the most thrilling parts of the history of this country. The time is not far distant when the whole South will appreciate this service in a way that it has not yet been able to do.

Marchette Chute

A LIFE OF WILLIAM SHAKESPEARE

ILLUSTRATED BY *Robert Sinnott*

NO WRITER has been more loved for his work than William Shakespeare. It is pleasant to know that the people of his own day loved him too, both as a writer and as a human being. He did not have an eventful life, but it must have been a happy one. Anyone who gave delight to so many people must have felt some of it for himself.

He was born in 1564, in the green, prosperous little town of Stratford in the southern part of England, and the town clerk marked down the day of his baptism as the 26th of April. The day was an important one for his father, John Shakespeare. For he and his wife Mary had had two little girls who died, and they must have hoped great things for the new baby boy.

Several little brothers and sisters followed and they all grew up together in a comfortable house on Henley Street. John Shakespeare was a glove maker, which was an important trade in those days, and he was very active in town affairs. He served for many years on the Town Council, and when William was four years old his father was elected to the highest position in Stratford and became the mayor. This gave him the right to wear a robe of scarlet and fur and to have the best pew in church and also, if he wished, to get himself a coat of arms.

Stratford was a busy town in those days, with so many people passing through that there was enough trade for four fine inns. Twice a year there was a fair, with people coming for miles around to do their shopping in Stratford and with plenty of pies and performing animals for small boys to enjoy. Even more exciting, from the point of view of the small boys, was the fact that traveling actors began to stop there.

The first company of actors came to Stratford the year that John Shakespeare was mayor. They came by wagon, with their drums and their glittering costumes, and brought the same plays that had been applauded in London. This was a period when there were no magazines or newspapers and only a few books, so that most of the excitement of story-telling and make-believe came through actors and acting. There were dozens of these acting companies traveling all over England, and wherever they went the people hurried to see them.

The life of a small boy in Stratford was not all play. The school hours were very long, lasting from seven in the morning until late afternoon, and since there was a law which said that all the children had to be home by eight o'clock in the evening there was not much time for games. Like all the other small boys in town, young William Shakespeare must have spent long hours in the upstairs room where Stratford had its school. It was a good school, using well-trained teachers and giving them higher pay than was usual, but like all the schools of the period it taught nothing but Latin.

Latin never interested Shakespeare very much. He knew the opening pages of his Latin primer by heart, but it was the English language that delighted him. English was not taught in the schools because it was a young language and still changing. There were no English dictionaries or books on English grammar for Shakespeare to study. That meant there was still room for experimentation and even for invention, and Shakespeare and his fellow writers had a whole world of words to explore when they left the schoolroom and started writing English poetry.

By the time Shakespeare was old enough to leave school, his father was not as rich or as influential as he had once been. He had even left the Town Council, although his fellow members hopefully kept his place open for him. There were money troubles and land troubles, and there were five children at home to clothe and feed.

If young William Shakespeare had done the usual thing, he would have gone into his father's business and settled down quietly in Stratford. That was what his school friends were doing, and perhaps his family hoped that Shakespeare would be like the rest. But he was not in the least like any of the rest or, for that matter, like anyone else in England. The greatest writer that England had ever known could not possibly have settled down contently as a small-town businessman.

He had every reason for staying in Stratford. When he was eighteen years old he married a woman, named Anne Hathaway, from a neighboring village and they had three children. First there was a little girl named Susanna and then there were twins, a boy and a girl. Shakespeare had a family to support by the time he was twenty-one, and everyone must have expected him to stay home and learn a trade.

Luckily for himself and for the world, Shakespeare did nothing of the sort. Instead, like so many other young Englishmen of his day, he left his quiet home town and went to the great, lively city of London.

London was a port city, and the river Thames brought the wealth of the world into its tangled network of narrow streets, where new ideas and foreign costumes jostled each other happily and every corner might bring a new adventure. In Stratford a young man could learn a trade and he could learn Latin. In London he could learn French or Turkish, how to write shorthand, or fence, or play a bass viol. He could see strange plants, like tomatoes from Spain, or corn from America. He could meet adventurous men who had fought in Holland, or sailed under great sea captains like Sir Francis Drake. He could visit the lions in the zoo, or the tombs of the kings in Westminster Abbey. He could hear fine music and see splendid processions, and he could find bookstalls piled high with books. In their pages he could get instruction on everything from cooking to mathematics, and there were story books to tell of the troubles of great folk of former days, like young Juliet of Verona or Queen Cleopatra of Egypt. Above all, Shakespeare could meet his fellow poets, since every young man in England who wanted to be a poet tried to get to London.

If a poet wanted to make a living in London he wrote plays. The actors had found that verse was easy to memorize and effective to deliver, and the best poets in England were supplying the London actors with beautiful rolling lines that brought waves of applause from the audiences.

In London everyone went to the theatre, and a city of a quarter of a million people was able to support a great many acting companies. At first the companies had used large halls or the yards of inns and had kept their costumes and properties packed up so that they could move them as quickly as possible. But when Shakespeare was twelve years old an actor named James Burbage decided that his company ought to have a home of its own and built the first theatre in England.

Burbage's building was not shaped like a modern theatre, which is a long, lighted box with a stage set into one end of it. His Theatre was a huge, gaily painted wooden circle, open to the sky. The seats curved around three sides of it, and if the customers could not afford more than a penny they were allowed to stand on the ground in front of the jutting stage. The acting area was built on several levels, ranging from the trap doors underneath the stage through which devils or witches could leap with an explosion of fireworks, to the topmost level from which birds or goddesses could be let down by pulleys. It was possible to put on a whole war in Burbage's Theatre, with the stage balconies serving as the walls of the besieged castle, and the actors using real swords and gunpowder.

The Theatre was a great success and other playhouses like the Curtain and the Rose were put up to compete with it. All of them were big, brightly painted wooden buildings that could hold more than a thousand people. The audiences were a fine mixture, from velvet-clad courtiers to workmen and their wives; and so many children came to laugh at the clowns and applaud the heroes that the show had to close early to get them home before dark.

An actor who worked in any of these theatres had to be well trained. He had to know how to fence, since most of the plays had fights in them, and he had to be athletic enough to take a fall from one of the stage balconies without hurting his expensive costume. He had to be able to remember a great deal of stage poetry, since a new play was put on every afternoon, and to recite it in a voice that could be heard at the back of a large open-air building. He had to be able to change his costume quickly, since he was often expected to take four or five parts in the same play. He had to know how to dance and sing, and how to play at least one musical instrument, and he had to be able to keep going, day after day in winter and

Midsummer Night's Dream—*Titania sleeping*

summer, in all the strenuous parts that the playwrights had written for him.

By the time he had reached his late twenties, Shakespeare had learned to do all these things and was a successful actor on the London stage. Only the very best actors were able to build a career in London; the lesser ones went abroad or worked in the smaller towns. And since Shakespeare was a London actor for about twenty years it is clear that he must have been a good one.

By this time also he was beginning to be known as a playwright. When he was twenty-eight, Shakespeare was attacked in print by another London playwright named Robert Greene, who felt that actors had no business writing plays too. Greene's publisher apologized for having printed the attack, especially since, as he explained, Shakespeare was as courteous in his behavior as he was excellent in his acting. It is clear that Greene had no reason to dislike Shakespeare personally. But the plays that Shakespeare had begun to write were so successful with the London audiences that some of the other playwrights were beginning to be a little afraid of him.

Shakespeare's earliest plays were full of variety. They were not all good since, like most great writers he grew slowly, but they showed that he knew how to put a story together and how to please an audience. He wrote a very popular series of plays on English history, full of blood and battles. He wrote a Roman tragedy, also full of blood, and a Roman comedy, full of jokes. He also wrote a light little comedy full of word-music, and in fact there was almost nothing that he was not willing to try.

In the same year that Robert Greene made his attack on Shakespeare, all the theatres in London had to be closed because of a plague. No one could get work as a playwright, so Shakespeare tried his hand at writing narrative poems instead. He wrote two of these story poems, which were printed by an important London publisher and dedicated to a prominent young nobleman. Both poems were greatly admired, and Shakespeare now had an opportunity to become a fashionable London poet instead of a popular London playwright.

In those days it was believed that plays had no value whatever as literature. If they happened to get into print they came out in cheap little pamphlets that did not even bother to mention the author's name. Nor did the writer get any money from the publisher, for the play he had written did not belong to him. It belonged to the acting company that had bought it, and the company could do whatever it liked with it. A poem, however, was different. It could be handsomely printed with the author's name in large type. It would be read by influential people and then handed down to their children so that the poet's name would be known in future generations.

Shakespeare planned to write a third poem, and then suddenly he changed his mind. Instead, he joined a company of actors that was just being formed and from that time forward he wrote nothing but plays. Shakespeare had evidently decided that he did not want to please publishers and noblemen. He wanted to please ordinary Londoners, using his poetry to bring them wonderful stories about people, and making them come alive on the stage. His place was in the theatre, and from that time on he never left it.

The company of actors that Shakespeare joined in 1594 was not quite like any other. All the acting companies knew how to work together, since they owned their plays and costumes and properties in partnership, but most of them were held together only by the fact that they wanted to make money. Shakespeare's company stayed in existence for half a century, outlasting every other acting company in London, because the men who made it up were not only business partners, but close and affectionate friends. They took care of each others' children and remembered each other in their wills, and they enjoyed working together because they loved one another.

The most famous actor in the company was Richard Burbage, the son of the man who had built the Theatre. He brought to life some of Shakespeare's greatest characters—Hamlet, Othello and King Lear—and if there had been a star in the company he would have been the star. But the actors worked together as equals, taking a large part one afternoon and a small part the next, and Shakespeare worked as hard as any of them. It is not known what parts he acted, except that he appeared in both comedies and tragedies, and a fellow poet who praised him for his courtesy spoke especially of the "kingly" parts he had played.

Shakespeare's company was made up of experienced actors who knew how to work together democratically, and who made the play as a whole more important than any of the people in it. It was very well equipped to present the plays that Shakespeare was now writing at the rate of about two a year, and his art expanded like a great tree that at last had room to grow.

The people of London were delighted with his new plays and flocked to the theatre where they were being shown. His first great success for the new company was the history play of *Richard III,* and the Londoners went around quoting the climax when Burbage, who played King Richard, shouted in his wonderful voice, "A horse! A horse! My kingdom for a horse!" Even more popular was *Romeo and Juliet,* the tragic story of two young lovers whose parents hated each other; and it was said that when a London boy wanted to make love to his girl he used Shakespeare's beautiful lines and talked "naught but pure Juliet and Romeo." Shakespeare gave the Londoners the fairies of *A Midsummer Night's Dream,* the excitement of Portia facing Shylock in the trial scene of *The Merchant of Venice,* and above all he gave them a fat and rowdy knight named Sir John Falstaff. Falstaff surged his outrageously funny way through a history play called *Henry IV* and pleased everyone so much that Shakespeare finally had to give him a whole play to himself.

Every year the London public loved Shakespeare more. But literary critics and university people felt that he had made a great mistake in deciding to write for ordinary people instead of doing narrative poems for the nobility. Shakespeare's name is mentioned many times in this period but almost always in praise of his two poems. His plays were only common theatre scripts and very few people felt that they were of any real importance.

Since Shakespeare was only a playwright, no one bothered

The Globe Theatre

to write down any news about him. A writer who liked his work made a complete list of all his plays, but no one kept his letters or wrote down any information about him. Unlike most writers of the period, Shakespeare did not become involved in London lawsuits or get sent to prison, and so there are no legal records about him. He spent his time writing and acting and, except for an occasional mention in a tax report or something like that, he left very few traces of his years in London.

In Stratford it was different. Stratford was a small town compared to London, and now that Shakespeare was a successful man in London his own family became increasingly important at home. Two years after Shakespeare joined the acting company his father managed to get the coat of arms he had dreamed of, complete with its silver falcon and its golden spear. The year after that William Shakespeare bought the second largest house in Stratford and soon he was buying large tracts of land in the surrounding countryside. Since he was busy in London his brother Gilbert handled the details, and the Shakespeare family became the large landowner that John Shakespeare had hoped it would be. But there was no son to inherit the Shakespeare land and carry on the family name, for William Shakespeare's little boy had died in Stratford when he was eleven years old.

Meanwhile Shakespeare went on writing plays. Like most of the playwrights of the period he did not make up his own plots, but picked up stories wherever he could find them. His plays about English kings and queens were based on a history book called Holinshed's *Chronicles,* and his great Roman tragedy on the murder of Julius Caesar came from a Greek writer named Plutarch. But in general most of Shakespeare's plots came from popular stories that could be found in anthologies on any bookstall, or else from old plays that he had seen.

The most famous story that Shakespeare took from an old play is *Hamlet.* The story of the prince of Denmark, who was commanded by his father's ghost to murder his uncle, had been popular for years on the English stage because it had an exciting plot full of poison and sword-play. Shakespeare decided to write a new version of the bloody old melodrama, and no one could have guessed that he was going to raise it up into one of the greatest and most loved plays ever written. Today, the fame of Shakespeare's wonderful prince has gone all over the world, and even in his own day the literary critics who had ignored his earlier plays had to admit that *Hamlet* was worthy of their attention. One well-known scholar of the period said that it would "please the wiser sort" and another said that it would "please all."

If Shakespeare had been anxious about his reputation as a writer, he could have put his plays into print as some of his fellow playwrights were beginning to do. But Shakespeare felt that his plays belonged to his company, not to himself, and he never worried about their safety. It was his company that guarded them so carefully and that was so proud of the man they called "our Shakespeare."

Not long after *Hamlet* was written the great Queen of England died. Elizabeth the First had been a magnificent ruler and she gave her name to a great age, The Elizabethan Age. But the last few years of her reign had been rather difficult, with a depression and high taxes, and a foreign war that no one seemed to be able to stop. All England was pleased when a cousin of hers was crowned as James the First, and the opening years of his reign were both peaceful and prosperous.

The new king enjoyed going to plays just as much as Queen Elizabeth had done, and he took Shakespeare's company under his special protection. They were now called the King's Men, and in the acting permit they were given, the name of Shakespeare occurs just above Richard Burbage's. Occasionally the King's Men had special duties to perform. For instance, when an important Spanish official came to London they served as attendants. But in general their chief business was what it had always been—to put on good plays.

The King's Men now owned a theatre of their own and they no longer had to perform in a rented playhouse as the other companies were doing. They had leased some land near the river Thames and erected the building themselves, using the heavy timber from Burbage's old Theatre, but adding many improvements. Their splendid new theatre was called the Globe, and all Shakespeare's plays were presented in it—*Hamlet* and the history plays and the comedies, and then the series of great tragedies that he wrote early in the reign of King James.

Shakespeare did not write these tragedies because of sadness in his private life. He was prospering in London, doing the work he wanted to do, and his family was prospering in Stratford. But every year his knowledge of people deepened, and he could see how easy it was for human beings to hurt themselves and others. He could see how the hero of *Othello* could become so frantic with fear that his wife did not love him, that he could decide to kill her. He could see how the hero of *Macbeth* could want power so badly that he committed murder to get it, and then had to go on with more murders, and still could never feel safe again. He could see how the hero of *King Lear,* old and spoiled and comfortable, could imagine no other kind of existence until he was suddenly thrust out into the cold winds of hunger and pain. And he could tell these stories, and others like them, in poetry so beautiful and so moving that nothing like it had ever existed in the world before.

During his last years in the theatre, Shakespeare went back to the lighter, almost fairylike plays he had written when he was a young man. The most famous of these is *The Tempest,* the story of an enchanted island with a fairy named Ariel and a monster named Caliban. The play is full of magic and it is difficult to stage in a theatre today. But the actors who owned the Globe had all the equipment they needed to show a storm at sea, or a banquet table suddenly being carried away through the air, and whatever Shakespeare wanted they were able to give him.

During these years in London, Shakespeare lived in hired lodgings, since his wife Anne apparently did not want to leave Stratford and make a home for him in the city. At about the time King James came to the throne, Shakespeare was living on the west side of London in the house of a man named Christopher Mountjoy. Shakespeare was very kind to Mountjoy's daughter and helped with the arrangements for her marriage.

In spite of his long, hard days in the theatre, he was not too busy to attend the "many conferences" that had to be held before her wedding.

Nevertheless, no one who worked as hard as Shakespeare did, can work forever. The company was becoming more active all the time, and in 1608, fourteen years after Shakespeare had joined them, they took over a handsome indoor theatre called the Blackfriars. Shakespeare was still acting, and he was listed as one of the "men players" who worked in the new theatre. But a short time later he retired. He visited London often and wrote at least one more play, but he spent his last years in Stratford in his handsome brick house that was called New Place. It had ten fireplaces, two orchards and a large garden, and from the windows Shakespeare could look across the street at the small upstairs room where he had once gone to school.

He died on the 23rd of April, 1616, just fifty-two years from the month in which he had been born. In his careful will he gave away his lands and his sword and his great gilded bowl, and he was buried in the old church where he had been baptized. There was nothing he could leave to his actor friends in London, since they already had all his plays, but he asked in his will that some money be set aside to buy memorial rings for "my fellows, John Heminges, Richard Burbage and Henry Condell." These were his three oldest friends in the company, and Shakespeare wanted them to wear the rings in memory of him.

Three years later Richard Burbage died also, and the company continued with Heminges and Condell at its head. All of Shakespeare's plays were still being acted both at the Globe and at the Blackfriars, but Heminges and Condell were afraid that the time might come when they would be lost. Half the plays were in print, but in cheap little pamphlets that were badly printed and wore out quickly; and it was quite possible that in a hundred years no one would know that William Shakespeare had ever written a line.

Heminges and Condell decided that something must be done to keep the plays of their friend safe. So they collected all

Hamlet—"*Good night, sweet Prince*"

thirty-six of them and had them printed in a large book that is now called the First Folio. They said they did not do this to make money, but "to keep the memory of so worthy a friend and fellow alive as was our Shakespeare."

Another friend of Shakespeare's named Ben Jonson wrote a poem to put in the front of the book. Like everyone else, Jonson had loved Shakespeare, and he gave his poem this title: "To my beloved, the author, Master William Shakespeare, and what he hath left us." Jonson also called him "gentle Shakespeare," and praised him for his courtesy, and in this Jonson was only saying what many people had already said. But most people still believed that Shakespeare was only a pleasant, popular writer, but Jonson knew better. He said in his poem that Shakespeare could be ranked with the greatest of the Greek dramatists and that his name would become known over the whole world.

"He was not of an age, but for all time."

Jonson was right. Today, everyone knows the name of William Shakespeare. His work is read all over the earth and has been translated into Italian, Norwegian, Japanese, and many other languages so that everyone can enjoy him. The people of England have shared him with everyone, and the Elizabethan playwright who worked so patiently and so carefully with his friends at the Globe is now conceded to be one of the greatest writers the world has ever known.

SHAKESPEARE

Agnes Lee

Because, the singer of an age, he sang
The passions of the ages,
It was humanity itself that leaped
To life upon his pages.

He told no single being's tale—he forced
All beings to his pen.
And when he made a man to walk the street
Forth walked a million men.

Laura Benét

HENRY WADSWORTH LONGFELLOW

ILLUSTRATED BY *Pelagie Doane*

HENRY WADSWORTH LONGFELLOW, poet of *The Children's Hour,* was born in Portland, Maine, on February twenty-seventh, 1807. His birthplace was a seafaring town and the house in which he was born looked out on the ocean. When he was a baby, his family moved to another house that had been his mother's old home. Of Portland he wrote:

> "Often I think of the beautiful town
>   That is seated by the sea;
> Often in thought go up and down
>   The pleasant streets of that dear old town,
> And my youth comes back to me,"

for he never forgot the "beauty and mystery of the ships. And the magic of the sea."

His father, Stephen Longfellow, was a successful lawyer. But his mother was fond of poetry, music and the out-of-doors, and taught Henry to love them, too. She was never very strong but she was a good mother to her four boys and four girls. The Longfellows were a big, happy family. Stephen, two years older, was the brother who was Henry's companion. They flew kites together, played ball and went swimming. In the bitter cold Maine winters they coasted and skated. When their lessons and a romp before bedtime were over, they would find their sleeping rooms as icy as the North Pole. But the children would plunge into good, deep feather beds and soon be warm and fast asleep. Often in the morning, ice in their pitchers had to be broken before they could wash.

As a child, Henry never liked loud noises or the sound of firecrakers, which made him cover his ears. Once he did take a gun and go hunting. He brought down a bird which turned out to be a robin. This grieved him so much that he never used a gun again. Portland had no theater but the children enjoyed the circus which came every year to their town. Henry Longfellow had plenty of books, for his father's library was a good one for those days. His favorite stories were the *Arabian Nights* and *Robinson Crusoe* and he loved *Don Quixote* and Irving's *Sketch Book.*

On Sundays, when Henry walked to church with his mother, carrying her footstool, all books except the Bible were strictly put away. On Sunday afternoons their mother read aloud to all the children from the Bible and, as it was illustrated, they enjoyed looking at the pictures. In the evening they all joined in singing hymns.

When he was only three years old Henry was sent to Ma'am Fellows' Dame School. She was stern and the children learned not to even smile during lesson hours. She must have had a switch on hand! Soon Henry was transferred to another school, where his teacher gave him the following splendid certificate. He was only six and a half at the time.

"Master Henry Longfellow is one of the best boys we have in school. He spells and reads very well. He also can add and multiply numbers. His conduct last quarter was very correct and amiable. June 30, 1813."

The war of 1812 between England and America touched the town of Portland when Henry was a child. The *Enterprise,* an American brig of war, fought and captured the British schooner, *Boxer.* Then she towed her prize into the harbor. The sad ending was that both commanders were killed in this battle and their bodies buried at the foot of Munjoy's Hill, in Portland.

At thirteen Henry wrote a poem on a place he knew, called Lovell's Pond. It had been a battleground between the French and Indians in their wars, so his poem was called *The Battle of Lovell's Pond.* It was published in the Portland *Gazette* and signed "Henry." A friend of the family, Judge Mullen, showed it to Henry's father. "This is very stiff," the Judge commented dryly, "and all copied, every bit of it." The boy's feelings were deeply hurt by the unjust criticism. But he went on writing verses. Fortunately, he was not too easily discouraged.

When he was fifteen he was ready for Bowdoin College in Portland, where his father was a trustee. He entered at the same time as his brother, Stephen. Since Henry was an excellent student, he made the sophomore class. There he met Nathaniel Hawthorne. The two young men were both very shy with each other at first but destined to be friends in later life, when Hawthorne sent his first book, *Twice Told Tales,* to Longfellow, then a professor at Harvard. Longfellow (as we will call him now) wrote a favorable review of it. His college mates and professors liked this young fellow. He was a good companion, sociable, cheerful and generous, envying no one. He had a fine head and wore his hair rather long. His eyes were a clear blue and these good features made up for a large nose. He was fussy about his dress, liked light vests and varied neckties. The young men of those days wore knee breeches and silk stockings and generally tied their long hair in a club.

While he was in college, Longfellow did a good deal of writing. Seventeen poems, many of which appeared in the *United States Literary Gazette,* were completed and later on five of them were included in his books. He stood high in his class as well, for he was a first-rate student, though in no way remarkable. When he graduated at barely nineteen, he was awarded the honor of delivering one of the English orations. Then, because of a translation he had made of one of *Horace's Odes,* read at an examination, young Longfellow received a further honor. He was elected to the chair of modern languages. The faculty required, however, that he travel in Europe for three years in order to be thoroughly familiar with the languages he would teach. The poet had made up his mind to be a writer as well as a teacher. But his father, who had wished his son to be a lawyer, did not favor the plan. So the son went to Europe in 1826, to fit himself for teaching.

He spent three years in France, Spain, Italy and Germany.

He took many a walking trip in order to mingle naturally with the people of these different countries and learn to know them as well as the tongues they spoke. This time was a good one for Longfellow. Travel and the contact with other minds broadened his mind and he gathered material for poems. *Outre-Mer* describes his experiences. The years abroad drew to a close, and at twenty-two the young man came back to Bowdoin to teach. Then he fell in love with a lovely but frail girl, Mary Storer Potter, and married her in 1831. Both were happy, for the new professor was a success with his classes, though his salary was never more than a thousand dollars for the year's teaching. For five years he taught languages at Bowdoin.

In 1835 a turn came in Longfellow's affairs. He was chosen by Harvard College to be its Smith professor of modern languages at an annual salary of fifteen hundred dollars. Again he was to go abroad for one year as a "refresher course" for his languages. His wife went with him. Though she was ailing, they traveled through Sweden safely. When they reached Rotterdam, in Holland, she was taken ill and died suddenly. Her death was a frightful blow to her young husband, but he was compelled to go on, study, travel and prepare himself for his new position.

In 1836, when his duties at Harvard began, Longfellow wandered about the town of Cambridge, looking for a room. He called at the old Craigie House, which pleased him. Washington had made his headquarters there. He was told by old Mrs. Craigie that she never rented rooms to students. "But I am a professor," he said and obtained her permission to live in the mansion. He selected the bedroom Washington had occupied, little knowing the house was to be his in later years.

Though he had become a professor, Longfellow did not neglect writing. Two years later, in 1838, *The Psalm of Life* appeared. Ministers gave it a great deal of attention, and parts of it were even sung as a hymn. But the author was paid nothing for the poem. About the same time his long prose romance, *Hyperion,* was published and collections of minor poems called *Voices of the Night* and *Translations and Ballads.* A rising critic,

called Edgar Allan Poe, condemned *Voices of the Night* very sharply. But Longfellow had become popular notwithstanding. Indeed, by 1854, when he was forty-seven, his books had sold so well that he had a good income and gave up teaching.

Meantime, on his return to Cambridge, he had met and become a warm friend of Charles Sumner. Longfellow, Sumner and three other young men, who called themselves "The Five of Clubs," gathered every Saturday afternoon to talk and relax together. These meetings continued for years and it was Sumner who influenced his friend to write poems on slavery.

Longfellow's life was again a happy one, for he was no longer lonely. When he traveled abroad at the time of his first wife's death, he had met the attractive daughter of a wealthy man, a Mr. Nathan Appleton. He had to court her a long time, but she finally consented to marry Longfellow and for eighteen years their life together went on placidly and joyously. The Craigie House, bought for them by his wife's father, became their home. Six children came. The three younger ones were those daughters named in *The Children's Hour* as "grave Alice and laughing Allegra and Edith with golden hair." The poet's home life was ideal and did much for his writing. He was now known as "The Children's Poet." In 1847 he wrote the romantic story of *Evangeline,* suggested to him by Hawthorne; and *Hiawatha,* the poem all school children know and love, and *The Courtship of Miles Standish,* one of his most dramatic pieces. He himself was a descendant of John and Priscilla Alden.

As an American poet Longfellow was reaching his prime. He was beloved by his countrymen, and honors began to crowd in on him. Then, without warning, in 1861 the second great tragedy of his life fell upon him. His wife died suddenly. . . .

In spite of the terrible loss of his wife, Longfellow went on gallantly and much of his most notable work was done in the later period of his life. When the War between the States broke out, his son Charles enlisted and was severely wounded but recovered. On his last trip to Europe in 1867, Longfellow, now the outstanding American poet, was heaped with honors everywhere he went. While in England, he visited the poet, Alfred Tennyson. Once when he was driving in London, a laborer came up to his carriage and said humbly, "I wish to shake hands with the author of *The Psalm of Life.*" That touched the poet deeply.

Now Longfellow was fast becoming a white-haired gentle

old man, though age laid its hand upon him lightly. Visits to him gave people pleasure; for he was always kindly in his manner and interested in anyone who took delight in his work. On his seventy-second birthday, the children of Cambridge presented him with a splendid armchair made out of the wood of his "spreading chestnut tree" that had stood by the village smithy. It was black and carved with the fruit and leaves of the horse chestnut and upholstered in green leather. It had a brass plate beneath the cushion with the inscription: "To the author of *The Village Blacksmith,* this chair, made from the wood of the spreading chestnut tree, is presented as an expression of grateful regard and veneration by the children of Cambridge. February 27, 1879."

Perhaps the poet appreciated this gift even more because one of his great-grandfathers had been a blacksmith. A poem, *From My Armchair,* was written to the children in reply.

He died at seventy-five and was buried in Mount Auburn. The whole land mourned for him.

What do we remember especially of Henry Wadsworth Longfellow as a poet? The variety of his subjects, the beautiful and musical English in which he wrote and the artistic quality of all his verses. He was influenced by the German lyric poets of his period. Sometimes he preached too much and spoiled the beauty of what he was describing by too obvious a moral.

All the outstanding writers of the time were Longfellow's friends; besides Hawthorne and Dickens, Thackeray, Oliver Wendell Holmes, Sumner, Agassiz, Emerson, and Lowell. He knew and admired Jenny Lind and the musician, Ole Bull. He outlived both Poe and Margaret Fuller, who had attacked his work.

Since most poets are apt to be poor and struggling, one can think of Longfellow as the exception. He always knew comfort and, in his later years, real ease, and his children were devoted to him.

SANTA FILOMENA

Henry Wadsworth Longfellow

Whene'er a noble deed is wrought,
Whene'er is spoken a noble thought,
Our hearts, in glad surprise,
To higher levels rise.

The tidal wave of deeper souls
Into our inmost being rolls,
And lifts us unawares
Out of all meaner cares.

Honor to those whose words or deeds
Thus help us in our daily needs,
And by their overflow
Raise us from what is low!

Thus thought I, as by night I read
Of the great army of the dead,
The trenches cold and damp,
The starved and frozen camp,—

THE "lady with the lamp" in this poem was the famous English nurse, Florence Nightingale.

The wounded from the battle-plain,
In dreary hospitals of pain,
  The cheerless corridors,
  The cold and stony floors.

Lo! in that house of misery
A lady with a lamp I see
  Pass through the glimmering gloom,
  And flit from room to room.

And slow, as in a dream of bliss,
The speechless sufferer turns to kiss
  Her shadow, as it falls
  Upon the darkening walls.

As if a door in heaven should be
Opened and then closed suddenly,
  The vision came and went,
  The light shone and was spent.

On England's annals, through the long
Hereafter of her speech and song,
  That light its rays shall cast
  From portals of the past.

A Lady with a Lamp shall stand
In the great history of the land,
  A noble type of good,
  Heroic womanhood.

Nor even shall be wanting here
The palm, the lily, and the spear,
  The symbols that of yore
  Saint Filomena bore.

Charles Lindbergh, author of *The Spirit of St. Louis*, became famous overnight in 1927 for the first flight made alone across the Atlantic Ocean from New York to Paris. This daring deed was acclaimed by all nations and did a great deal to stimulate interest in aviation. During his many years in the United States Air Corps he made several good-will tours to Mexico and South America. He did valuable research for the war department in World War II and afterwards continued as a civilian consultant on aircraft problems.

Charles A. Lindbergh

NEW YORK TO PARIS

ILLUSTRATED BY *Paul Strayer*

At New York we checked over the plane, engine, and instruments, which required several short flights over the field.

When the plane was completely inspected and ready for the trans-Atlantic flight, there were dense fogs reported along the coast and over Nova Scotia and Newfoundland, in addition to a storm area over the North Atlantic.

On the morning of May 19th, a light rain was falling and the sky was overcast. Weather reports from land stations and ships along the great circle course were unfavorable and there was apparently no prospect of taking off for Paris for several days at least. In the morning I visited the Wright plant at Paterson, New Jersey, and had planned to attend a theater performance in New York that evening. But at about six o'clock I received a special report from the New York Weather Bureau. A high pressure area was over the entire North Atlantic and the low pressure over Nova Scotia and Newfoundland was receding. It was apparent that the prospects of the fog clearing up were as good as I might expect for some time to come. The North Atlantic should be clear with only local storms on the coast of Europe. The moon had just passed full and the percentage of days with fog over Newfoundland and the Grand Banks was increasing so that there seemed to be no advantage in waiting longer.

We went to Curtiss Field as quickly as possible and made arrangements for the barograph to be sealed and installed and for the plane to be serviced and checked.

We decided partially to fill the fuel tanks in the hangar before towing the ship on a truck to Roosevelt Field, which adjoins Curtiss on the east, where the servicing would be completed.

I left the responsibility for conditioning the plane in the hands of the men on the field while I went into the hotel for about two and one-half hours of rest; but at the hotel there were several more details which had to be completed, and I was unable to get any sleep that night.

I returned to the field before daybreak on the morning of the twentieth. A light rain was falling which continued until almost dawn; consequently we did not move the ship to Roosevelt Field until much later than we had planned, and the take-off was delayed from daybreak until nearly eight o'clock.

At dawn the shower had passed, although the sky was overcast, and occasionally there would be some slight precipitation. The tail of the plane was lashed to a truck and escorted by a number of motorcycle police. The slow trip from Curtiss to Roosevelt was begun.

The ship was placed at the extreme west end of the field heading along the east and west runway, and the final fueling commenced.

About 7:40 A.M. the motor was started, and at 7:52 I took off on the flight for Paris.

The field was a little soft due to the rain during the night, and the heavily loaded plane gathered speed very slowly. After passing the halfway mark, however, it was apparent that I would be able to clear the obstructions at the end. I passed over a tractor by about fifteen feet and a telephone line by about twenty, with a fair reserve of flying speed. I believe that the ship would have taken off from a hard field with at least five hundred pounds more weight.

I turned slightly to the right to avoid some high trees on a hill directly ahead, but by the time I had gone a few hundred yards I had sufficient altitude to clear all obstructions and throttled the engine down to 1750 R.P.M. I took up a compass course at once and soon reached Long Island Sound where the Curtiss Oriole with its photographer, which had been escorting me, turned back.

The haze soon cleared, and from Cape Cod through the southern half of Nova Scotia the weather and visibility were excellent. I was flying very low, sometimes as close as ten feet from the trees and water.

On the three hundred mile stretch of water between Cape Cod and Nova Scotia I passed within view of numerous fishing vessels.

The northern part of Nova Scotia contained a number of storm areas, and several times I flew through cloudbursts.

As I neared the northern coast, snow appeared in patches on the ground and far to the eastward the coastline was covered with fog.

For many miles between Nova Scotia and Newfoundland the ocean was covered with caked ice, but as I approached the coast the ice disappeared entirely and I saw several ships in this area.

I had taken up a course for St. Johns, which is south of the great Circle from New York to Paris, so that there would be no question of the fact that I had passed Newfoundland in case I was forced down in the North Atlantic.

I passed over numerous icebergs after leaving St. Johns, but saw no ships except near the coast.

Darkness set in about 8:15 New York time, and a thin, low fog formed through which the white bergs showed up with surprising clearness. This fog became thicker and increased in

height until within two hours I was just skimming the top of storm clouds at about ten thousand feet. Even at this altitude there was a thick haze through which only the stars directly overhead could be seen.

There was no moon, and it was very dark. The tops of some of the storm clouds were several thousand feet above me, and at one time, when I attempted to fly through one of the larger clouds, sleet started to collect on the plane, and I was forced to turn around and get back into clear air immediately and then fly around any clouds which I could not get over.

The moon appeared on the horizon after about two hours of darkness; then the flying was much less complicated.

Dawn came at about 1 A.M. New York time, and the temperature had risen until there was practically no remaining danger of sleet.

Shortly after sunrise the clouds became more broken, although some of them were far above me, and it was often necessary to fly through them, navigating by instruments only.

As the sun became higher, holes appeared in the fog. Through one the open water was visible, and I dropped down until less than a hundred feet above the waves. There was a strong wind blowing from the northwest, and the ocean was covered with white caps.

After a few miles of fairly clear weather, the ceiling lowered to zero, and for nearly two hours I flew entirely blind through the fog at an altitude of about 1500 feet. Then the fog raised and the water was visible again.

On several more occasions it was necessary to fly by instrument for short periods; then the fog broke up into patches. These patches took on forms of every description. Numerous shorelines appeared, with trees perfectly outlined against the horizon. In fact, the mirages were so natural that, had I not been in mid-Atlantic and known that no land existed along my route, I would have taken them to be actual islands.

As the fog cleared I dropped down closer to the water, sometimes flying within ten feet of the waves and seldom higher than two hundred.

There is a cushion of air close to the ground or water through which a plane flies with less effort than when at a higher altitude, and for hours at a time I took advantage of this factor.

Also, it was less difficult to determine the wind drift near the water. During the entire flight the wind was strong enough to produce white caps on the waves. When one of these formed, the foam would be blown off, showing the wind's direction and approximate velocity. This foam remained on the water long enough for me to obtain a general idea of my drift.

During the day I saw a number of porpoises and a few birds but no ships, although I understand that two different boats reported me passing over.

The first indication of my approach to the European Coast was a small fishing boat which I first noticed a few miles ahead and slightly to the south of my course. There were several of these fishing boats grouped within a few miles of each other.

I flew over the first boat without seeing any signs of life. As I circled over the second, however, a man's face appeared, looking out of the cabin window.

I have carried on short conversations with people on the ground by flying low with throttled engine, shouting a question, and receiving the answer by some signal. When I saw this fisherman I decided to try to get him to point towards land. I had no sooner made the decision than the futility of the effort became apparent. In all likelihood he could not speak English, and even if he could, he would undoubtedly be far too astounded to answer. However, I circled again and closing the throttle as the plane passed within a few feet of the boat, I shouted, "Which way is Ireland?" Of course the attempt was useless, and I continued on my course.

Less than an hour later a rugged and semi-mountainous coastline appeared to the northeast. I was flying less than two hundred feet from the water when I sighted it. The shore was fairly distinct and not over ten or fifteen miles away. A light haze coupled with numerous local storm areas had prevented my seeing it from a long distance.

The coastline came down from the north, curved over toward

the east. I had very little doubt that it was the southwestern end of Ireland, but in order to make sure I changed my course towards the nearest point of land.

I located Cape Valentia and Dingle Bay, then resumed my compass course towards Paris.

After leaving Ireland I passed a number of steamers and was seldom out of sight of a ship.

In a little over two hours the coast of England appeared. My course passed over Southern England and a little south of Plymouth; then across the English Channel, striking France over Cherbourg.

The English farms were very impressive from the air in contrast to ours in America. They appeared extremely small and unusually neat and tidy with their stone and hedge fences.

I was flying at about a fifteen-hundred-foot altitude over England and as I crossed the Channel and passed over Cherbourg, France, I had probably seen more of that part of Europe than many native Europeans. The visibility was good, and the country could be seen for miles around.

People who have taken their first flight often remark that no one knows what the locality he lives in is like until he has seen it from above. Countries take on different characteristics from the air.

The sun went down shortly after passing Cherbourg, and soon the beacons along the Paris-London airway became visible.

I first saw the lights of Paris a little before ten P.M., or five P.M. New York time, and a few minutes later I was circling the Eiffel Tower at an altitude of about four thousand feet.

The lights of Le Bourget were plainly visible, but appeared to be very close to Paris. I had understood that the field was farther from the city, so continued out to the northeast into the country for four or five miles to make sure that there was not another field farther out which might be Le Bourget. Then I returned and spiralled down closer to the lights. Presently I could make out long lines of hangars, and the roads appeared to be jammed with cars.

I flew low over the field once, then circled around into the wind and landed.

After the plane stopped rolling I turned it around and started to taxi back to the lights. The entire field ahead, however, was covered with thousands of people all running towards my ship. When the first few arrived, I attempted to get them to hold the rest of the crowd back, away from the plane, but apparently no one could understand, or would have been able to conform to my request if he had.

I cut the switch to keep the propeller from killing some one, and attempted to organize an impromptu guard for the plane. The impossibility of any immediate organization became apparent, and when parts of the ship began to crack from the pressure of the multitude I decided to climb out of the cockpit in order to draw the crowd away.

Speaking was impossible; no words could be heard in the uproar, and nobody apparently cared to hear any. I started to climb out of the cockpit, but as soon as one foot appeared through the door I was dragged the rest of the way without assistance on my part.

For nearly half an hour I was unable to touch the ground, during which time I was ardently carried around in what seemed to be a very small area, and in every position it is possible to be in. Everyone had the best of intentions, but no one seemed to know just what they were.

The French military flyers very resourcefully took the situation in hand. A number of them mingled with the crowd; then, at a given signal, they placed my helmet on an American correspondent and cried: "Here is Lindbergh." That helmet on an American was sufficient evidence. The correspondent immediately became the center of attraction, and while he was being taken protestingly to the Reception Committee via a rather devious route, I managed to get inside one of the hangars.

Meanwhile a second group of soldiers and police had surrounded the plane and soon placed it out of danger in another hangar.

The French ability to handle an unusual situation with speed and capability was remarkably demonstrated that night at Le Bourget.

Ambassador Herrick extended me an invitation to remain at his Embassy while I was in Paris, which I gladly accepted. But grateful as I was at the time, it did not take me long to realize that a kind Providence had placed me in Ambassador Herrick's hands. The ensuing days found me in situations that I had certainly never expected to be in and in which I relied on Ambassador Herrick's sympathetic aid.

These situations were brought about by the wholehearted welcome to me—an American—that touched me beyond any point that any words can express. I left France with a debt of gratitude which, though I cannot repay it, I shall always remember. If the French people had been acclaiming their own gallant airmen, Nungesser and Coli, who were lost only after fearlessly departing in the face of conditions insurmountably greater than those that confronted me, their enthusiastic welcome and graciousness could not have been greater.

In Belgium as well, I was received with a warmth which reflected more than simply a passing curiosity in a trans-Atlantic flight, but which was rather a demonstration by the people of their interest in a new means of transportation which eventually would bring still closer together the new world and the old. Their welcome, too, will be a cherished memory for all time.

In England, I experienced one final unforgettable demonstration of friendship for an American. That spontaneous wonderful reception during my brief visit seemed typical of what I had always heard of the good sportsmanship of the English.

My words to all those friends in Europe are inadequate, but my feelings of appreciation are boundless.

LINDBERGH FLIES ALONE

Editorial, *New York Sun,* May 21, 1927

Alone?

Is he alone at whose right side rides Courage, with Skill within the cockpit and Faith upon the left? Does solitude surround the brave when Adventure leads the way and Ambition reads the dials? Is there no company with him for whom the air is cleft by Daring and the darkness is made light by Emprise?

True, the fragile bodies of his fellows do not weigh down his plane; true, the fretful minds of weaker men are lacking from his crowded cabin; but as his airship keeps her course he holds communion with those rarer spirits that inspire to intrepidity and by their sustaining potency give strength to arm, resource to mind, content to soul.

Alone? With what other companions would that man fly to whom the choice were given?

Mathilda Schirmer

ALBERT SCHWEITZER: THE DOCTOR IN THE JUNGLE

ILLUSTRATED BY *Hardie Gramatky*

ALBERT SCHWEITZER was reading the monthly report of the Paris Missionary Society. Suddenly an article drew his attention. The French Colony of Gabon in Equatorial Africa needed workers, especially doctors.

As he read, he remembered the missionary meetings at his father's church when he was a boy. What was it they had called the Gabon? "The most unhealthful spot on earth." They, too, had talked about the sorry plight of the natives. The climate was hot and humid; insects and termites destroyed property, animals, and man. Primitive peoples, even cannibals, lived in the area. Famines occurred often. Worst of all, the people were subject to all kinds of disease.

He put the magazine aside, but within a few days he sent letters to his family and his friends. He told them that he had decided to study medicine and that later he would go to Africa as a doctor.

He expected people to be surprised. After all, he was now thirty years of age and had done a great deal during his life. He was a minister, a musician, a writer, a philosopher, a teacher, and a lecturer. In all these fields he had gained fame and honors. But he did not expect his friends to protest as much as they did.

Some said, "You are a minister. Why not go there and preach?"

Others said, "You are a great musician. You should not bury your talents."

Still others said, "If you want to help through medicine, why not stay in Europe and give concerts and recitals? With the money you raise, you could send many doctors out there, instead of just yourself."

But there was one person who understood him. She was Helene Bresslau, who was to become his wife. He told her that when he was twenty-one he had been home during summer vacation, and as he thought over his life he felt he had been very fortunate. He had enjoyed a happy childhood, good health, pleasure in music, and success in his studies and work. Then the thought came to him that he should not accept all these blessings without giving something in return. He did not know what he would do, but he decided to continue with art and science, which he loved, until he was thirty. Then he would devote his life to some direct service to mankind.

"My search is over," he announced.

"I will take a course in nursing," she said. "Then you won't be able to get along without me."

During the next six years Albert Schweitzer studied medicine at the Strasbourg University. He also continued to preach, to write, and to give organ concerts. After his graduation he spent a year as a hospital intern, and later went to Paris to study tropical diseases. Then Dr. Schweitzer felt he was prepared to go to Africa.

However, he wanted to raise his own funds and support and build his own hospital. All he asked of the Paris Missionary Society was some land on their grounds. They consented, and also promised him two buildings, one a clinic, and the other, a house for himself. By soliciting funds and giving recitals and concerts he raised enough money to operate the hospital for about a year.

At last, in 1913, almost eight years after he had announced his decision, Dr. Schweitzer and his wife left for Africa.

When they arrived at Lambarene, the missionaries greeted them heartily and escorted them to their home. As they lit the kerosene lamp, a huge black spider crept down the wall and flying cockroaches swarmed in the air. The battles that the

Schweitzers were to fight against insects, nature, and disease had begun.

In the morning the Schweitzers had two big disappointments. The building of corrugated iron that they had been promised had not been built, and the interpreter whom they were to employ was in his village, busy with a lawsuit. Sick people began arriving, although the mission had sent word that only serious cases could be cared for until the supplies arrived. Dr. Schweitzer treated as many of them as he could, but he had to work under the hot sun and sudden downpour.

He decided that his greatest need was some sort of shelter. The only thing he could find was an old hen house, no longer in use. With the aid of his wife, by sweeping and cleaning and whitewashing, they made it habitable.

Then, among his patients, he found Joseph Azoawani. Joseph could speak many African dialects, and French. He became the doctor's assistant. He often made the doctor laugh by his reports. He had once been a cook, and since he knew anatomy by the names of cuts of meat, he would say a patient had a pain in "the right leg of mutton" or "upper left cutlet."

At last the supplies arrived. With them came the gift of the Paris Bach Society to Dr. Schweitzer, a zinc-lined piano with a special pedal attachment. Many times, when he was overtired, or discouraged, he spent time at the piano, playing Bach and all the other music he loved.

However, he did not have much time for music in the jungle. A native told him, "Here among us, everybody is sick." From one to two hundred miles around, canoes sailed along the Ogowe, bringing sick people to him. His first operations were successful, as well as many of his treatments. As his reputation spread among the natives, more people came. After a few months he was treating as many as forty patients a day.

The natives gave him the name of "Oganga," or fetishman, a magic worker. They called pain "the Worm" and thought that it was an evil spirit that was in their bodies. Oganga was able to drive it out. He did other mysterious things. During operations he used anesthetics. The natives could not understand this.

HARDIE GRAMATKY

One girl wrote, "First of all he kills the sick people. Then he cures them, and after that he wakes them up again."

There was more to being a doctor in the jungle than healing. Dr. Schweitzer became carpenter, foreman, builder, architect, and even judge when the need arose. He got permission to build his hospital, but he was not able to get any work out of the laborers he hired. He worked with them, doing hard manual labor, but when he was not there they did nothing. Finally, the mission loaned him two mechanics, and the building was completed early in November. It had four rooms: a consulting room, operating room, a dispensary, and sterilizing room. The next month they built a waiting room, a shed for housing the patients, and a hut for Joseph. These were made like the native huts, of unhewn logs and raffia leaves. Mattresses were made of dried grass.

As more patients streamed in, other problems arose. At last, Dr. Schweitzer wrote a set of rules that was read aloud every morning. One was: "Patients and their friends must bring with them food enough for one day. . . ." However, the kind-hearted doctor could not refuse those who came empty-handed. He would take care of their hunger as well as their illness.

Another rule said: "All bottles and tin boxes in which medicines are given must be returned." In the damp atmosphere, medicines had to be kept in these containers, or they would spoil. Many times Dr. Schweitzer grew angry with patients who claimed to have lost their bottles. He would exclaim to his wife, "How I look forward to the day when I shall have a sufficient supply of such things!" And in their letters home they would both plead for more bottles, corks, tin boxes, and tubes.

Both Doctor and Mrs. Schweitzer worked hard, season after season, until the doctor realized that they had to take a rest and have medical treatment themselves. They left Joseph in charge and sailed to Cape Lopez, where they both recuperated. Then they sailed back to Lambarene.

When they returned, they learned that Europe was at war. Not long afterward they were declared prisoners of the French. Dr. Schweitzer and his wife were Alsatians, but Alsace was at that time owned by Germany. Therefore, the French considered them enemy aliens. They were not permitted to practice medicine; they were not even permitted to speak to the natives or their guards.

Many another man would have been at a loss, but Dr. Schweitzer used this time profitably and wrote a book. He also practiced on his piano.

One day an order came to send all aliens to France as prisoners of war. So it was that the doctor and his wife left Africa.

The Alsatians were permitted to return home after a period of internment. By this time, both Dr. Schweitzer and his wife were ill and overtired. When he reached his father's house in Gunsbach, he was a very sick man.

After the Armistice, on November 11, 1918, health and hope slowly came back to Albert Schweitzer, and he was made happy by the birth of a daughter, Rhena. Slowly the European world called him back to his early talents, to his lecturing, and his organ playing. Again he reached the international fame that had been his before going to Africa. Again, he decided to return to the Gabon. There were many teachers and musicians in Europe, but at Lambarene there was no doctor now.

This time there were two important differences. Helene, his wife, was too ill to accompany him, and besides, it would not do to take the child to Africa. And this time there was more support, for many people had heard of the work he was doing in Lambarene and had formed societies to aid him.

It was 1924 when Dr. Schweitzer returned to his hospital. He knew it would be overgrown by jungle, but it was worse than he had imagined it could be. He had to start all over, clearing, rebuilding, and repairing where he could. He had to treat the sick who had heard that he was back and had come for help to "our doctor."

Some of the people in Europe who heard about his work were doctors and nurses. They, too, decided that they would like to help the Africans, and joined him. Even with assistance, the doctor was busy every minute. Then something happened that made him want to build a larger hospital on a different site.

The biggest industry in the jungle was lumbering. Many of the natives worked for the timber dealers after the war. They neglected their plantations, and so a famine resulted. With it came an epidemic. Soon the hospital was overflowing with patients.

One day Dr. Schweitzer went to see the District Commissioner to get a concession for new land. That night he called his staff together and told them of his plans to build a new hospital. He told them of the new land he had gotten and what it would mean—a new hospital, plenty of space to cultivate food, better living quarters, and other improvements. The whole staff was excited about the plan and cheered heartily. There was only one regret for Dr. Schweitzer. He would have to stay until the work was done, and not see his wife and child for at least another year. It was July, 1927, before he could join them again.

From that time on he divided his time between Europe and Africa. During the Second World War he was at his hospital, although times were very difficult, and he could not get many

The Doctor in the jungle

supplies. He was often discouraged, but he did the best he could. At last, the war was over and he was able to return to Europe.

In 1949 he went to America for the first time to give a lecture at a conference in Aspen, Colorado. Many people were happy to meet him because they had read the books he had written, had heard the recordings he had made, and had heard about his work.

Now aged seventy-five, he again returned to Africa. Sailing once more up the Ogowe he must have remembered another canoe trip many years ago, when he discovered his basic principle of ethics, "Reverence for Life."

"A man who has become a thinking being . . ." he wrote, "accepts as being good: to preserve life, to promote life, to raise life which is capable of development to its highest value. . . . A man is ethical only when life, as such, is sacred to him, that of plants and animals as that of his fellow men, and when he devotes himself helpfully to all life that is in need of help."

Dr. Schweitzer was awarded the Nobel Peace Prizes for 1952 and 1953.

Nicholas Nirgiotis

MARIE CURIE: DISCOVERER OF A HIDDEN TREASURE

ILLUSTRATED BY *Helen Prickett*

"CAN I trust you, my little one, not to break my precious glasses?" Professor Sklodovski spoke to his younger daughter with tenderness as he cautioned her to be careful with his laboratory equipment. But despite her age, the professor did not have to worry about his daughter's respect for the queer-looking jars and odd shaped glass tubes that filled his laboratory.

At the age when most little girls would be playing with dolls, Marie Sklodovski was spending her time in the large room which her father, a teacher of physics and mathematics, used for a classroom. After classes she helped him dust the tables and shelves, and wash the glass tubes and jars of the laboratory. And she listened with curiosity and excitement to what her father told her about the wonders of the world and about the forces that made it move.

It wasn't all very clear to her then, but Marie realized that through science she could find out more and more about the world she lived in. The simple, understandable words of her father had moved her to wonder and to search for knowledge, and she retained this fascination for knowledge and research all her life. Later, she was to make the greatest discovery in modern science—a discovery that gave new stimulus to medicine, physics, and chemistry.

Marie learned to read before she was ready for school by peeking behind the backs of her brothers and sisters while they studied their lessons. At the age of sixteen she was graduated from high school with a gold medal for excellence. She wanted to be a teacher, but women were not allowed to enter the university in her native Poland. There was only one thing to do. She and her sister Bronya must take turns helping each other through some school outside Poland. Marie accepted a position as tutor while Bronya went to Paris to study medicine, with the understanding that Bronya was to send for her when she had completed her six years of medical training. Marie was twenty-four when she arrived in Paris, eager to start her new life.

Paris was not, however, the marvelous place Marie had dreamed about. Far away from home and with very little money, she felt discouraged for the first time in her life. And she was handicapped in another way. Being a woman, she found it impossible to obtain the kind of work she best liked to do—assisting in a laboratory. She had, however, faced difficulties before and her persistence and patience had always been rewarded. Marie was finally taken on as assistant in a chemical laboratory to clean the various instruments and care for the furnace. She soon proved to her employers how valuable she could be to them. Supporting herself in this manner, Marie was able to win two degrees. In her four years at the university she received one in mathematics and one in chemistry.

Soon Pierre Curie, a brilliant young professor, met Marie and before long asked her to marry him. For their honeymoon in 1895 they went on a bicycle trip in the country. So began the wonderful partnership of two great scientists whose hard work and heroic struggle was to be crowned at last by success.

Marie began to teach at the university, to work under Pierre in his laboratory, to cook the meals, keep the clothes in order, and go to market before morning classes. Her daughter Irene, who also was to become a famous physicist and winner of the Nobel prize, was born the next year, and spent her first years in the Curie workroom among her parents' test tubes. Marie's second daughter, Eve, who later wrote a wonderful biography of her famous mother, was born eight years later.

A year after the Curies were married, the German scientist Roentgen discovered X-rays, beams of light which could pass through wood and other solid bodies and could even show the bony skeleton of the human body. It was also noticed about this time that the substance known as uranium gave off, without the help of an outside light, a strange glow which, like X-rays, passed through solid bodies. What was even more strange, it was next discovered that pitchblende, the mineral from which uranium was extracted, gave off rays even more powerful than pure uranium. There was no doubt that an element other than uranium existed in pitchblende, which possessed great energy, and Marie Curie undertook its discovery.

The Curies, for Pierre soon joined his wife in her search, met with difficulties from the beginning. A rare mineral, pitchblende was found only in Austria and was very expensive. The Curies could not afford to buy the tons of pitchblende they needed for their experiments with their small salaries. Fortunately, however, they didn't lack resourcefulness. After its use in the manufacture of glass, what remained of the pitchblende was considered useless and was thrown away. This refuse the Curies could have for a reasonable price and the cost of transporting it to France. Their laboratory was a damp and leaky shed with an open courtyard outside it, but here they worked with patience, determination, and skill.

Pierre and Marie labored day after day in their drafty, leaky laboratory, spending long hours over their difficult problem. The days became months and the months years, and slowly radium began to unveil itself. When the Curies realized that success was close at hand, they redoubled their efforts, and often would not resist the urge to return in the evening for one more look at their precious work. And so it was that one evening, four years after their experiments began, that Marie and Pierre decided to return to the shed they had left only a few hours before. They walked in silence, all the way to their leaky laboratory, each deep in his own thoughts. It was dark when they arrived. The squeaky door admitted them with some protest. Pierre, as was his habit, moved toward the lamp when an excited cry stopped him abruptly. "Pierre . . . look!" Marie was pointing to the shelves along the wall. A light strong enough

to read by gleamed from the glass receivers in the darkness. It was a magical moment to be enjoyed and remembered forever. In silence Marie and Pierre sat, their faces toward the light of radium.

Thus after four years of arduous toil the Curies were rewarded with a thimbleful of grayish white powder which looked like common table salt. It was radium, the most marvelous of all radioactive substances, an element which burned with a ray that could penetrate flesh and bone and even an inch-thick iron plate.

The Curies now found themselves famous not only in France, but throughout the world. But these modest workers wanted nothing for themselves, only the chance to go on with their research, to explore the possibilities of their discovery, and to investigate how radium could best serve mankind. "What we discover belongs to the world—to anyone who can use it," said Marie Curie.

So much pitchblende was needed for so little radium, and pitchblende was so expensive, that the Curies had to overcome great problems to produce enough of the precious element they had discovered. Nevertheless, they continued to teach and work, putting their skill, knowledge, and experience to good use. Eventually, with the help of other medical men, they discovered that radium by destroying diseased cells cured tumors and certain kinds of cancer. "Curietherapy" is still used today in cancer treatment.

One day in 1906, when Pierre was hurrying across a busy Paris street, he was struck by a passing truck and was killed instantly. Marie continued with courage and devotion the work they had begun together, and even took his teaching position at the university—the first woman ever to hold such an important post. When World War I began in 1914, Marie organized ambulance units which carried X-ray equipment to the front to aid the wounded close behind the lines.

In 1921 Marie Curie, the only person to have won the Nobel prize twice, visited the United States where all the universities paid tribute to her. One of the university presidents said what was in everyone's mind: "The discovery of radium by Madame Curie had world-wide interest, all the more important because it gave new hope to those suffering from certain incurable diseases. That hope is being realized today!"

Mabelle E. Martin

GEORGE WASHINGTON CARVER

ILLUSTRATED BY *Rod Ruth*

DARK NIGHT had settled over the Carver plantation. In a tiny cabin back of the big house sat Mary, the colored slave, rocking her sick baby boy. Suddenly she heard galloping horses coming down the road. She was terrified. It might be the night riders who stole slaves and took them down the river to sell to other plantation owners! "Hush, baby, hush," she whispered, as she started to run for her master's big house. But she was too late. The riders grabbed her and the baby and carried them off.

The Carvers were angry and unhappy, for they were very fond of Mary and her baby. Mr. Carver offered a large reward for their return. Mary had already been sold, and they never saw her again, but the baby was finally found and brought back to them. He was still very ill, and only Mrs. Carver's careful nursing kept him alive.

It was the custom in those days for a slave to take the family name of his master, so the little lad became known as George Washington Carver. He grew into a puny little fellow with pipe-stem legs, bony fingers, and a pinched little face. He was sick a great deal. His voice was high-pitched and cracked, and he stuttered. He was ten years old before he could talk so people could understand him. This made him shy and, when he was not working, he amused himself by wandering through the woods. He dug plants and brought them back for his own garden. He talked to the plants as he worked among them, and felt that they could understand him, even if people couldn't.

He didn't know then that his interest in the soil and in growing things was later to make him famous.

George must have been about seven or eight when he began peeking in at the schoolhouse door. He couldn't understand or accept the fact that Negroes didn't go to school. Mrs. Carver gave him a spelling book, and he tried to teach himself, but it was too slow. There was so much to learn and, anyway, spelling books didn't tell you "why" about everything. Gradually Mr. Carver came to realize that the young boy was really in earnest, and when George was eleven, Mr. Carver sent him to a distant town, where there was a school for Negro children. It took George all day to travel there on foot. When he arrived he had no place to stay, so he slept that night in a hayloft. The next day he went to school. The children laughed at his squeaky voice and funny clothes, but he was happy—until school was out. Then he went from house to house trying to find a place to work for room and board. Nobody seemed to want him, and he spent that winter attending school in the day and sleeping in the barn at night, half frozen, half starved. Finally a colored woman, Aunt Mariah Watkins, took him into her home. She was a good mother to him. She taught him to wash and iron, cook and bake, sew and clean house. He had a natural talent for doing things with his hands and soon learned how to crochet, hemstitch, and knit. For two years he lived with Aunt Mariah, helping at home and attending school. By then he had learned everything the school taught, and he had also learned that Negroes were supposed to do the kind of work that needed little or no education.

But George would not give up. He had heard of a high school in Kansas that taught both white and colored children. And so at the age of thirteen he left Missouri and traveled with a family moving to Kansas. Their wagon was so loaded with household goods that he had to walk most of the way. Once there, he had no trouble finding work, for Aunt Mariah had taught him well.

He did such excellent work in high school that, when he graduated, he was offered a scholarship at a university. But when he presented his letter at the university, he was told that

Rod Ruth

they did not admit Negro students. In despair he turned to homesteading in western Kansas and tried to forget his thirst for knowledge. Then he heard of a little school in Iowa where he could go on with his studies. Once there, he set up a laundry in a woodshed and earned his way through school by caring for the other students' clothes. From there he went to the State Agricultural College at Ames, Iowa, where he did such brilliant and painstaking work that they put him in charge of the greenhouse when he graduated. At last he had exactly what he wanted! He could grow plants and study plant life. He had a good income and could live a good life.

But fate had other plans for the little slave boy. He received a letter from Booker T. Washington, head of the Negro school at Tuskegee, Alabama. "I cannot offer you money, position, or fame," wrote Mr. Washington. "The children, barefoot, come for miles over bad roads. They are thin and in rags. You would not understand such poverty. These people do not know how to plow or plant or harvest. I am not skilled at such things. I teach them how to read, to write, to make shoes, good bricks, and how to build a wall. I cannot give them food, and so they starve."

But Mr. Washington was wrong. Carver did understand such poverty. Had he not suffered through it in his fight to become educated? And what good was his education if it could not help others like him? So he left his fine position and his fascinating work, and journeyed to Alabama.

Here he found problems, indeed. The southern farmers had grown cotton for so long that the soil was worn out. The crops were growing poorer each year. Carver advised them to grow peanuts to enrich the soil. "Peanuts!" exclaimed the farmers. "What would we do with peanuts?"

Carver answered that question, in time, by showing them that from peanuts they could make milk, cheese, butter, candy, ice-cream powder, pickles, mock oysters, and flour. In addition he showed them how to make more than 300 non-food products from peanuts, including plastics, paper, insulating boards, dye, ink, soap, shaving lotion, and linoleum. He did this by separating the chemicals in the peanuts and combining them in a new way to create new products. He was developing a new science—chemurgy. It has done a lot to change farming and increase the wealth of farmers, who now are raising the raw materials from which plastics and synthetic rubber are made.

Up to then most farm crops were intended as food for men and animals. But the farmers produced more food than was needed, and the surplus went to waste. Here was a way of using that wasted food, of turning it into money. Henry Ford, the automobile man, was one of the leaders in this movement. He and Carver became fast friends. Carver used soybeans to make a plastic which Ford used in his cars.

It is not surprising that, in 1940, George Washington Carver was chosen as the man of the year who had contributed most to science. He died in 1943 at about the age of eighty.

And so ends the story of the sickly little Negro slave, who strove for education against almost impossible odds, who arrived at a position of ease and importance, and then had the courage to give it up in order that he might be of service to his people. In so doing, he has been of service to the whole world—a countryman to be proud of!

THE STRUGGLE

Arthur Hugh Clough

Say not the struggle naught availeth,
   The labour and the wounds are vain,
The enemy faints not, nor faileth,
   And as things have been they remain. . . .

Not by eastern windows only,
   When daylight comes, comes in the light;
In front the sun climbs slow, how slowly!
   But westward, look, the land is bright!

THOMAS JEFFERSON, the third president of the United States, was born in Shadwell, Virginia. He is perhaps best remembered as the author of the *Declaration of Independence*. Most of his life was spent in various capacities serving the interests of the United States. He is responsible for the founding of the Democratic Party and the purchase of Louisiana. Throughout his life he was a great statesman and a champion of independence. Monticello, his beautiful home where he died in 1826, is now a memorial.

Sonia Daugherty

THOMAS JEFFERSON

ILLUSTRATED BY *John Merryweather*

THE STREETS of Philadelphia were full of people: young men in new militia uniforms, ladies in silks and laces, riding in sedan chairs, workmen in rough homespun, peddlers, hawkers, and many strangers from the thirteen colonies. A man with a wheelbarrow pushed his way through the crowds to knock at one door after another. No one paid attention to him as they hurried on their way. But now and then, men stopped at street corners to talk, and to ask the question that was on their minds—*What would King George do if the colonies declared for independence?* The Continental Congress was holding meetings at the State House. No one knew what would come out of these deliberations.

Mrs. Graff was polishing her candlesticks when the man with the wheelbarrow stopped to knock at the door of her new brick house. Who could it be, knocking so loud, she wondered.

"Have you anything made of lead?" the man asked when she came to the door.

"I have none for sale, if that's what you want," said Mrs. Graff. She was about to shut the door when the man put his foot in the doorway.

"I've not come to buy or to sell," he said. "It's to be donated."

"Donated?" Mrs. Graff looked indignant. She was a newly married housekeeper, proud of her spick and span brick house and her precious possessions.

"To make bullets," explained the man, displaying a badge under his coat. On it was printed—"Sons of Liberty."

Mrs. Graff looked at the badge, and from the badge to the wheelbarrow piled high with all kinds of utensils. "Bullets?" she repeated in a dazed voice. She wanted to cry, but it was no use. She knew that if she refused to give him anything, he might report that she was for King George and therefore a Tory. Unpleasant things happened to Tories these days; some were even known to have been tarred and feathered. She went to the cupboard and brought out her polished candlesticks. The man threw them into the wheelbarrow, and trudged away to knock on other doors.

"Bullets," muttered Mrs. Graff; all kinds of fearful thoughts came into her head. She went out to sit on the white stone step to watch for her lodger. She would ask him about it. He would know, she reasoned. He had come all the way from Virginia to sit in the Continental Congress with the delegates from the thirteen colonies.

But Thomas Jefferson had left his apartment early to walk in the cool of the morning and prepare his thoughts for the debates.

A short man with a sallow face overtook Thomas Jefferson as he neared the State House. "To my mind," said the man by way of greeting, "there's no need for further debate."

"I am of the same opinion," said Jefferson with a quiet smile.

"Richard Henry Lee stated it clearly in his proposed resolution: that the Congress should declare that these United Colonies are, and of a right ought to be, free and independent states. Why do we wait to make our declaration?" demanded Samuel

Adams in a peppery voice. "In Massachusetts we're ready for the revolution. We've proven it at Bunker Hill." He pronounced the word "revolution" in a ringing voice as if he liked the sound of the word. In his mind it stood for a brave free world.

Jefferson smiled. He chose his words with great care. The word "revolution" was not mentioned at the meetings at the State House. They called the king a tyrant, they spoke of misrule by the English Parliament and talked of independence and of liberty. Only at the tavern over their dinner was the word "revolution" mentioned.

"What are we waiting for?" Samuel Adams repeated the question as Jefferson remained thoughtfully silent. "Are we waiting for King George to hang us, before we make up our minds?"

"In Virginia they think the declaration's been made," said Jefferson at last. "But there are those colonies who are only half convinced, as you know. We wait for them. We must be of one mind about so great a matter."

They had come to the State House now. The delegates were arriving, greeting each other with sober faces, each one thinking his own thoughts.

It was a warm June day. From the near-by stables came the smell of horses and the buzz of flies. The debate started where it left off the day before—"If it comes to war, we may be caught and hanged as rebels and then the condition in the colonies will be worse than it is now," argued one of the delegates.

John Adams stood up and began to speak. Jefferson listened in silence. He was not as eloquent a talker as John Adams. He could write his thoughts much more clearly than any of them; but just now John Adams was saying what he would say if he were to stand up and talk.

"Richard Henry Lee of Virginia has stated it clearly for us all in his proposed resolution," called out one delegate from a side seat.

"Let the resolution be read," called out another voice.

The secretary, Charles Thomson, read the resolution in a clear loud voice ". . . Resolved that these United Colonies are and of a right ought to be free and independent states . . ."

A solemn silence followed, and then suddenly president John Hancock called for a vote. The resolution was passed, with loud ayes, but there were a few ayes that sounded a little faint; the delegates looked at each other half fearful, half triumphant.

The die was cast. The Declaration of Independence must now be written out and presented to the people.

Mrs. Graff went about with a long face. She missed her candlesticks. But that was not all she had on her mind. If war came, the redcoats, she reasoned, were sure to win. There were plenty of them in the colonies and more in England. They were trained soldiers; they had arms and ammunition. Her husband was a bricklayer and her brothers were farmers. If it came to war, what would they know about shooting and killing? When Henry, her young nephew, brought her eggs from his father's farm late one afternoon, she began to tell him about her candlesticks, and about the Sons of Liberty.

But Henry was much more interested in asking her questions about her lodger—"Is it true that Thomas Jefferson's name is written on the King's list of outlaws in England?" he asked her.

Mrs. Graff looked more alarmed than ever. "Who told you?"

"Reginald said so. Reginald heard his father tell a man that Mr. Jefferson would be the first one hanged for a rebel. His name was on the King's list for a long time now because he wrote a paper. 'Summary Views from Virginia' it was called, he said. It made King George angry, and he called Jefferson a dangerous rebel. Reginald said Jefferson is a wicked man. He owns lots of slaves and he beats them with whips."

"Reginald's father is a Tory, that's the reason he talks like that," frowned Mrs. Graff. "You'd better keep away from Reginald, or you'll get into trouble."

"What if he is a Tory? He lets me ride his horse and hunt with him. I don't care who is a Tory and who isn't," said Henry.

Bob, Jefferson's slave, came into the kitchen now. He filled a large pitcher with water to have it ready for his master when he came back from the State House. Henry followed the young Negro up the stairs to the two-room apartment, a sitting room on one side of the stairs, a bedroom on the other side.

"Is it true Mr. Jefferson beats his slaves with a leather whip?" asked Henry, standing in the doorway.

"No sir, never nobody ever been beat in Monticello." Bob looked amazed at the question. "No, sir," he repeated, "Massa be gen'le, he be kind—"

"How many slaves has he?" asked Henry, watching Bob smooth the bed, and arrange towels on the washstand.

Bob showed glistening white teeth in a proud smile. "We has thousan' and mebby two thousan'. We has a big house on top o' mountain. It sure is cool up there, we has big trees, and we has flowers, and we has birds a singin'. Monticello we calls the place," Bob wagged his head in pride. "An' we has ho'ses, fines' ho'ses in the whole wo'ld, we has."

"I heard say that your master came on horseback all the way from Virginia, but I don't believe it," said Henry.

"Massa shure did come ridin' his ho'se all the way, he shure did," smiled Bob. "We has the ho'se in the stable waitin' to bring massa home. An' me, I'm waitin' too," he added with another smile.

Henry looked around the small sitting room with its plain furniture, and wondered what made Jefferson want to leave his fine house and come to this place, and get mixed up with rebels, and be hanged maybe, when he could be up there on his mountain with slaves and horses and all kinds of fine things.—"What's in that box?" he asked, trying to open what looked like a wooden box on the table.

A firm footfall could now be heard on the stairs. The next instant a tall slender gentleman entered the sitting room. Henry took his hand off the box, and looked down on the floor.

"I am pleased to find a visitor," said Thomas Jefferson in a friendly voice. "I see that you are interested in that box," he added with a slow smile.

"I thought there might be pistols in there," stammered Henry.

"It holds something more deadly than pistols," said Jefferson with a shake of the head.

"More deadly than pistols?" Henry repeated the words, greatly puzzled.

Jefferson took a key from his pocket and unlocked the box.

"It's a desk," exclaimed Henry, much amazed. "I never saw a desk like that."

"That's because there isn't another one like it—I designed it, and had it made," explained Jefferson. "Very convenient; can be used on horseback if necessary." He sat down in a chair, the desk unfolded on his lap to show Henry how he used it.

Henry stared at the sheets of paper covered with fine writing. "But that's only paper," he said at last, no longer frightened.

Jefferson sorted the papers in silence for a while. "Only papers?" he stacked the shining white sheets carefully one on top of the other—"What's written on these pages is our ammunition. It is ideas we really fight with, and when an idea is true and right, it is more powerful than swords and pistols. If you understand this, you'll fight on the right side always."

Henry felt almost awed as he stood there, looking at Jefferson's pale face so kind and genial. He did not understand exactly what it was he was saying, but he knew, somehow, that what he said was wise and true, and that he was a great man.

"Thank you, sir," he said, backing out of the room. Never again would he believe what Reginald said about Thomas Jefferson. He came down the stairs two steps at a time. Let Reginald be a Tory; he, Henry, would be on Jefferson's side from now on.

"You shouldn't be going upstairs to Mr. Jefferson's rooms, he doesn't want to be disturbed," scolded Mrs. Graff.

"I'm going to join the Sons of Liberty as soon as I'm old enough," said Henry by way of an answer.

Mrs. Graff shook her head and sighed. Her husband told her in secret, that he had heard Mr. Jefferson was writing a declaration of rights up there in their sitting room. Mr. Jefferson was a very fine gentleman, anyone could see that. He gave her no trouble; but she was not at all sure that it was quite safe to have him in their house. No one knew which way the tide might turn. And now her young nephew was talking about wanting to join the Sons of Liberty. What had Jefferson said to Henry to make him turn about like that, she wondered uneasily. "You'll be sleeping on the third floor right over his sitting room while you are visiting us; don't you go disturbing him," she warned.

Thomas Jefferson was also thinking about Henry as he settled down to work at his small desk on his lap. The boy was an upstanding, promising young person. He and many others like him might have to take a gun in their hands before long to back up what he was writing here on these sheets of foolscap. He rose to pace the floor, his face clouded now. Ever since the beginning of time, blind and selfish men had forced brave men to fight for freedom and justice. Each time the choice had to be made anew. The vision came when the need was greatest and the hearts of men were willing; and always, there were enough brave men to carry the banner of progress, and to fight for it.

His quill moved slowly over the white paper, writing and rewriting. What he was writing here must proclaim their cause,

make it clear to themselves and to the world— ". . . When in the course of human events, it becomes necessary for one people to dissolve the political bands which have connected them with another, and to assume, among the powers of the earth, the separate and equal station to which the laws of nature and of nature's God entitle them . . ."

The house was steeped in stillness. The scratching of the quill on the paper sounded like a voice. He was meeting the future: a great nation mighty in youth and freedom. He must not say too much nor too little. He wished for a moment that both

Benjamin Franklin and John Adams, who were appointed to write this declaration with him, were present now. But the aged Benjamin Franklin, busy on many other committees, delegated the task to the two younger men, and John Adams declared that he had argued so much for independence, his name must have become odious to the people, and insisted that Jefferson was the proper man to compose this paper for he had greater felicity of expression.

Jefferson had accepted this task with fear and trembling; the purpose of this declaration was too sacred to make it less than great. Again he paced the floor, weighing each phrase and word. Franklin and Adams had approved his first draft; he must choose words with no doubtful meanings. Each word must be a sword to pierce the thickness of the flesh.

It was warm in the room. He opened the window and the door to make a draught. The candles sputtered in the feeble breeze. He held the pen suspended above the paper and read aloud what he had written—". . . We hold these truths to be self-evident—that all men are created equal; that they are endowed by their Creator with certain unalienable rights; that among these are life, liberty and the pursuit of happiness . . ."

In the room above, Henry lay awake on the narrow bed. It was too warm to sleep, but that was not the only reason he was awake. His thoughts circled round and round; something strange had happened to him. He did not know what it was and it frightened him a little. Through the open door he could hear the scratching of the pen on the paper and the low voice reading something he did not altogether understand. But the words excited him. They made him feel brave. He wished with all his might to be a man. But no matter, he would certainly fight on Mr. Jefferson's side as soon as he was old enough, he promised himself as he fell asleep at last.

Henry's father had a small farm not far from the city. He was neither for the Tories, nor against them. He sold milk and eggs to his neighbors and he didn't care whether they were Tories.

When Henry came home from his visit, and began to tell his father about Thomas Jefferson, and what he said to him, Henry's father told him to mind his own business, and chop wood for kindling. Henry chopped wood, but his thoughts went back to the papers in the small desk Mr. Jefferson showed him. He remembered every word Jefferson said to him, and how he looked. It was hard not to talk about it, and he was glad when Reginald came sauntering by on his sleek horse and stopped to talk to him.

"We might go hunting next week maybe," offered Reginald.

"I've got something better to do," said Henry.

"Better than hunting?" Reginald looked very surprised. "There isn't anything better than hunting."

"Yes, there is," said Henry. "But you wouldn't know," he added with a mysterious air.

"What are you talking about?" cried Reginald, much annoyed.

"You wouldn't understand because you're a Tory," said Henry.

"I certainly am a Tory. We're subject to the Crown of England, aren't we?" demanded Reginald.

"I'm for freedom, like Mr. Jefferson," said Henry proudly.

"You mean you're for the rebels?" Reginald got off his horse in his excitement. "You're crazy, you'll be hanged by the neck with all the other traitors as soon as they're caught."

"Then I'll be in good company—better company than the Tories," said Henry doggedly.

"You traitor!" shouted Reginald, red in the face with anger.

"You old Tory!" shouted Henry. "I'm going to join the Sons of Liberty and help tar and feather all the Tories we find."

"You will, will you?" Reginald struck Henry in the face. The next minute they were pounding each other with their fists. Reginald's fists were not as tough as Henry's. He was getting the worst of it.

"I'll have my father put you in jail," he cried, trying to stop his nosebleed with his fine white cambric handkerchief.

"You better tell your father to hide under the bed before the Sons of Liberty smear him with tar and stick feathers all over him, and you too," cried Henry.

"You'll be flogged and put in jail," threatened Reginald.

But when Reginald told his father about Henry, his father remained silent, his face pale with apprehension. Half his help at his elegant store on Chestnut Street, he suspected, were rebels, and were secretly wearing badges of Sons of Liberty. No one knew these days what might happen to anyone.

At the State House, the Continental Congress was discussing the now completed Declaration of Independence. Jefferson listened in silence: let them pick and argue, let them tear it apart, he had spoken for the people. It was their voice as well as his. He knew their mind, he had listened to their complaints and to their hopes. They were of a mind to be a free, independent country. What would they do with this freedom? Would they know, all of them together, how to shape this new nation into a great nation?

Franklin, sitting near by, watched the younger man with a smile of sympathy. Was he perhaps troubled by the arguments over his composition? He came over to sit beside Jefferson.

"I'll tell you a story," he offered with a droll smile. "A man I knew opened a hat store, and hung a sign over the door. It had a picture of a hat and read 'John Thompson, hatter, makes and sells hats for ready money.' When he asked his customers for their opinion of his sign, one said the word 'hatter' should be omitted because the words 'makes hats' told he was a hatter; another customer said the word 'makes' should be left out because customers wouldn't care who made the hats; another one said the words 'for ready money' should be left out as everyone who bought a hat expected to pay. The sign now read 'John Thompson sells hats.' Why have 'sells hats' on the sign? asked a friend. Nobody will expect you to give them away, and why have the word 'hats' when there is a picture of a hat on the sign? So now all there was left was the picture of a hat and the name John Thompson."

Jefferson listened with an amused smile. Franklin was telling him this story, he realized, not only to take his mind off the debate over his composition but to make him see that the important things in the declaration would remain. That was, after all, what mattered. Let them argue about this word or that word; the Declaration of men's rights was now complete, and it was to be proclaimed to the world.

The weighing of words ended at last. Solemnly, and in a loud voice, John Hancock called for a vote. The room rang with aye, aye, but not all the ayes were loud and glad, some were low and timid.

The Declaration of Independence was adopted.

"We may hang for this," muttered a few low voices.

"Aye, we may hang for this, but if we don't hang together we shall certainly hang separately," said Franklin. He was fond of repeating this pleasantry.

John Hancock laughed louder than any of them. The British Parliament interfered with his importing and exporting; now he would be free of their interference at last. But there was no time to waste on more talk. The Declaration must be printed as quickly as possible. John Hancock gave the order to send it to the printer immediately. Special messengers on horseback were to carry printed copies to every city, town and hamlet to be read aloud in public. The printer worked all night to have enough copies ready for all the commanders in the army to read to troops in every courthouse in the colonies.

Jefferson was now free to go home to his beloved Monticello. He went shopping on Chestnut Street in the handsome stores he much admired. He bought presents, and paid the bill for the seven pairs of gloves he had bought for his wife. He paid for a thermometer he had bought when he first arrived. He felt gay and buoyant. He bought a ticket for two shillings, to see some monkeys on exhibition.

Bob, his young slave, packed his bags and waited patiently. But Jefferson remained in the yard of the State House to listen to the public reading of the Declaration.

An eager crowd was waiting to hear the reading. The young Navy officer looked around at the expectant faces, his eyes solemn and serious. His voice rang out clear and strong in the solemn silence ". . . We hold these truths to be self-evident, that all men are created equal, that they are endowed by their Creator with certain unalienable rights, that among these are life, liberty and the pursuit of happiness . . ."

A loud shout went out from the crowd when the reading

ended. Singing riotous songs, the crowd broke into the State House, dragged the king's coat of arms from the hall, and set fire to it in the square. Everybody was shouting and singing—bonfires were lighted, guns saluted, bells rang—

Standing somewhat apart, Jefferson watched the crowd, his serious eyes alight with a strange smile. Young Henry spied him in the crowd, and came up to stand beside him. The ringing of the great bell on the steeple of the State House swelled the din of the many-throated voices of the people. One could hardly make out what anyone said. A man with a white beard, standing near by, edged his way towards Jefferson and called out—"Did you know, sir, the words that are molded on the top of the bell?" and without waiting for Jefferson to answer he added, "It's a verse from the Bible. It's been there since 1751 and it says 'Proclaim liberty throughout *all* the land unto all the inhabitants thereof'— It's a prophecy, sir, I guess."

"And so it is," exclaimed Jefferson.

Henry looked up at the bell in wonder. "To think it has all been written there and we didn't know it," he said in a voice of awe.

"Some of us knew it," smiled the old man as he edged away through the crowd. Henry moved nearer to Jefferson and displayed his badge of the Sons of Liberty he was wearing on his chest. "I'm going to fight, sir, as soon as they'll let me," he said proudly. "I'm going to be in the militia."

Jefferson shook the boy's hand and walked back to his rooms for final preparations to go home. But he did not sleep that night. Bells rang all through the night and people sang around bonfires until their voices grew hoarse. Jefferson went out to walk in the streets. He was going home, his farm needed looking after—things were in a muddle there after so long an absence, but his thoughts were not on his own affairs this night.

He listened to the songs and the tolling of bells and feet dancing on sidewalks. This was the lusty voice of a new nation, the United States of America; a democracy shouting its freedom. He wanted to savor it, taste it, and remember this to the end of his days.

THEODORE ROOSEVELT's motto, "Speak softly, but carry a big stick," was a typical example of the man himself. His childhood was overshadowed by sickness and only through determination was he able to build up a strong body. Soon after he was graduated from Harvard he entered politics and before long was appointed Secretary of the Navy and did a great deal in building up a strong fleet. As leader of the Rough Riders he again distinguished himself during the Spanish American War. Following this he was elected Governor of New York and later vice-president. On McKinley's death he was sworn in as president of the United States. He was responsible for the construction of the Panama Canal, the Russo-Japanese treaty, the conservation law, and the Navy's first trip around the world. After completing his term he spent much of his time hunting, traveling, and writing until his death in 1919.

Julian Street

THEODORE ROOSEVELT

ILLUSTRATED BY *John Merryweather*

IN THE early years of World War I, when German aggressions against the United States were piling up, and we were trying to talk our way out of trouble instead of meeting strength with strength, I was one of a little group of men who used to go for stimulus and comfort to Theodore Roosevelt.

"Let's go to Oyster Bay and take a treatment," we would say when we felt sunk, and always when we had been with the old, tawny lion of Sagamore Hill for a little while, his courage and vitality would flow into us, and we would light up with the holy fire.

The man who had been the youngest and most versatile of American presidents was then a private citizen without a party backing, but as always he was the leader of a spirited element in the nation. Up and down the land he went, preaching straight Americanism and the old heroic virtues without which no nation can be great. But the nation was slow to hear.

He spoke to me of that.

"The average man," he said, "does not want to be disturbed. He doesn't want to be called upon to leave his business and his family and do a distinctly unpleasant duty. That is natural enough. Nevertheless, you can appeal to the two soul sides of that man. If you appeal to his deepest sense of duty, to all that he has of strength and courage and high-mindedness, you can make him shake off his sloth, his self-indulgence, his short-sightedness, or his timidity, and stand up and do and dare and die at need, just as the men of Bunker Hill and Trenton and Yorktown and Gettysburg and Shiloh did and dared and died."

Love of country was the predominant passion of Theodore Roosevelt's life. It was he who first perceived this nation's larger destiny and led us toward it. We must be strong. He advocated universal military training for young men for national safety, discipline, and health. He founded the modern American Navy, and having done so was not content to see it rust. When Europe was slow to recognize our increased stature Roosevelt compelled attention to it. With territorial aspirations, Germany sent a squadron to Venezuela, but Roosevelt reasserted the Monroe Doctrine and backed it with the fleet. So that the navy could be switched quickly from ocean to ocean he built the Panama Canal. To advertise American power he sent a fleet of sixteen battleships around the world. The first "courtesy call" made by this fleet was on truculent Japan, and the effect upon Japan was salutary. "Perdicaris alive or Raisouli dead" was his formula when an American citizen was held for ransom by a Moroccan brigand, and Mr. Perdicaris was quickly set free.

In 1905 he wrote his English friend Cecil Spring-Rice: "My object is to keep America in trim so that fighting her shall be too expensive and dangerous a task lightly to be undertaken by anybody."

Stupid people used to call him bloodthirsty and say he wanted war, when what he wanted was strength to avoid war. Long before 1917 he was considering an organization of nations for peace. "We must strive for peace always," he said, "but we must never hesitate to put righteousness above peace. . . . National righteousness without force back of it speedily becomes a matter of derision."

His statesmanlike foresight continues to be revealed. Innumerable instances might be cited, but I select as an example the fact that in the fall of 1914 he said that if Germany subjugated England she would probably ally herself with Japan and within a few years make a joint attack on the United States.

Once I asked him if he thought he had genius.

"Most emphatically not," he answered, and spoke of occupations at which he wished to excel but according to his statement did not excel. He said he was not a first-rate horseman ("My hands aren't good"), or boxer ("My arms are too short"), or shot ("I'm blind in one eye"), or orator ("I haven't a good voice"), or writer ("Except perhaps that I have a good instinct and a liking for simplicity and directness"). Yet he was the former colonel of Roosevelt's Rough Riders, had supplied the Museum of Natural History with its famous collection of African big game, was one of the most formidable political campaigners this country ever saw, and an author who, if he had achieved nothing else in life, would have earned fame through his books.

"If I have anything at all resembling genius," he said, "it is the gift for leadership. Men will follow me." And he added, "To tell the truth, I like to believe that by what I have accomplished *without* great gifts I may be a source of encouragement to American boys."

His thought for American boys was characteristic, for he had a special tenderness for children. As a child he had struggled with ill-health, and his rugged body had been built up only by sheer determination. And that was what he wanted all of us to have—the kind of determination that makes a people strong and rugged and virile and united. Throughout his mature life he urged those qualities upon us, and sometimes he was abused for doing it.

Thinking of this I once said to him that I did not see how he had kept from becoming cynical about mankind.

"I am not cynical," he replied, "because I have observed that just when our people seem to be altogether beyond hope they have a way of turning round and doing something perfectly magnificent."

As our little group used to go in the old days to Theodore Roosevelt for stimulus and comfort, those of us who remain turn to him in memory. Often it seems to me I know, as if I had just been talking with him, what he would think and feel today.

His first thought would be for the men of Wake and Midway and the Philippines, those all too few heroic men whose deeds belong to history and the poets.

His next thought would be for us, and it would be colored with uneasiness lest our traditional feelings of safety from attack make us incredulous and complacent, so that we take too long to reach the point of "doing something perfectly magnificent."

And perhaps he would repeat to us the message delivered in a speech he made in 1899:

"I preach to you, then, my countrymen, that our country calls not for the life of ease, but for the life of strenuous endeavor. The twentieth century looms before us big with the fate of many nations. If we stand idly by, if we seek merely swollen, slothful, ease and ignoble peace, if we shrink from the hard contests where men must win at hazard of their lives and at the risk of all they hold dear, then the bolder and stronger people will pass by us and will win for themselves the domination of the world.

"Let us therefore boldly face the life of strife, resolute to do our duty well and manfully; resolute to uphold righteousness by deed and by word; resolute to be both honest and brave, to serve high ideals, yet to use practical methods. Above all, let us not shrink from strife, moral or physical, within or without the Nation, provided we are certain the strife is justified; for it is only through strife, through hard and dangerous endeavor, that we shall ultimately win the goal of true national greatness."

Constance Buel Burnett

MARIAN ANDERSON: A VOICE IN A HUNDRED YEARS

ILLUSTRATED BY *Matilda Breuer*

A SINGING voice has been described as a gift of God. It is the one musical instrument which cannot be bought or handed down to future generations. The famous violins of Guarnerius and Stradivarius are a heritage of the centuries. They still sing for us with matchless tone, but the use of a beautiful voice is permitted to but one favored individual. Its possession alone will not make a great artist, unless he is spiritually and mentally endowed to make the highest use of his gift.

A hundred years ago, in Sweden, the child-soprano Jenny Lind indicated early that she was destined for an extraordinary career. Here in America another child-singer has made history. Little Marian Anderson, born in the Negro quarter of the city of Philadelphia, was found to possess a contralto of magnificent range and quality. Her musical intelligence and her devotion to her art have made her one of the great singers of our times.

No famous voice has had a more favorable environment in which to develop than that of Marian Anderson. Music is a natural expression of her race, and no people have finer vocal equipment.

Marian Anderson remembers, with a kind of affection, the white marble doorsteps of the houses in Philadelphia where she grew up. By scrubbing them, she once earned enough money to buy a violin.

The daily scouring of the family doorstep is a ritual familiar to many a Philadelphia child, and Marian liked to hear the swish of her mother's scrubbing brush and see the swirl of soapsuds over the wet stone. For rhythm was a language she understood before she understood speech.

Rhythm talked to her in many tongues. Now it ticked inside her father's watch. At other times it puffed and sang from the kettle's spout on her mother's stove, or tapped a lively beat on the pavement whenever a horse went by, or passed like thunder down the street on the rumble of wheels. Any rhythmic noise is, for a canary, an invitation to song, and so it was for Marian.

She raised her voice in a babbling accompaniment to her mother's housework, feeling the impulse to sing whenever she heard the sweep of the broom or the hum of the sewing machine. Very soon, however, she learned to memorize and carry a tune.

An aunt sang frequently in the Anderson home, and shortly her little niece was imitating the melodies she heard. But harmony excited Marian even more than melody. She thrilled under the impact of its resonance rolling out of her grandmother's small pedal-organ, and from the throats of men and women singing Negro spirituals.

All during infancy she was unconsciously absorbing musical impressions, and then, when she was about three, she made a discovery that was equally important to her development. Her mother had told the child to sit quietly in her high chair while she herself prepared breakfast in another room. Marian had always been permitted to trot about the kitchen. Often she had been allowed to stand on a chair and stir the breakfast porridge with a wooden spoon. This morning, the ways of grown people seemed inexplicably cruel. She screamed with indignation. Then something strange happened she never forgot.

A flowered border decorated the wallpaper of the room in which she sat. Marian saw the flowers each time she threw back her head and opened her mouth to get her breath. Suddenly she became alert and watchful, even though she went on crying as loudly as ever. The flowers were moving. They were swaying in time to her crying—they were dancing! Marian brushed away angry tears and stared. As she gazed, the forget-me-nots smiled

She would scour a doorstep for any pay

at her, a large chrysanthemum nodded its head, and a blue rose was suddenly transformed into a prince with a plumed hat. The prince bowed to a purple lilac, and the lilac turned into a curtsying lady. Then all the flowers danced and sang.

When her mother came back from the kitchen, the little girl was singing happily, nor did she ever again mind being left alone. A door leading to an imaginative world had swung open for her and was never to shut. All those who are destined to become artists must find this door, each in his own manner.

It was well for this embryo artist that she found it early, for two little sisters were born, and Mrs. Anderson had to take in washing to help support the growing family. Marian was left more and more to her own resources. She says now that no toy had any real interest for her until she had invented some rhythmic kind of use for it. Instead of playing house with her dolls, she gave them singing lessons.

Mrs. Anderson, who had been a schoolteacher, watched her little daughter's growing absorption in music with keen interest. She knew that hers was no ordinary voice, for Marian had warm contralto notes unusual to a child, as well as high notes that climbed effortlessly up to high C.

Probably her parents did not dream at this time of a career for her. Mr. Anderson was a small dealer in coal and ice, and music lessons were costly. At the Baptist church, however, she would be given musical training of a sort, and opportunities to sing.

As soon as Marian was enrolled in the children's choir, the parish became aware of the child with the remarkable voice. She was natural and unafraid before an audience, and the neighborhood soon found they could count on little Marian Anderson to attract a crowd for their benefits and concerts. She made her first public appearance in the Union Baptist Church, singing a duet with another child. She was contributing her share to the musical life of the community when she was only six.

It was at this time that she longed to own a violin, and one day she saw one hanging in the window of a pawnshop. Its price was only $3.45!

Young as she was, Marian knew of the wonderful violins made by Stradivarius. She knew also what a pawnshop was, and that people desperately in need of money left their most treasured possessions there. It was possible that this violin might be a Stradivarius. Then and there she determined it was to be hers.

Armed with her mother's pail and scrubbing brush, she rang the bell of every house on her street. She would scour a doorstep for anything a housewife was willing to pay. It was a long, anxious wait before she collected the necessary amount, for she received only five or ten cents for her labors—and in the meantime what was to prevent some wealthier person from buying the violin?

Perhaps the pawnbroker saved the instrument for the child who came to his shop daily to gaze wistfully at it from the street. At all events, it was still there when finally she emptied a stockingful of pennies, nickels, and dimes on his counter.

"At last you have come for the violin!" The storekeeper counted out the money carefully. "You buy it for yourself? You are too small to play."

His shrewd eyes narrowed with curiosity.

Marian held the violin close. She had no answer for him because she had a burning question of her own.

"Is it a very fine violin? Is it—a Stradivarius?"

The pawnbroker rubbed his chin. Naïve customers were rare visitors in a pawnshop. With great seriousness he examined her purchase.

"You want me to be honest, yes? Well—" he leaned confidentially over the counter—"it is not a Strad, no, but it is an exceptionally fine fiddle—and what a bargain, *hein?* No extra charge for the bow and case!"

Blissfully Marian carried the violin home and began laboriously to teach herself to play. She drew the bow timidly over the strings at first. It made her tremble to hear tones so like a human voice vibrating under her fingers. After days of experimenting she actually discovered the location of notes, and practiced constantly for months until the strings, worn out, snapped one by one.

By that time, however, the violin had served its purpose of satisfying a great hunger. Now she was a big girl—eight years old—and she had already earned her first concert fee of fifty cents, and posters announcing her appearance in concerts featured her as the "ten-year-old contralto"! No one hearing the ripe quality of that young voice would have believed her age, anyway.

Marian was going to public school now with all the other children on the street. Teachers found the wide-eyed little girl, with the alert listening expression, an intelligent, eager pupil. But there was one time in the morning when it seemed impossible to hold her attention. This was during music period in the adjoining schoolroom.

"Marian, go to the blackboard, please, and write the multiplication table as far as you can remember."

"Yes, Miss Jones."

Reluctantly Marian rose. It wasn't that standing at a blackboard disconcerted her—she was too used to an audience for that—nor were sums really difficult for her. But the melancholy strains of *My Old Kentucky Home* in the next room were like strong hands, tugging at her will to concentrate and weakening it.

"Five times six are thirty," she wrote on the blackboard while she listened to the singing. The five table was easy, she could remember it automatically. While she wrote she hummed under her breath. But by the time she reached six times seven, the stream of melody flowing in through the closed doors swept her completely away from the multiplication table. She stood motionless, the chalk suspended in her hand.

"You may sit down, Marian. Who will carry on from here?"

Practically the whole class waved a frantic assent to the teacher's question, but Marian scarcely noticed. Her mind and heart had already joined the nostalgic chorus in the other room. "*Weep no more, my lady—oh, weep no more today!*"

It was a mystery to the music teacher how little Marian Anderson contrived, each year, to know all the songs of the class to which she had been promoted before they were taught her.

When an upright piano was purchased by her father and mother, her excitement was as intense as the day she brought her violin home from the pawnshop. Her parents still could not afford to give her lessons, but she attacked the problem of teaching herself as confidently as she had the task of learning the violin.

She had a paper chart, an exact replica of the keyboard, with the names of the scales and the notes printed on it. Every night, when her father came home, she could hardly wait to show him what she had learned that day. Only when she saw his big thumb easily span two notes did she know slight discouragement, to think how long it would be before her own hand could stretch an octave.

She was twelve when her father died, and then it was necessary for someone to help her burdened mother earn a living for the family. As often as Marian could get engagements, she appeared as an assisting artist to other performers, and the people of her district loyally filled the halls, more interested in hearing the little girl who had grown up in their midst than in listening to visiting musicians.

For Marian, singing was too natural to seem more than an easy method of earning a living. It was not until she met and heard the famous Negro tenor, Roland Hayes, that she fully realized the potentialities of her voice and the responsibility such a gift might entail.

Watching the tall, slight man, who waited on the platform with such quiet dignity for applause to hush, she saw he was there for only one purpose—not to exhibit Roland Hayes, but to demonstrate the art of sensitive, beautiful singing. Music, as he presented it that day, was a shrine to which one brought humility and the fruit of selfless labor. It was a lesson she never forgot.

Roland Hayes sang often in Philadelphia after that, and if the concert was a local affair, Marian, now a girl of fifteen, was occasionally asked to sing a group of songs on the same program. She remembers the day when, in the artists' room during an intermission, he placed before her a copy of the well-known duet, *A Passage Bird's Farewell* by Eugene Hildach.

"Do you sing it?" he asked, smiling and sure of her answer.

Marian nodded, too excited for speech, but her face grew radiant.

"Good! Shall we finish the program together then?" suggested Roland Hayes, and earned a very young singer's heartfelt gratitude.

Because she was keenly aware of the problems of unequal opportunity confronting her race, Marian saw Hayes as something more than a distinguished singer. His international reputation made him a representative of his people. Every performance he gave forced recognition from his audience of the great latent capacities in the Negro. A career for one of her race, at this period, was more than a personal triumph, it was a crusade —a crusade in which she herself could enlist.

Circumstances were fast shaping Marian's future now, for at the time she was gaining vision and inspiration from the example of Roland Hayes, an eminent educator, Dr. Lucy L. W. Wilson, principal of the South Philadelphia High School for Girls, aided and encouraged her. Dr. Wilson invited her to her home and introduced her to prominent music lovers. Soon Mrs. Patterson volunteered to give her singing lessons for a year.

After that, the members of Marian's own district shouldered the responsibility of further lessons for the young girl who had sung so often at their music festivals. Nickels and dimes poured into a Fund for Marian Anderson's Future. From that time on, assistance was always at hand. The Philadelphia Choral Society invited Marian to give a concert under its auspices, and as a result she was offered two years of study with Miss Agnes Reifsneider. When that course was finished, her friends raised another fund, enabling her to study with the well-known teacher, Giuseppe Boghetti, who coached her for her first important appearance, at the Lewisohn Stadium with the New York Philharmonic Orchestra. She was chosen from among three hundred contestants for this honor, and the Philadelphia Orchestra shortly after offered her an engagement. Marian Anderson was launched on her career.

But though a career may be begun successfully, fame is not always waiting around the corner. It took ten more years of steady work and growth before she was acclaimed on two continents as a great singer.

Although she had won honors, her reputation was still in the making. To establish her in the foremost ranks would mean spending immense sums in publicity. Marian had no wealthy financial backing, and her racial background made her acceptance by the general public in the United States somewhat unpredictable.

Engagements dwindled and then became difficult to procure. It was evident that Marian's case was not to be different from that of many other American singers, who had first to establish a European reputation before they could win outstanding success in their own country.

Marian worked for a year with the well-known coach, Frank La Forge, before she ventured a trip to Europe. For three years then she went back and forth across the Atlantic. All this time travel was widening her experience and outlook. It was a period of quiet but fruitful growth. Her knowledge of languages and her repertory of foreign songs increased. Her art was expanding into fuller, richer expression.

In the year 1931, while she was in Berlin, Marian made a connection which was to start her at last on the road to spectacular success. She held an audition one day before a group of concert managers. In the audience sat Kosti Vehanen, Finnish pianist, accompanist, and friend of the Swedish impresario, Helmar Enwall, who had sent him on a special mission to Berlin for the purpose of hearing the Negro contralto about whom German managers were beginning to talk.

"She has a hundred colors in her voice," Vehanen reported back enthusiastically to Enwall, "and her stage presence has unusual dignity and individuality. She sings the songs of her own race with extraordinary feeling."

"Add to that the strange coincidence of her Scandinavian name! I believe I shall risk trying her here," decided Enwall, and engaged her on the spot.

Enwall booked her cautiously at first. The introduction of an unknown Negro singer was an experiment, but because the singer was Marian Anderson and because Scandinavian audiences are notably intelligent, the experiment proved a success. Soon all Scandinavia proclaimed the discovery of a new, sensational artist. By the end of her third concert season there she was filling hundreds of engagements, and Enwall was planning the long European tour which was to make her famous on the continent.

The next five years were a series of triumphs, singing to packed houses in the major cities of Europe.

"A voice like yours is heard once in a hundred years," Arturo Toscanini assured her in Salzburg, and news of the master's pronouncement was flashed back to America.

The great Finnish composer, Sibelius, in whose house she was invited to sing, paid her a graceful compliment. Coffee was to have been served at the end of the evening, but when Marian had finished her last group of Finnish songs by Sibelius, her host jumped to his feet and countermanded the coffee.

"Champagne!" he called enthusiastically to the servant. Then turning to his guest, "Let us have more Marian Anderson—and less Sibelius!"

Kosti Vehanen became her coach and accompanist, following her engagement by Helmar Enwall. The two artists were sympathetic, and the association proved a long and successful one, lasting over a period of ten years. Mr. Vehanen toured the continent with her, and remained her accompanist on her triumphal return to New York and on many subsequent American tours. His book, *Marian Anderson—a Portrait,* is a valuable record of her spectacular rise to fame.

All over Europe she was being acclaimed, and now her native land prepared to give her belated recognition. She was engaged for a concert at Town Hall in New York City, in December, 1935.

Her return was fraught with emotional significance for Marian. The friendship of distinguished people in Europe and the absence of race prejudice had been a moving and heartening experience. While she did not expect the same reception from her fellow countrymen, she hoped as she had never hoped for anything before that she might justify to Americans the artistic reputation earned abroad.

Unfortunatly, a painful accident lent added tension to the situation. She lost her balance during a storm on the Atlantic crossing, and in falling, fractured her foot. For a time it seemed as though she might have to cancel her New York appearance. But she was used to overcoming obstacles. So long as her voice was unimpaired, she would allow nothing to interfere with its use.

She insisted on fulfilling her promise to sing at the ship's concert although she had to be carried onto the platform. There were two more weeks for further recuperation before the concert at Town Hall, but Marian tried to walk too soon and had to hobble on to the stage before the curtain was raised.

No announcement of her injury had been made to the public. She wanted no appeal for leniency on this occasion of her homecoming. When the curtain rose, she stood erect and slim in the long silver gown which hid the plaster cast on her foot. She had to lean heavily against the piano to keep her balance. For further support, she counted on reserves of courage that had been hers since childhood.

On this night the New York critics and the public received their first indisputable evidence that Marian Anderson was a great artist. The sustained power and beauty of her phrasing in the Handel group indicated what was to come. People relaxed in their seats for an evening of utter enjoyment.

As song followed song, it became apparent that there were seemingly no limitations for this contralto singer. The flow and magnificence of the Handel arias changed to enchanting delicacy and tenderness in the Schubert lyrics, and no one had yet heard *Death and the Maiden*, by Franz Schubert, sung as she sang it, with a tone so floating and transparent it seemed an unearthly echo from some other world.

She closed the concert, as she had many others, with John Payne's *Crucifixion.* A moving quality of this spiritual is its stark simplicity. She sang it reverently, with closed eyes and in a

M. BREUER

hushed voice. Hers was the voice of a whole people now, the muted tragic accents of a race that has known bondage.

So great was the success of this concert that Marian had to sing twice again that season in New York, both times to crowded audiences in Carnegie Hall. Then, as soon as her foot was entirely mended, she was off to Europe once more. Her reputation was drawing her far afield, to the Soviet Union, to Africa, and to South America. When she returned home at last, she was scheduled for the longest and most intensive tour ever made by a singer in this country.

Scarcely a year went by now that she did not receive some outstanding tribute. She was awarded the *Grand Prix du Chant* for the best recorded voice on the continent, and America conferred upon her an Honorary Doctorate of Letters from Howard University in Washington, and another from Temple University. A little later she received the Spingarn Medal, and twice she sang at the White House, once for the President and his guests, and then before the King and Queen of England.

The little girl, born obscurely in the Negro quarter of Philadelphia, was realizing her dream of becoming a worthy representative of her race.

It was characteristic of her that all during the strenuous campaign of building a career, she longed at the same time for a retreat, a place where she might find relief from the strain of frequent public appearances. That desire has been fulfilled. She has a country home now that faces rolling meadows and blue hills. Its green acres offer the seclusion an artist needs for study and growth.

Marian Anderson was married July 17, 1943, in Bethel, Connecticut, to Orpheus Fischer, an architect, who was her childhood sweetheart. The singer's mother, and a sister who acts as her secretary, contribute much to family life when she is at home. The management of her house and gardens is a welcome diversion from the arduous professional schedule she keeps, and even while traveling she enjoys domestic activities. A sewing machine is an important item in her luggage. While on tour, yards of curtain lengths have been stitched for the many windows of the big white house on the wooded hill.

Adulation, that unhealthy adjunct of all spectacular careers, has left her untouched. To say merely that she is modest, however, is not enough. It leaves out all that contributes to her dignity. For behind Marian Anderson's achievement are an exalted purpose and a deep humility, ennobling impulses that make her a regal figure when she steps before an audience.

Marian Anderson hoped—and believed—that her career was an effective answer to those who denied her people equality with other races, and she never expected, nor wished, to be involved in a controversy. Nevertheless an unhappy occurrence in the spring of 1939—the refusal of Constitution Hall in Washington for her concert, presumably on the ground of her race—thrust her into the glare of a publicity from which she shrank but could not retreat. The story was featured in newspaper accounts throughout the country and public indignation was aroused. At the invitation of the Government, and with the special co-operation of the Department of the Interior, it was arranged that Miss Anderson should give her recital out-of-doors on Easter Sunday in front of the Lincoln Memorial.

The event was impressive and epochal. A great throng, attracted not only by the notoriety given the incident, but eager to pay tribute to a great singer, was massed in the large park between the Lincoln Memorial and the Obelisk. Washington spring weather was at its best. The lawns were green, cherry trees were in full bloom, and the long, transparent pool which reflects the Obelisk mirrored the late afternoon clouds.

On the platform were members of the Cabinet, of the Supreme Court, Senators and Congressmen. Secretary Ickes opened the ceremonies.

"Genius draws no color line," he said. "She has endowed Marian Anderson with such a voice as lifts any individual above his fellows, and is matter of exultant pride to any race. And so it is fitting that Marian Anderson should raise her voice in tribute to the noble Lincoln whom mankind will ever honor."

When he finished, silence held the vast audience waiting for the singer to appear. She came slowly, emerging from the white pillars of the Lincoln Memorial. For a moment she stood motionless at the head of the long flight of marble steps. Looking out over the sea of faces below her, she must in that instant have lost all sense of personal identity, and remembered with a great lift of the heart that those listening thousands would hear in her the Voice of a People.

In the flowing lines of a concert gown, Marian Anderson is statuesque. She was so that afternoon. Black velvet etched her sharply against the pale stone of the monument. She walked with raised head and a still dignity that brought throbbing emotion to more than one throat. Kosti Vehanen was already at the piano on the high platform built at the base of the Memorial. A row of amplifiers were like waiting sentinels across the front of the stage. She sang under the evening sky, and there was a glory in her face beyond the glory of the setting sun.

Since that historic occasion, Marian Anderson has been twice honored. In 1941 she was presented with the Bok Award for outstanding service to the City of Philadelphia, a sum of $10,000 which she promptly established as a fund to defray the costs of educating promising musicians without regard to race, creed or color. In 1944, she was awarded an Honorary Doctorate of Music by Smith College.

Those who have the good fortune to meet Marian Anderson are struck by her simplicity. She is as sincere and humble a servant of her art now, as when she scrubbed doorsteps to earn the price of a violin. Her life's purpose is well epitomized in the words of a Negro spiritual which she quoted at the close of her acceptance speech of the Bok Award:

"I have opened my mouth to the Lord and I won't turn back. I will go, I shall go, to see what the end will be."

Jean Henri Fabre, the great French naturalist, has been called "the Insect's Homer." When he looked at a wasp nest he saw its decorative twisted cords that looked like gold lace. He saw its modern stucco front, its porch, vestibule, nurseries, galleries, dining rooms, and well-filled pantries. When he looked at crickets and ants and bees they showed him how they hunted their food and how they fought their battles. They showed him their loves, their secret mysterious acts. They even showed him how they died. No other naturalist gained such a knowledge of the little creatures of the grass. What real but fairylike tales he told about them! He told about the spider who becomes a flying machine, the wasp who heroically battles the caterpillar, the praying mantis who scares the victim until it can't move, and he told about the tarantula lurking in her donjon tower and waiting for her prey.

Fabre, born of poor parents, peddled lemons, worked with a gang of laborers, and was so poor he had a hard time getting through school. He taught a primary school at 19, and later, when he married and became the father of a large family, he was a poor college professor. Then, after a forty-year struggle, he retired happily to a humble home in Serignan where he remained for the rest of his life. In this insect paradise he wrote books that later became famous. They were books that finally brought this great scientist fame and a pension from the French government. They brought him, too, a tribute from his friend Darwin who said, "He is a savant who thinks like a philosopher and writes like a poet."

Irmengarde Eberle

HENRI FABRE: A PLACE OF HIS OWN

ILLUSTRATED BY *Kay Lovelace*

HENRI had roamed far and wide over the countryside in the years since he had lived at Orange, so he knew where to look for a place he could buy. He drove over to Serignan, a very small village about four and one half miles northeast of Orange.

He came to a stretch of dry, flat land which was a part of an abandoned farm. A stone house, long empty, stood among the wild growths. All around it in the more fertile sections lay the farms of neighboring peasants. Gently undulating hills ranged to the north. Mount Ventoux raised its huge bulk beyond the broad plain and the low hills to the east. . . .

Henri went into the village and sought out the owner, who was very glad to get rid of this waste land, which no farmer would even consider because the soil was so scant and the rocks so abundant. So the matter was settled, and Henri at fifty-six at last had a place of his own, the outdoor laboratory he needed.

A few weeks later, in May, the Fabres moved to the new place. . . .

Henri Fabre called his place at Serignan his *harmas*, for that is the Provençal French name for a stony wild piece of land that farmers cannot use.

Workmen had been employed to repair the house, and to build a high stone wall all around the land. Fabre wanted the place completely cut off from the road, and from the gaze or the trespassing of strangers. It would be a private park for the family, their cats and the dog, and for the undisturbed lives of insects and plants.

Carpenters and plasterers were working all over the house, as the family unpacked the household goods. But the mother and her girls did not mind; they were so glad to be in this place of their own.

Marie said to Algaé, "It does me good just to look at your father out there on the grounds. He's so content, so at peace. . . . He can build something here that no one can take away."

Henri was really content. He went out day by day to look at the beautiful wild plants of the near-by meadows and roadsides—the thyme and lavender. He dug them up and planted them on his own small piece of land. He bought seeds of other plants he liked, which were not native to the region, and planted these, too, with loving hands. He was up before sunrise, listening to the bird songs, watching the insects as they roused from slumber. He looked often toward Mount Ventoux, beautiful and mighty in the mysterious glow of sunrise or sunset, or in the shimmering light of noonday.

Wandering over his grounds he decided he needed an artificial pool where he could study fresh-water animals and plants. So he began to build one, asking advice of the laborers who were still working on the house and wall, and set to work. . . .

He spent hours, too, in arranging his laboratory. The room to the left on the ground floor was set aside for this. His cases containing specimens of insects, shells, plants of all kinds, were set up. His small wire insect cages, the glass jars with gauze covers, and his old microscope were set on a long, plain, walnut wood table. . . .

His friends often sent him insects or plants that they thought would interest him. One day a case arrived containing two great crabs, or sea-spiders. The masons and carpenters came close, wondering at them as they were taken out of the box. One of them, by the name of Favier, said he knew what they were; that he had eaten them in some distant land when he had been a soldier in the service of his country. It was evident from the tone of his voice, and the way he held his shoulders as he talked that he was proud of his career and of his knowledge of the world. . . . Henri Fabre was amused and attracted by the colorful personality of the man; and hereafter he often called Favier and asked him to help him with some special job. . . .

Insects soon began to find Fabre's *harmas* a heaven, for while elsewhere farmers were doing all they could to exterminate them, here they were welcomed and encouraged to make themselves at home. When certain insects did not come of their own accord, Henri Fabre and Favier went out with pocket trowel and spade or net, and caught them and brought them into the grounds. In such ways certain wasps and wild bees, crickets, spiders, scorpions, various kinds of flies and beetles, all unknowing, became the living specimens of this amazing outdoor laboratory. And before Favier left, some years later, for reasons of importance to himself, the outdoor laboratory was in fine condition, thriving with plants and insects.

In the late winter of 1880, the end of the second year at

Serignan, a letter arrived from Charles Darwin, which started a series of new experiments. Darwin said he was very much interested in Fabre's findings about the ability of mason bees to find their way back to their nests when removed several miles in distance. He had read Fabre's descriptions of his experiments at Orange, as he had reported them; and he was eager to hear of more tests that might show how the insects were able to do this: whether they sensed the direction in which they were carried even when in closed paper twists, or whether the magnetism of the earth gave them a sense of direction. He suggested that Fabre, while he carried the bees around in their container, should do something to destroy their sense of direction, and then study their return flights.

Henri Fabre was interested in Darwin's suggestion; and shortly he undertook a number of experiments, choosing the mason bees of the walls to work with.

These insects abounded in this part of the country. There happened to be none on the Fabre *harmas*, but on neighboring farms they built such heavy and many celled masonry nests on the tiles of the roofs of houses and barns that the roofs sometimes sagged with them. Henri Fabre suggested to a farmer that he would take down whole tiles of his barn on which the bees had built, and replace them with new ones. It seemed sheer foolishness to the farmer for a man to offer to do this work for nothing, but it was all to his good, so he of course gladly agreed. . . .

Then as spring advanced, Henri and those of the family who were at home watched the nests day by day. The bees broke from their cells and flew out into the world; and almost immediately began to repair the old cells or build new ones beside them or on them. They stored them with food in preparation for laying their eggs and bringing up another generation of bees.

Henri waited until the bees were at their busiest. Then he prepared his mixture of gum arabic and chalk again and set it near the bees' nests. He dipped his straw into the mixture and with it made a white dot on the back of a bee. The bee was so busy putting a lump of masonry into place in her cell-building that it hardly noticed it. He captured a number of them by putting a small glass test tube over them, and from this transferred them into paper horns.

Leaving Antonia at the nests to watch for the returning marked insects, Fabre set out with his bees in their paper horns in a closed tin box. His dog came along as usual. It was just after the noon meal that he started. He carried the bees a quarter of a mile in one direction, then he turned and walked about the same distance in the opposite direction. He put the box in a sling of cloth and whirled it about, and performed similar acts to destroy the bees' sense of direction.

Finally, after a long walk in still another direction and a last whirl of the box, he released the bees in a meadow a little over two miles from the house. He looked at his watch and saw that it was two-fifteen, and then started home. When he got home one of the marked bees had already arrived. Antonia said she had seen it come to its nest at two-thirty. It had taken this bee just a quarter of an hour to find its way home, after all the changes of direction Fabre had made and the whirling it had been subjected to. Two more returned later. Some others may have returned, but with their white marks gone.

Next he marked the bees with red so that he could distinguish them from those of the day before if any of the marks remained, and made a new experiment. Another day he released forty-nine marked with a blue spot. Of these seventeen returned, in spite of all confusing elements introduced. He made numbers of experiments, and was convinced that he was not jumping at a conclusion when he stated that he did not think the bee's capacity to find its way home was based on sensing the direction in which he was carried, but that sheer instinct brought it back. The "insects' genius," he called it.

He wrote to Darwin, telling him the results of his experiments. Darwin was enormously interested and asked if Fabre would try attaching a very small magnet to his bees, to see how this would affect them. Perhaps earth magnetism had something to do with their finding their way back. Fabre tried to do this for Darwin, but approached the idea with doubt.

He magnetized a tiny broken-off part of a needle and glued it to a bee, but just as he had thought, the bee went nowhere till it had scraped off the small metal particle. It rolled and scraped on the ground, and rolled again. When it was rid of the needle point it flew directly home.

The experiments with the bees continued, with many variations. Meanwhile Henri was also at work on the second volume of the *Souvenirs*. . . .

People of the near-by farms and the village often helped Fabre by bringing him interesting things they found. The children especially were alert and eager. They knew Henri Fabre was studying creatures, and they liked him because he always answered them kindly and fully when they asked him questions. They often came running with a branch or leaf covered with insect eggs, or with a pupa dug up from the ground while spading in orchard or garden. Now and then these gifts turned out to be of real value to Henri. He always showed such keen appreciation that the children took delight in looking for things he wanted.

The years at the *harmas* were great years for Jean Henri Fabre. Studying his insects right on his own land all the time, his knowledge grew more complete, and his reports on them grew into further volumes of his fine books, the *Souvenirs Entomologiques*. As each came out, his fame grew among men of intelligence and discernment in the fields of the natural sciences and of the arts and letters. It grew quietly but steadily and strongly. . . .

It was these living plants and creatures that Fabre loved. It was in the study of the living insects that he added so much to the world's knowledge. The infinite variety of life, the slow unfolding of its mysteries, had filled his heart and mind, in spite of hardship, with joyful zest.

Ragna Eskil

JACQUES CARTIER

ILLUSTRATED BY *John Merryweather*

JACQUES CARTIER, who was to discover the great land of Canada, had the sea in his blood. He was born in the little town of St. Malo, on the coast of Brittany, in one of the most exciting times in history—the Age of the New World's Discovery.

He was just a year old when Columbus sailed across the Atlantic the first time, and only six years old when Cabot, in 1497, discovered the rich fishing banks of Newfoundland. Both these discoveries meant much to St. Malo, for St. Malo men made their living from the sea. Soon some were off to the new Spanish lands, but more sailed time and again to the cod banks where the sea so swarmed with fish that they hauled them up "with baskets let down with a stone." And when the mariners came home, the St. Malo boys would crowd to hear their tales—young Jacques the most eager of all. He would wish he could hurry the years so he would be old enough to go, too. But he would not be a simple seaman, he said. He'd be an ocean pilot! This was about the most daring ambition a boy could have in those days.

We don't know how young he was when he became a pilot, but the church register in St. Malo shows that he was a master-pilot at the time he married pretty Marie des Granches in 1519. By the time he was forty-two years old, he was rated the greatest pilot in all France. He had sailed the coast of France, been to the Mediterranean and parts of Africa, and historians are sure he had sailed to South America because, in his letters from Canada, he compared the trees and plants there with those of Brazil. Also, he had piloted ships to the cod banks. And when France was at war, he had been a roving corsair, hunting the sea for enemy ships of his country.

He was strong, brave, intelligent. As a commander, he seems never to have had trouble with his crews, and in Canada the Indians held great feasts for him whenever he came. They would give him presents of fish and eels, and bread they had baked by putting ground corn mixed with water on hot stones and covering it with pebbles. And they gave him and his men valuable furs. The Indians didn't have stockpiles of furs in Cartier's time. It was later when the fur traders came that the Indians went in for wholesale killing of fur animals.

So it wasn't surprising that when Francis I, King of France, decided that he, too, like the rulers of Spain, Portugal, England and Holland, would send an expedition to try to discover a western Passage to the Far East, he chose Cartier to lead it. Italy then controlled the Mediterranean, the only inside route to these fabulous lands, and wouldn't let any other country use it. While people now knew that the earth was round instead of flat, they still hadn't learned that America was a separate land with the Pacific Ocean lying between it and Asia. And Francis figured that if Cartier could find a backdoor passage, so to speak, to the rich cities of India and China, France could get a share, too, of the fine silks, porcelains, precious stones and spices which the Orient produced. It was a venture worth taking.

All the people in St. Malo were out that April morning in 1534 when Cartier and his company of sixty men set sail. They had two small boats, loaded with several months' provisions, firearms, and with trinkets and steel knives and hatchets to give the natives, if they should meet any. It was a gala occasion. Only Cartier's wife and the families of the crew were sad—explorers met many dangers, and would the men come back? Before embarking, the mariners attended church, and then they went aboard, with the townspeople waving and wishing them good fortune.

They had a fairly easy trip across the Atlantic and beyond the fishing grounds to the tip of Newfoundland. But at the Straits of Belle Isle, they met a severe storm and it was only Cartier's fine navigating that got them through. When they came into the Gulf of St. Lawrence with its islands, the first time white men had seen this area, Cartier was both disappointed and jubilant. He was disappointed because, while he kept sailing around for weeks, trying out this passage and that between islands, he could of course find none that led to India and China. But he was delighted with the wooded islands and shores he saw.

"It is the fairest land that may possibly be seen, full of goodly meadows and trees," he wrote in the journal he was keeping to show Francis. When he went on shore "to see closer the goodly sweet and smelling trees that were there," he wrote: "We found them to be cedars, yews, pines, white elm, ash, willows, with many other sorts of trees to us unknown, but without any fruit. The grounds where no wood is are very fair, and are full of peason (peas), white and red gooseberries, strawberries, blackberries and wild corn, which seemed to have been sowed and ploughed."

They saw strange sights, too—"fishes shaped like horses" (walruses) and a huge school of white whales tumbling in the water. "They were headed like greyhounds, and were as white as snow, and were never before of any man seen or known." They caught a polar bear, and "its flesh was as good to eat as any heifer of two years."

Luckily, before they had to turn back, Cartier discovered the mouth of the St. Lawrence River, and even sailed up it "until land could be seen on either side." However, provisions were getting low, and reluctantly he gave the return order. But he felt confident the king would authorize another voyage, for this might be the passage!

On their way to the Straits, they passed the lovely Gaspé shore and at a favorable spot they anchored for several days to get their ships in shape for the Atlantic crossing. Some roving Indians were here, too, who thought the white men were gods

and gave them presents of everything they had. Cartier, in turn, gave the women trinkets and the men steel knives, which pleased them mightily, for their tools were of stone.

Here, with the Indians looking on, Cartier had a huge cross, thirty feet high, erected, on which he had emblazoned an inscription which claimed this territory for the King of France. An artist later made a painting of this scene, as he imagined it from Cartier's account. All the later French explorers erected crosses, too, whenever they took possession in the king's name of new territory.

Like Columbus, Cartier made two other trips to the land he discovered—one the following year when he had three boats and 121 men and stayed over the winter, and one in 1541 when he stayed about the same length of time.

On the second trip, he sailed up the St. Lawrence to where Quebec now is and where the Indians had a village they called Stadacona. He anchored here for the winter, and while part of the men built a fort, he took others with him on an exploratory trip to Hochelaga, the largest village in the whole region. Montreal is built on the same site. Both these villages had stockades around them. The Indians were friendly and they exchanged gifts. The woods were in autumn color, and Cartier enjoyed their beauty. But he was becoming convinced that here was no passage to the Far East.

The French had a miserable time that winter. They froze in the subzero cold; their food ran low. Scurvy developed because of the lack of vitamins; many men died, and many more were horribly sick. But an Indian told Cartier that if the men would drink a concoction made by boiling spruce boughs in water, they would be cured. And they were well within a week. But all were glad to sail home when the ice broke.

His third trip, in 1541, was to establish a settlement, but nothing came of it for the settlers wouldn't stay. And it wasn't until Champlain came some sixty years later that a French settlement in Canada really took root.

In appreciation of his great service to France, the king gave Cartier a manor near St. Malo, and he spent his last years there. He had no children of his own, but he was fond of children, for the church records show that he was godfather to twenty-seven boys and girls! So he must have been well liked by the townspeople.

He died in 1557.

William Oliver Stevens

JANE ADDAMS

ILLUSTRATED BY *Kay Lovelace*

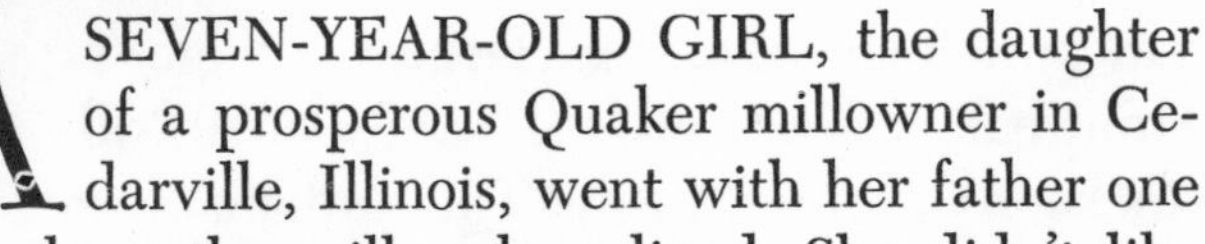

A SEVEN-YEAR-OLD GIRL, the daughter of a prosperous Quaker millowner in Cedarville, Illinois, went with her father one day to a district where the millworkers lived. She didn't like what she saw and smelled.

"Papa," she asked, "what makes people live in such horrid little houses?" Her father tried to explain how it was that some persons were so poor that they had to live in houses like these.

"Well," said the child, "when I get to be big I'm going to have a big house, but it isn't going to be between other big houses; it's going to be between horrid little houses like these." That little girl was Jane Addams, and the story of her life is that of her big house set between "horrid little houses like these."

Her mother died when she was too young to remember her, and all the child's love and devotion were centered on her father. He was such a magnificent man, admired and respected by everyone, rich or poor. He had been the friend of Abraham Lincoln when that great man was only an obscure lawyer, and still treasured Lincoln's letters, beginning, "My dear Double-D'ed Addams." One of Jane's earliest memories was that of seeing all the houses draped in black on the news of Lincoln's assassination. This was when she was not quite five years old.

Jane suffered a slight curvature of the spine in her childhood, and she thought of herself as such a homely, crooked little thing that she didn't want strangers to think of her as the daughter of her wonderful father. Often, after Sunday meeting, she would contrive to walk home with her uncle instead. But one day, when she was out shopping with her uncle on a crowded street, her father came out of a bank and, seeing her, lifted his hat with a courtly bow. "Why, how do you do, my dear?"

"Papa," she said to him afterwards, "aren't you ashamed of me?"

"Why, you foolish child, I'm *proud* of you!"

After that her life's ambition was to be worthy of his pride. But she never lost her self-effacing modesty.

Jane Addams was always a great reader. Her father encouraged her by paying her five cents for each one of *Plutarch's Lives* that she could report on clearly, and, after that, ten cents for each one of the lives of the signers of the Declaration of Independence. Soon she needed no payments. One summer vacation she read all of Gibbons' *Decline and Fall of the Roman Empire.* But she never forgot "those horrid little houses." While still in her teens she determined that her life should be one of service to the underprivileged. At first she thought that she would be a doctor, and in 1877 she entered medical college. But her spinal trouble returned to plague her and lay her flat on her bed. Her doctors ordered her to give up a medical career and go to Europe for rest and travel for two years.

One midnight she was sitting on top of a sight-seeing bus in London, riding through the slums. She saw an auction of decayed vegetables going on from a huckster's wagon surrounded by a pitiful rabble. One man bid on a superannuated cabbage for tuppence, and then and there he wolfed it down raw. That glimpse of slum life determined Jane Addams' career. When she was back in America, she and her schoolmate and traveling companion, Ellen Starr, moved in on the Chicago slums, to do battle against suffering, sickness and crime.

It was in January, 1889, that Jane Addams rented a big, shabby mansion that had been built by a pioneer citizen of Chicago, named Hull, in 1856, on South Halsted Street. When Jane and her friend took over, that section of the city was the heart of the slum district. The house had been not only a private home but, in after years, a factory office, a secondhand furniture store and a home for the aged. There was much repair work to be done before it could be used, and in came the painters and carpenters. When their work was done, Jane furnished the old house just as if it were in a respectable quarter of the city, with fine pictures, carpets and chairs. Then she gave out an invitation to her astonished neighbors, "Come in and see us."

In those days, out of a million inhabitants in Chicago, 750,000 were foreign-born. On one side of Hull House was a colony of about 10,000 Italians; to the south, as many Germans, with Russian and Polish Jews in the side streets; farther south was a great Bohemian settlement and to the northwest French Canadians; directly north were the Irish. The whole area was a mess of rotten tenements, filthy stables and outhouses, dives and saloons.

All these various races and nationalities hated each other. Their first instinct was to suspect that this rich young American woman must have some mean purpose against them; why else should she come down to live among them? But Jane Addams persisted and, by-and-by, as her deeds of kindness became the talk of the neighbors, all the distrust vanished. It was a tough assignment that she had made for herself, but her life motto was, "Always do what you are afraid to do." She fought corrupt politicians in behalf of clean streets, and she had to fight crime and evil in all forms, rooted deep in her district. For instance, when she moved into Hull House, the drugstores were selling cocaine to teen-agers freely!

It is a long story, for she labored there for forty years. The one old house expanded into a group of thirteen buildings. The fame of her work spread all over the world. Echoes of Hull House were heard in the slums of many other great cities. Thousands of miserable men, women and children were made healthier, happier and better because of her.

Jane Addams had no thought of herself. One day a group of her admirers held a meeting and passed a resolution to the effect that she buy herself a new hat at once. One night she awoke to find a burglar in the room. The man, knowing that he had been discovered, dashed for the window. "No, no," said

she calmly. "You'll hurt yourself trying to get away by the window. Go out by the door."

After the First World War broke out, Jane Addams was in the forefront of the women's movements to bring about peace. In 1915 she was elected President of the International Congress of Women at the Hague in Holland. As the head of one of two delegations, she went from one warring country to another, striving to end the war by negotiations. She had made warring nationalities in Chicago forget their hatreds, why not do the same in Europe? But the official gentlemen sitting in the various capitals were harder to deal with than the "bums" of South Halsted Street. Since she opposed our own entry in the war, she was expelled from the D. A. R., and denounced by many newspapers and speakers. But the Secretary of War, Newton Baker, came to her defense; and after the war Mr. Hoover sought and obtained her aid for the women and children among the victims of the war. In 1931 she was awarded, along with Dr. Nicholas Murray Butler, the Nobel Peace Prize. On that occasion the Norwegian Chairman of the Committee of Award addressed her as "America's Uncrowned Queen."

When Jane Addams died suddenly at the age of seventy-four, the whole civilized world joined in tribute. A European wrote of her as "the one saint that America has produced." And she was a saint, indeed, worthy to stand with the shining names of the past; fearless, unselfish, an angel of mercy to the outcast and miserable during her entire active life. "Inasmuch as ye have done it unto the least of these . . ." Jane Addams selected for her ministry the very least of these, the most wretched and degraded of humanity. She wrote many books and articles, made many speeches; but, as someone said, "her masterpiece is her life."

She was given a public funeral in the courtyard at Hull House, and for two days her body lay in state in Bowen Hall. During that time, both day and night, about fifty thousand people filed past to pay her reverence. Many were weeping and many knelt a moment to offer a prayer. They all realized that they had lost their best friend and were inconsolable. One old Greek turned to a resident of Hull House who stood near. "She Catholic? She Orthodox? She Jewish?" To each question the resident answered, "No." "Oh, I see," he said with a smile, "she *all* religions."

Walter Ransom Barrows

LEONARDO DA VINCI

ILLUSTRATED BY *Robert Sinnott*

I HAVE a way of constructing light and portable bridges, to be used in pursuit of, or in retreat from the enemy, proof against fire, and easy to fix or to remove. For sieges, I can remove the water from the ditches, and make an infinite variety of scaling ladders and other engines suitable to such purposes. I have also portable bombs, excellent for throwing showers of small missiles, and with the smoke thereof causing the enemy great terror. I can make mortars and fieldpieces of useful shape, entirely different from those in use now. In time of peace, I believe I could equal any man in works of architecture. I can design buildings, whether public or private, and also conduct water from one place to another. Furthermore, I can execute works in marble, sculpture, bronze or terracotta. In painting, too, I can do what may be done, as well as any other man whomever he may be."

This was part of a letter written by a man of thirty, in applying for a position with the Duke of Milan. His name was Leonardo da Vinci (Vin-chi). He was one of the most gifted men who ever lived. He was supreme in art, science, mathematics, engineering, geology, geography, astronomy, anatomy and biology. He discovered secrets of nature not revealed until hundreds of years later. He is said to have even designed an airplane. But he is best known for his painting, ranking with the greatest who ever lived.

He was born in 1452 at a little town in Italy, named Vinci, about four miles from Florence. As a boy he made drawings of faces, animals and flowers and, when his father, a lawyer, showed them to his friend the artist Verrocchio, he was so impressed that he accepted Leonardo as a pupil in his studio. Verrocchio was a painter, sculptor and goldsmith, and a fine teacher. Leonardo entered the workshop at the age of thirteen and remained there for twelve years learning the essentials of art.

Stories went around about the young apprentice. He was ambidextrous, drawing with his left hand and painting with his right. His strength was so tremendous that he could bend a horseshoe as if it were a coil of lead. He was very fond of animals, often buying caged birds and then setting the birds free.

At this time we can picture Leonardo, brilliant and charming, often walking through the streets of Florence, his golden hair falling over his rose-colored cloak. We can see him joking, laughing, singing and talking to the eager crowd that followed him. We can see him studying the different expressions on the faces of these people, ready to jot them down in his sketch book always hanging from his waist.

After his apprenticeship was finished, he worked as an independent artist for a few years and then entered the service of the Duke of Milan. Here he painted, with exquisite taste, his great pictures, full of wonderful lights and shades, his great pictures of people whose faces always revealed some hidden emotion. It was at the command of the Duke that he painted his famous "The Last Supper." It was painted on the damp walls of the refectory in the Church of Saint Mary of the Graces. It is perhaps the most famous painting in the world—a picture of Christ and his disciples, when Christ says, "One of you shall betray me." We remember the simple background of this painting and we shall never forget the varied expressions of the disciples at this dramatic moment. Dampness and neglect caused the picture to deteriorate. Napoleon's soldiers are said to have thrown their boots at Judas Iscariot. But an Italian genius did a fine job of restoration in the early 1900's and the picture is now in fair shape.

A few years later Leonardo painted his other masterpiece, the "Mona Lisa," which is also called "La Gioconda." It is a picture of a Florentine noblewoman and is considered perhaps the finest portrait ever painted. Against a background of rocks and water, Leonardo painted this lady that all the world has wondered over,

Leonardo painted the "Mona Lisa" that all the world has wondered over

this lady with the puzzling eyes and the secret smile. You can see the famous Mona Lisa smile today in the Louvre, the big art museum in Paris.

Besides working on commissions for various churches and municipalities he worked awhile for Pope Leo X. His last years were spent in France where he was a guest of the king, Francis I.

He could paint no longer, for his hands were paralyzed, but his mind was still active and he wrote his thoughts and speculations in his famous Note Books.

He died in 1519 at the age of 67—one of the greatest men who ever lived.

Marjorie Gordon

LUDWIG VAN BEETHOVEN

ILLUSTRATED BY *Henry Pitz*

"LUDWIG," said the Duke, "you know how much faith I have in you. I don't want to be too severe, but never again must you disturb a chapel service with such jokes!"

Ludwig van Beethoven nodded solemnly, but he found it hard not to smile as he remembered the joke. The thirteen-year-old musician was assistant to the chapel organist at the Court of Duke Max Franz. He had bet Herr Heller, the chapel's solo tenor, that he could throw him off key during his solo by playing variations of the song on the organ. Herr Heller had very confidently accepted the bet, but what confusion there had been as the celebrated singer faltered and stuttered through his song, unable to remain on key! Beethoven had won his bet, but he understood the Duke's anger.

"I won't do it again, Your Excellency," he promised.

Ludwig wished to keep his position in order to help support his parents and his two brothers, Carl and Johann. He also played the clavier, an early form of the piano, at the Court Theatre. He played in the orchestra and even conducted it when the regular leader was busy.

These important positions, however, did not demand too much from the young boy, for Beethoven had begun to study music at the age of four! When his father had seen that his son was a musical genius he had given him the best music lessons available. He was hopeful his son could earn money by giving concerts, as young Mozart had. So for many hours a day Beethoven had practised the harpsichord, clavier, organ and the violin!

When he was only eleven Beethoven had made a successful concert tour and for many years he was more famous for his fine playing than for his great compositions.

Then when Beethoven was sixteen his father decided to send him to Vienna to play for the famous Mozart. When Beethoven arrived at Mozart's house he was very nervous, and decided that the best way to please the master would be to play his own compositions. Mozart, however, had so often heard his own works that he sat stonily throughout the performance, and even yawned! In desperation, Beethoven finally asked him to give him a theme upon which he could improvise. Then as his fingers dashed along the keyboard, inventing brilliant variations upon Mozart's theme, the older man sat up in surprise.

"Some day the world will hear of this boy," he said.

Back in Bonn, Beethoven again took up his duties. His mother died, and the loss was hard to bear. At this time, though, he met the happy van Breuning family, who were to remain his friends all his life. With them he went on many excursions, and spent happy days picnicking in the woods. Beethoven always loved to wander in the woods and fields, and there ideas came to him for many of his great compositions.

At the age of eighteen, Ludwig left Bonn to live in Vienna for the rest of his life. Joseph Haydn had come to visit Bonn, and had been so impressed with a cantata the young musician had written that he offered to give Beethoven lessons himself if he would come to Vienna. So Beethoven became Haydn's pupil. In Vienna he soon became famous as a pianist and as a composer as well, for now he really began to create great music.

Although Beethoven mixed with the highest society in Vienna, he refused to accept patronage, and remained independent even when he had very little money. He was the first musician to assert his equality with all men, and to refuse to bow before nobility. As a result, many members of Viennese society were prejudiced against him, and they thought that his free way of speaking and acting was rude. The nobles at Prince Lichnowsky's, however, where he gave his first performance, forgot his rude manners when they heard his beautiful music.

Besides ten early trios Beethoven wrote many violin and piano sonatas. These helped to establish the piano as the expressive and versatile instrument which we know today. His best known piano sonatas are the *Pathetique* and the *Moonlight* sonatas.

Perhaps as famous as his sonatas are his nine symphonies. His Third Symphony, the *Eroica,* was originally written in honor of Napoleon, for Beethoven thought that Napoleon believed in the freedom and equality of all men, as he did. But when Beethoven heard that his hero had declared himself Emperor of France, he almost destroyed his symphony. Fortunately his friends urged him to save it. But he changed his dedication, for Beethoven had no sympathy with tyrants.

One day when walking in the woods Beethoven heard a yellowhammer singing in a tree above him. The song began to suggest a tune, and he quickly got out his notebook and began to write what became his famous Fifth Symphony in C Minor. During World War II the opening phrase of this symphony was discovered to spell a V in Morse Code. So this musical phrase became known throughout the world as V, the symbol of Victory.

Besides his great symphonies, Beethoven composed an opera, *Fidelio*, a beautiful mass, the *Missa Solemnis,* and sixteen string quartets. Today they are recognized as great masterpieces.

When he was only thirty years old, Beethoven began to lose his hearing. In later years this great genius could not hear his own music when it was played. But inside his head he did hear the magnificent pieces. Altogether he wrote one hundred and thirty-eight works which are loved by the whole world.

Beethoven not only helped to develop the musical forms of the sonata and symphony, but he expressed in his music the strength and joy which he felt in living. Music was his life, and despite the many hardships which he knew, he saw much happiness and beauty around him. Through his great genius he was able to create works which expressed his belief in life, and so to give his vision of beauty and triumph as a gift to the world.

Ragna Eskil

LOUIS JOSEPH, MARQUIS DE MONTCALM

ILLUSTRATED BY *John Merryweather*

"WE WANTED to see this famous man who tramples the English under his feet. We thought we should find him so tall that his head would be in the clouds." So spoke an Indian chief from faraway Lake Superior to General Montcalm. "But you are a little man, my father. It is when we look into your eyes that we see the greatness of the pine tree and the fire of the eagle."

Well might the chief address Montcalm so eloquently. When the general had come to Canada a few months before to command the French army against the English in the Seven Years' War, the Indians, who were allies of the French, made fun of him behind his back. For General Montcalm was a short man. But after they had seen him win the battle of Oswego, they changed their tune, and his reputation was carried from tribe to tribe.

Indeed, so many Indians came to see him that he was pressed for time to go through the ceremony of greeting them. He wrote his mother in France from Montreal: "Ever since I have been here, I have had nothing but visits, harangues and deputations of these gentry. The Iroquois ladies, who always take part in their government, came also, and did me the honor to bring me belts of wampum, which will oblige me to go to their village and sing the war-song. . . . Yesterday we had eighty-three warriors here."

To sing the war-song in an Indian lodge meant the giving of lengthy orations, often lasting several hours, both by the visitor and the host. So it isn't surprising that Montcalm found these ceremonies burdensome. But the Indians were highly sensitive to any slight, and he didn't dare offend them. In that wild, unsettled country, the Indians were invaluable for scouting, and if the French had flouted them, they would have gone over to the English. They would not have remained neutral.

However, Montcalm could never get reconciled to the Indian savage methods of warfare and especially the way they treated prisoners. Once he threw himself among them, crying, "Kill me, but spare the English who are under our protection." Montcalm always respected the bravery of the troops who fought against him, and when he won a battle and they had to surrender their fort, he would allow them the honors of war—to march out with banners flying and drums beating, under protection of an escort of his own men. Just before this was to happen, he would call the Indian chiefs together to get their promise not to molest the beaten enemy. But, try as he would to hold them in line, the Indians never would keep their promise. When he could, he would pay the chiefs for their prisoners to save them from atrocities.

Montcalm, like certain great generals of our time, hated war. He entered the army when he was only fifteen years old because he thought it his duty, and he had taken a brilliant part in campaigns in Germany, Bohemia and Italy before he came to Canada in 1756—he was then forty-four years old. He had a genius for strategy and command. As he once said, "When I went to war, I did the best I could." And it was because his best was so good and the situation so critical, that France chose him to be commander-in-chief in Canada. For, in the Seven

Years' War, France and England were fighting for nothing less than the possession of North America. Whichever country lost would lose everything it claimed on this great continent. It was a huge responsibility.

Montcalm came to Canada but had to leave his mother, his wife and his six children, as well as his beautiful chateau in Southern France. He and his wife would send long letters to each other on every boat that sailed between Canada and France. He wanted to know everything that happened to them, and he would write about scenes and events in Canada. He would write constantly, "I live only in the hope of joining you all again."

An incident which happened when he was a schoolboy is interesting. His family was comfortably well-to-do, and he studied with a tutor who lived a short distance away. Montcalm had a quick temper, and when the tutor wrote to the elder Montcalm complaining that the son "has great need of docility, industry and willingness to take advice. What will become of him?" young Montcalm thought he had better write his father his own ideas of what his aims should be.

This is what he wrote: "First, to be an honorable man, of good morals, brave, and a Christian. Secondly, to read in moderation; to know as much Greek and Latin as most men of the world; also the four rules of arithmetic, and something of history, geography, and French and Latin *belles-lettres*, as well as to have a taste for the arts and sciences. Thirdly, and above all, to be obedient, docile, and very submissive to your orders and those of my dear mother; and also to defer to the advice of M. Dumas (the tutor). Fourthly, to fence and ride as well as my small abilities permit."

Montcalm had been winning the battles in 1756 and 1757, but in 1758 things began to go badly for the French, through no fault of his. France was waging war in several directions and couldn't send the supplies and men that were needed.

Meanwhile, the English had been getting stronger and, under the push of Prime Minister Pitt, were determined to win. They sent over an increasing number of trained regulars, and the

American colonials supplied unstinted help. And then the British got a tremendous asset in the arrival of Brigadier-General James Wolfe. He was to prove as fine a military genius as Montcalm, and was as fine in character. It was largely through his strategy that Louisburg fell in the summer of 1758 and, with its fall, England got control of the entrance to the St. Lawrence. The way was now open for Wolfe to transport an army, accompanied by a flotilla of ships, to besiege Quebec in June of 1759.

This is one of the important sieges of history. The English and the American colonists had recaptured Oswego and other fortifications the French had held, and Montcalm knew that if Quebec were taken, France had lost the war. Wolfe, of course knew this, too, so it was one great general against another. The siege went on for weeks and weeks, Wolfe battering day and night from the river and the island below. But Montcalm held.

Then, just as Wolfe was about to withdraw before winter set in, he took one desperate chance. He had discovered a secret path (it was covered by bushes) up a steep cliff that led to the plains of Abraham outside the city. Under cover of night, his patrol got up that, killed the guards, and the army followed. It was a complete surprise and, as we know, the French lost, and in the Treaty of Paris, England got everything France had owned in North America.

But the battle brought two great tragedies. Wolfe died on the battlefield. Montcalm was mortally wounded, and when the surgeon told him he had perhaps twelve hours to live, he said, "So much the better. I am happy that I shall not live to see the surrender of Quebec."

And he addressed this note to the English commander: "Monsieur, the humanity of the English sets my mind at peace concerning the fate of the French prisoners and the Canadians. . . . Do not let them perceive that they have changed masters. Be their protector as I have been their father."

He died at dawn and lies buried in the Chapel of the Ursulines in Quebec.

WITH his election to the Virginia House of Burgesses, Patrick Henry's public career was launched. Many years later Thomas Jefferson was to say, "After all, it must be allowed that he (Patrick Henry) was our leader in the measures of the Revolution in Virginia, and in that respect more is due to him than to any other person. . . . He left all of us far behind."

Powerful advocate of the rights of the common man, Patrick Henry was a determined and resourceful proponent of a bill of rights both for Virginia and for the federal government. When his colony became a state, he was elected the first Governor of Virginia. During Washington's administration he declined to serve as Secretary of State in his Cabinet and, because of failing health, later had to refuse the post of Chief Justice of the United States Supreme Court. But the title that stuck to him always was "Virginia's man of the people," the man who said, "Give me liberty or give me death."

Julia M. H. Carson

PATRICK HENRY ENTERS PUBLIC LIFE

ILLUSTRATED BY *DeWitt Whistler Jayne*

YOUNG PATRICK HENRY had not been practicing law a great while in Virginia before there was talk of running him for public office. Patrick himself made no move to bring this about but no young lawyer with a country practice could fail to recognize the broadening of reputation that might follow such public service. Then suddenly, in the spring of 1765, the neighboring county of Louisa had a vacancy in the House of Burgesses and ignoring county lines, as was often done, they elected Patrick Henry of Hanover County to fill the vacancy.

When he was told of his election by a small delegation, Patrick Henry accepted with friendliness but without undue pride. "I will do my best," he said, "to represent Louisa County in so distinguished an assemblage."

The men who had come to tell him liked his straightforward self-possession and the erect way he held his head when he spoke of serving them. It straightened their own spines and made them feel it was a fine thing to have some part in government. As they rode away they congratulated themselves again on the good choice they had made.

Patrick watched them out of sight, then crossed the porch with long strides and burst into the sitting room where his wife, Sally, was spinning and their three small daughters—Martha, Anne, and Betsey—were working on bright-colored samplers. "I'm going to Williamsburg!" he cried. "To represent Louisa County!"

"Patrick! Oh, I'm so glad!" Sally gathered up her billowing skirts and ran to him while the treadle of the spinning wheel went up and down of its own momentum and then slowed to a standstill. Patrick caught her about the waist and danced the length of the room with her while the little girls squealed with delight, and spun around in circles themselves from a general sense of excitement. "Ride us on your back three-at-a-time!" they clamored as he released their mother, laughing and breathless.

"What? Carry children on my back?" he demanded in mock dismay, screwing his face into an amazed grimace that delighted them afresh. "Don't you realize it is problems of state I should be shouldering now?"

They laughed at his teasing voice, even though the words meant nothing to them, and clambered onto his long back as he got down on his hands and knees.

"A fine load, this, for a burgess!" he protested, jogging at a wonderfully rough gait around the room. But the glance he threw Sally showed her how pleased he was.

The next day he swung saddlebags containing fresh linen, hand-fashioned stockings, and very little else, across the broad back of his horse, Shandy, and cantering down the dirt road turned toward the capital. He wore his usual buckskin breeches and a new homespun coat that fitted him none too well. In the stirrups were the snug but sturdy boots of an up-country planter. Under the tricorn, pulled firmly down on his brown wig, were thoughts, up-country in form, perhaps, but of a scope far transcending the Piedmont, the tidewater, and even Virginia itself.

The House of Burgesses had been in session for some weeks when Patrick Henry turned Shandy down Duke of Gloucester Street. Though he had been in the town before, he was impressed now as though for the first time with the fine street that ran its length, with the college at one end and the capitol at the other. He reined Shandy to the side of the road suddenly as several coaches lurched past over the ruts. A fan of muddy water splashed out of a puddle by the iron tire and one of them wet Shandy's forelegs. Patrick reined him in calmly, observing meanwhile that the coaches were of excellent construction—probably English. A swift glance through the lowered windows showed him laughing ladies in silks and elegantly tailored Tuckahoe gentlemen.

Stories of the social life of Williamsburg during the sessions of the burgesses were current through the colony and Patrick knew that Governor Francis Fauquier, driving about town behind six white horses, was the titular center of the elaborate festivities. He had heard too of such men as Peyton Randolph, the Attorney-General, Robert Carter Nicholas, the outstanding lawyer, and George Wythe, a renowned Latin and Greek scholar as well as a distinguished debater—the man who had refused to examine him for the bar. He knew such men held places of vast influence in the colony though without the prestige, possessed by the Governor, of royal prerogative. It was they and their friends who held undisputed sway in the House of Burgesses and though all of them had joined in the dignified petitions to the Crown and Parliament, asking that a stamp tax—latest of British proposals—be not levied on the colonies, it was common knowledge that many of these wealthy plantation owners had hearty regard for the forms of aristocratic authority. Control of the House of Burgesses they took for granted as their right. It was true that as the frontier was pushed westward, as

up-country lands came into cultivation, rural representation steadily increased. But it was not articulate representation, whether from Louisa, Hanover, or newer counties. When it came to polished oratory, to holding the floor, the tidewater members were not seriously challenged.

Patrick Henry took his seat in May. Washington, already in his place, bowed a grave welcome to the newcomer across the intervening benches. Patrick returned the bow with a pleasant smile. It was a pleasure to have this chance to see the intrepid Indian fighter at close range. He had been greatly interested in the current stories about Colonel Washington, all of them emphasizing the man's calm strategy and his reckless personal courage. Though his formal education had been no more extensive than Patrick's own, men of affairs respected his sound judgment.

Patrick spent his first evening as a burgess walking about the town. There was gaiety in the air. Principal houses showed the soft glow of many candles and through unshuttered windows he could have seen groups of carefully groomed gentlemen and ladies with high white hair, their brocades gleaming in the yellow, wavering light.

But he did not look in the windows or, if infectious laughter drew his eyes automatically to the houses he was passing, he gave scarcely an edge of thought to what he saw. Already the business of the colony was engrossing him. By chance upon his arrival he had fallen into conversation with a group of up-country men as he was seeing to the stabling of his horse. At first their talk was of the rumor that a stamp act had finally passed the British Parliament. Patrick had asked a few sharp questions about this rumor but they knew only the barest hear-say. All they could tell him definitely was that no such act had as yet been reported to the House.

"And there better be no stamp act!" cried a printer emphatically, banging one fist into the palm of the other hand and clamping ink-stained nails upon it. "The newspaper trade will be ruined if every sheet has to have a stamp stuck on it!"

Several days later—it was May 29, 1765—a greatly diminished House gathered in the capitol building at the end of the Duke of Gloucester Street. Many members had gone home, the call to supervise their rapidly growing crops more compelling than their sense of obligation to sit out a legislative session that appeared to have nearly run its course.

It was still a few minutes before the convening hour as Patrick joined the burgesses gathering outside and crowding the outer doors.

"Well, Mr. Henry," a pleasant voice greeted him from over his shoulder, "it looks as though from now on we lawyers will have to lick innumerable stamps for our legal documents. The Stamp Act has passed in spite of our petitions to Parliament and the Crown."

Patrick looked around into the clear eyes of one of the outstanding spokesmen for the tidewater interests. "So it has passed," he repeated with great interest. "Will the matter be brought up today for discussion?"

"It's passage will probably be noted. Beyond that there is not much one can do—"

"Not much one can do?" Patrick Henry protested.

The older member gave no indication he heard the amazement in Patrick Henry's voice at such violation by His Majesty's Government of Virginia's clear constitutional rights—unless it was evident in the tightness with which he pronounced the words, "Since the tax is now the law of the land, Mr. Henry."

Patrick bowed slightly, entered the legislative chamber, and thoughtfully took his seat. In a few moments the Speaker's gavel fell and the session began. Slumped in his seat, one leg thrust forward at a comfortable angle, Patrick Henry followed the dignified and temperate comments on the Stamp Act. Men in velvet and fine ruffles were stressing the point that the entire situation had changed now the act had been passed and was, therefore, no longer a theoretical proposal. In spite of his respect for the experienced burgesses about him, Patrick felt his disagreement growing with each speech.

Impatiently he moved in his seat. Then reluctantly he had to acknowledge to himself they spoke the truth when they said that not one of the colonies had raised its voice officially against this legislation. Was Virginia, like the other colonies, he demanded hotly of himself, going to submit without protest?

He looked from one member to another, studying their faces. How wide a line, he wondered, divided these tidewater planters from the British? Were their interests almost identical? Actually the Stamp Act would not be financially onerous—probably averaging little more than a shilling per head. But he saw it as delicate bait on the strong, sharp hook of British self-interest. Once the colonists swallowed this without protest they would be fairly caught in Parliament's claim of her unlimited right to tax. Britain was staggering under a great war debt. What more natural than that her ministry should seek means to foist as much of it as possible onto the American colonies? This mild Stamp Act was an entering wedge. Once the colonists accepted it, they were doomed to increasing subservience to Britain. Once they accepted it they tacitly consented to treatment Englishmen at

home would never tolerate: taxation without representation.

Almost docile though the House seemed this morning, Patrick Henry did not believe that even the wealthiest, the most highly polished burgesses, in their innermost thoughts, wanted servile subservience to Parliament. Elegant though their way of living might be, they as well as his up-country colleagues were men of a new, young country. Freedom under just laws, personal liberty, the full self-respecting rights of Englishmen were part of their tough fiber. What they needed now was to be shown the full implication of tame acceptance of this act.

Pulling toward him an old copy of a lawbook, Patrick turned to a blank flyleaf. Blowing away the bits of leather crumbling from its covers, he dipped his quill and began to write. When he was through he passed the book, with the several resolutions written in his distinctive hand, to George Johnston, the member from Fairfax.

"Will you second them," he asked with an eyebrow raised in inquiry, "when I propose them?"

Johnston read them through, then nodded.

"Mr. Speaker," said Patrick Henry, getting slowly to his feet. As he made a halting start, the burgesses turned in their seats in some surprise to face this newcomer in their midst. He began mildly, reasonably, in a measured tone. He described the recent setbacks the colonies had suffered due to British legislation. He spoke of the smallness of the stamp tax—a tax in the nuisance class.

Then he pulled his spectacles down from their perch on his high forehead and raising the lawbook began to read what he had written on the flyleaf—words that came to be known as "the Virginia Resolves."

At the word "resolves" Patrick Henry looked up and saw several of the leaders of the House sitting suddenly straighter in their seats. Disapproving glances were being exchanged here and there. He knew they were thinking it was completely out of place for any member but themselves to propose resolves for endorsement by the whole House.

Nevertheless with stern insistence in his voice he made them listen, his flexible voice making them feel the full impact of mounting tension. Then, at the conclusion, his voice rang out as had no other in that assemblage: "Resolved, therefore, that the General Assembly of this colony have the only and sole exclusive right and power to lay taxes and impositions upon the inhabitants of this colony; and that every attempt to vest such power in any person or persons whatsoever, other than the General Assembly aforesaid, has a manifest tendency to destroy British as well as American freedom."

For the fraction of a moment after he sat down there was the tense stillness that rides the center of a typhoon. Then in storming temper the accustomed leadership was on its feet: Peyton Randolph, Pendleton, Nicholas, Wythe, and others. Who was this terrible new member? Such bold power must not be allowed to grasp the authority that was theirs. It was on the verge of doing so. Fear, not unmixed with panic, flung bitter words in his direction. The unmitigated presumption of him! In that plausible, compelling voice of his, he had had the temerity to place Virginia's law-making power above the British Parliament. It was seditious. But more immediately disturbing to red-faced gentlemen, interrupting each other to gain the floor, was his self-confident assumption that it was he who would show the burgesses the path the colony was to take.

Dignity demanded that they meet this upstart's challenge to their ascendancy by crushing arguments on the merits of the proposition and to this end much sound logic was expounded. Lending Patrick a hand in the swift debate, his seconder, George Johnston, proved a formidable reasoner. But merely to counter on the proposition itself did not satisfy the burgesses who were smarting under the young man's cool attitude that he knew best what Virginia's stand should be. Unconsciously they envied him his sureness and unconsciously, too, some may have responded to the fundamental justice of his resolves, little as they liked to give ground to such a novice.

In the heat of debate they attacked him personally with lashing sarcasm and open ridicule—

"Perhaps the clowning actor from up-country does not know

that in civilized countries a law when passed by the highest law-making body of the realm is not subject to review by homespun jurists."

"Our talkative young friend—elected from Louisa County, we believe—not by his neighbors in Hanover where he lives. Perhaps his neighbors know his seditious tendencies too well to want him as their representative."

"Our buckskin orator, so safe in his up-country haunts from British chastisement."

"Doubtless it is too much to expect that one whose 'larnin' is —shall we be kind and say—not extensive should comprehend the intricacies of jurisprudence."

This last sally brought Patrick Henry to his feet with almost a jump of exaggerated awkwardness. "Mr. Speaker, if I may make so bold—" He sent his voice through his nose in exaggeration of the effete nasal whine of his attacker. Up came his hand in a disjointed gesture so subtly copying the preceding speaker and so comical that a titter of amusement ran around the room. The solemness of Henry's face did not change, however, nor was there a sound in the room as he went on in the same whine but using up-country pronunciation, "If I may make so bold as to say so, Mr. Speaker, naitural parts is better than all the larnin' upon the yearth."

Then with a quick rousing of his posture his commanding voice cut their laugh so short it took their breath and riveted startled eyes upon him. Torrents of eloquence poured from him in a voice not seemingly remarkable but with a hypnotic hold on every individual in the room. The true inwardness of liberty, the symbols that laws must be for the soul's deep integrity—words of plain speaking and full meaning—words as clearly spoken as those from Virginia's most polished gentlemen. With a crescendo of conviction that would brook no interference the force of Patrick Henry's belief in the freedom that was to be America's beat upon his hearers, reducing them to maleability in his hands.

Here was tyranny to be repulsed. Here was a threat to the rights of man that no true Britisher should tolerate. Parliament and the King had gone too far. They had usurped rights not belonging to them. "Caesar had his Brutus," Patrick Henry's voice was deep and full of mounting fury that was more threatening because he held a tight rein on it—"Charles the First his Cromwell"—the gathering volume was like a cataract—"and George the Third—"

"Treason!" shouted the Speaker crashing his silver mace.

"Treason, treason!" rang through the House.

But even as they spoke they were held by a grip that did not falter. Never taking his eyes from the Speaker's face, Patrick Henry drew himself erect and, impervious to interruption, "George the Third," he thundered with stern authority, "may profit by their example! If this be treason, make the most of it!"

The vote on his resolves was being taken. Patrick Henry listened without moving a muscle. It would be very close. Would they fail and Virginia lose this chance to stand against arbitrary government? The count went on. Burgesses here and there were keeping tally. Patrick counted in his head.

Before the results were officially announced, Patrick knew the resolves had carried, though with the very slimmest margin. He grinned across at his seconder and nodded slightly, then let all signs of triumph sober from his face as the clerk announced that the resolves had passed.

Hard, loud talking burst forth on all sides as the House broke up with adjournment. Red, defiant faces passed him while upcountry men crowded close to clap him on the back or shake his hand. Now and then a tidewater planter followed their example. Over their heads Patrick saw Tom Jefferson in the doorway. Tom gave him a broad smile of congratulation. Between them Peyton Randolph strode angrily from the Chamber biting out between his teeth, "By God, I would have given five hundred guineas for a single vote!"

"Mr. Henry—" Patrick turned, recognizing the courteous but rather formal voice of Colonel Washington. "Mr. Henry, you have put Virginia at the head of all the colonies."

Mathilda Schirmer

HOWARD PYLE: GREAT AMERICAN ILLUSTRATOR

ILLUSTRATED BY *Paul Strayer*

HOWARD PYLE stood back from his easel and studied the picture he was painting. It was a dramatic scene, showing a group in a lifesaving station interrupted at their card game by a man bursting into the room. He points toward the stormy sea and shouts that there is a wreck in the offing.

For six weeks the young artist had worked on this painting, but he still was not entirely satisfied. Today, however, he had to take the picture to the publishers, Harpers, to try to sell it. He needed money. All he had in his pocket was five cents.

He used the nickel to pay his carfare, but what a disappointment awaited him! The art director was out of town and wouldn't be back for two days. Leaving the picture with the publisher, Howard walked back to his studio. Now he had no money and no food, and he had to wait two long days before he would know if his picture would sell. He couldn't face his friends, although they would have been glad to help him. There was nothing to do but start working on something new.

Finally, the two days passed, and early in the morning the hungry young man set out for the office. Timidly he greeted the art director with questioning eyes. Was it accepted?

"Mr. Harper liked your picture and wants to use it in our *Weekly*," the art director said. "We can give you seventy-five dollars for it."

The young man left the office with the money in his pocket. The first thing he did was to go to Delmonico's, a New York restaurant famous for good food, and enjoy a big dinner. The work and poverty for those weeks had been worth-while after all.

Up to this time Howard Pyle had been insecure and unsure of himself. He had always liked to draw, but although he studied drawing and painting, he did not do art work for a living. Instead, he worked for his father who had a leather business. They lived in Wilmington, Delaware, and Howard spent his leisure time enjoying himself with the other young people.

Then, in 1876, he visited the little island of Chincoteague off the shores of Virginia, while on vacation. He was fascinated by the wild horses on the island, and when he returned home he wrote about everything he had seen: how the horses were penned and branded, how the people lived and how they worked. He illustrated his article with sketches which so delighted his mother that she persuaded him to submit them to *Scribner's*.

They were accepted, and one of the owners was so enthusiastic that he urged Howard to come to New York and use his talents in writing and drawing.

It was a hopeful young man who went to the big city, but he soon found that, in order to earn his living, he would have to work hard, and study more. Furthermore, he knew that he would have to decide between writing and drawing.

He was able to sell some fables, along with pictures to illustrate them, to *St. Nicholas* magazine, but he did not receive much for them. He also sold sketches to *Harpers*, but the art editor gave them to professional artists to do over.

Finally, Howard made up his mind. He would give all his time to drawing and work towards becoming an outstanding illustrator. It was a slow process, but Howard stuck to his decision. He gave up all social engagements, even the theater, which he loved, and spent long hours drawing. And then at last he was rewarded. He sold his picture, "The Wreck in the Offing."

He stayed in New York three years longer, and then he returned to Wilmington. He loved this city and he cherished the memories of his childhood there. When Howard was a boy, the Pyle family had lived just outside the city in a quaint stone house, one part of it dating from 1740. In front was a terraced lawn, and on one side was a grove of trees, and on the other a flower garden. Howard always remembered the flowers, the birds, and the sunshine in that garden.

He once wrote that when he was very, very young he was so inspired with its beauty that he decided to write a poem. He got pencil and paper from his mother and went out, but only then did he realize that he didn't know how to read or write.

However, Howard's mother used to read to him, and she also gave him famous paintings to look at. When he learned to read, he would draw pictures of the way he imagined the characters. Robin Hood, King Arthur, Robinson Crusoe, fairies, and goblins appeared on his slate, or on the leaves of his books.

One of Howard Pyle's own pictures

Now that he was a man, once again he drew these story-book people, but this time he put them in the pages of books. He not only drew, but he re-wrote the stories about them, for he found that he could be both an author and an illustrator. They became popular, and boys and girls were thrilled by the adventures of the medieval heroes and pored over the glowing, zestful pictures. He wrote other original stories about knights and their fair ladies, two of which have also been great favorites with boys and girls for many, many years: *Men of Iron* and *Otto of the Silver Hand.*

In Wilmington he met his own fair lady. A group of young people planned a picnic, and for entertainment they wanted singing. They needed a tenor and Howard volunteered. The first rehearsal was held at the home of the Pooles. Howard arrived early and was greeted at the door by Anne Poole. Although they had never met, and in those days it was improper for a young lady to speak with a young man without being introduced, she welcomed him in. By the time the others arrived, the two were chatting like old friends. The following year they were married.

Howard and his wife continued to live in Wilmington, but in the summer they went to Rehobeth, on the eastern coast. It was there that Pyle's vivid imagination was stirred by stories of pirates that led him to do research into the lives of Captain Kidd, Edward England, and other pirates. As a result he drew marvellous pictures and wrote exciting adventure stories about them, such as *The Rose of Paradise* and *Jack Ballister's Fortune.*

Besides pirates, fairies, and knights, Howard Pyle was interested in the story of America. Some of the most important events of the Revolutionary War had taken place where he lived. He studied the history of the colonies and learned about the campaigns, but he also found out about the clothes that were worn, and the utensils that were used, and other information he needed to make his pictures accurate. Thus he became one of the greatest authorities on early America.

As his reputation grew, many young artists clamored to study with him. For a while he taught at Drexel Institute in Philadelphia, and at summer school in Chadd's Ford, Pennsylvania, where his studio was in an old mill directly across from where Washington and Lafayette had made their headquarters. He was such a great teacher that hundreds of artists wanted to study with him. However, teaching began to take too much of his time and energy, so he gave it up to spend all his time in Wilmington, with only a few of the most promising young people as his students. Many of them became famous. Among them are Jessie Wilcox Smith, N. C. Wyeth, and Maxfield Parrish, as well as the Children's Hour artist, Paul Strayer.

He would tell a student, "You must live your best and work hard." He not only told them this, but his own life was an example of this advice.

Howard Pyle has been called the founder of the national school of art, for he believed that American men and women were able to develop themselves here. Howard Pyle never studied abroad, and it was not until he was in his late fifties that he went to Italy. He himself felt his real life's work was just beginning. He was there for a little more than a year when he died suddenly in Florence.

A fine artist, writer, and well-loved teacher, he scoffed at the suggestion of artistic temperament. He said:

"A successful artist is just like any other successful man—conservative, provident, and normal. He does his work and takes care of himself and his credit. Titian, the Venetian, industrious and ambitious, had ministers and kings for his friends and companions. Leonardo da Vinci, whose 'Last Supper,' the wall-painting at Milan, has made him immortal, was a brilliant architect, sculptor, engineer, scientist, and musician. Raphael, tremendously practical, was not only the architect of St. Peter's, but was an able archeologist and an authority on the antiquities of Rome. Michelangelo wrote poetry, drew plans for splendid buildings, and was one of the most learned anatomists of his time. The 'old masters' were sensible men. So are the young masters, whether they be artists, lawyers, doctors, or preachers. Nor is any great achievement the completed effort of an inspired instant. Nothing worth-while is done without toil, and toil compels one to be sober-minded and careful."

Mabel L. Robinson

LOUIS AGASSIZ

ILLUSTRATED BY *Lynd Ward*

"WHO IS Louis Agassiz?" you ask. And you do well not to say who *was* he, because he captured the only way to live endlessly, through the living growth of the projects into which he poured his life. Nor did this work come as a product of everlasting grind. Never did a man have more fun doing the things he wanted to do. When he and his men, after gruelling hours of mountain climbing, reached a shining peak, they fell to wrestling and dancing until the chamois scattered through the snow. Agassiz could come back from the Jungfrau, tired perhaps, but as gay and proud as if he had the peak in his pocket.

Nor was his life wholly concerned with adventures though no man liked them better than he did. They were always secondary to some search, some discovery, some project. But the combination with adventure, which he usually managed, fed his rich vitality so that to the end of his life he kept his love of living and his magnetic hold upon people.

When you come upon a man who has done exactly what he wanted to do with his life, and realize how splendid can be the force of that uninhibited effort, you are quite right to want to know how this force was born and nurtured. Proverbs may seem catch phrases to you, but they rise from the hard experience of the race, and there never was a truer one than, "The boy is father to the man." You are young now, but within you lie the qualities which will quicken and grow with care until you are the kind of adult you want to be.

So to understand a man who was a scientist, an explorer, an educator, we are farsighted if we look back to his youth. Back at the beginning of the nineteenth century, a young pastor, Rudolphe Agassiz, and his wife, Rose, lived in the Swiss mountains. The life was harsh, and one after another their babies died, until the young pair could bear the place no longer.

They came to Motier, and here they built a new life. And here on May 28th, 1807, the fifth child was born, equipped to hold to his life and make of it a great gift to mankind. Jean Louis Rudolphe Agassiz was his name, and they called him Louis. The heart of his mother beat high and strong again with the strength of her boy. Rose Agassiz somehow knew that here was no ordinary child entrusted to her care. She loved the other children who came later, but through her long and useful life Louis was her very heart.

There in the Swiss mountains the boy grew up, knowing them as much his home as the quiet parsonage where he lived. With his brother, Auguste, he made endless collections of animals, rocks, plants, for which his mother always allowed room. Board, too, for many animals needed feeding. The yard was a small enclosed museum. And this way of living was a sound and active prophecy of the future of young Louis Agassiz.

So, too, were the qualities of the boy which grew with him into the man whom nobody forgot once he had had the luck to know him. Tremendous vitality carried the boy along on its swift current through project after project until Auguste and his parents could follow no longer. But a little out of breath, they still watched him eagerly, intently. As did the boys of the village.

For Louis had that strange, intangible quality which has endless power for good or evil, the dangerous, lovely quality of charm which swung him on his irresistible way through all his life. He was a born leader, and part of his leadership lay in his intelligent directorship, and part in the charm which drew his followers after him. Here was a gang of boys who were not mischief-makers, and who, to their own surprise, got excited about such ordinary things as fish, stones, shells. Louis could keep ahead of them in everything else, so why not listen to him when he burned with excitement over a new find?

Together they explored the regions about them which had seemed so familiar and ordinary. From them they extracted new and endless possibilities for adventure and for amazing collections which must be valuable because Louis said so. Anyway it was fun to risk their necks going after them, and to see in Louis's glowing dark eyes the astonishing reward for their success. Not a bad prophecy of the way Agassiz handled his scientific affairs later.

So here you have the boys' gifts which he could use even to the last strong beat of their power, or discard in a search for something the world values like comfort of living, riches. Here was an intelligent mind, eager to make use of its strength and rejoicing in the excitement of feeling the brain at work. Here was a strong body which delighted in its own activity. Here was charm, that magnetic quality which drew men to him. Here was a love for the earth and everything which grew from it, and passionate curiosity about how it all came about. And sometimes these gifts fought with each other, because no man is perfect. If Louis's excitement and curiosity about one project were demolished by another, he deserted the first and left it for someone else to finish. But after all, his new interest was usually an outgrowth of the old and more important.

Now as with ourselves when we are grown, let us see where gifts and temperament led the youth into the adult. The question of school and education is always a part of the problem of growing up. Here in Motier was no good school, but Louis had the luck to have a father who was an inspired teacher as well as a pastor. For the first ten years of his life he had as modern a training as our own educators could have devised. And perhaps that early training in outdoor practice of indoor theory helped to make him the inspired teacher which he, himself, grew into.

The College of Bienne was only twenty miles away, and there Louis and Auguste spent four good years, coming home for holi-

days and festivals easily enough by walking the twenty miles. No hitch-hiking came their way! But they grew strong through the quickened life which the new order demanded.

At Bienne the emphasis had been on classics. Now at fourteen Louis could no longer resist the driving force of his urge to understand the mysteries of the life of land and sea. At Lausanne he could work with men who knew some of the answers. For two years he studied natural history with professors who judged him as their equal, and gave to him all that he asked.

But there were four children in the Agassiz family now, and the salary of a pastor was small. Louis understood and agreed to their proposition that he become a physician. After all, this was a profession based on science. And it ought to allow him time for outside explorations. He would try it.

A medical training meant the University of Zurich where Louis could have two years more to find out about animals, plants, and rocks, which would not deflect him too much from human diseases. He entered at seventeen, and with his entrance the walls of the dark laboratories seemed to expand, the grim, hard-working students to discover laughter. For as ever, Louis swung work into play through his vitality and charm. With effortless enjoyment he won companions, professors, and prizes in learning and in sports. His early equipment increased in strength and achievement.

Two years at Zurich, then a year and a half at Heidelberg, and Louis was just past twenty, and in love. His close friend, Alex Braun, had a sister, a pleasant, sensitive girl who helped the boys with their drawings, when they came home for week-ends. But when Louis to his astonishment and dismay fell ill of typhoid, the Braun family took him in and Cily helped to nurse him. To the boy who had never known dependence, she became the pivot on which his life turned. And since no illness could devastate his charm, Cily loved him tenderly.

So now with no money, unfinished education, and no possible prospect of a home, Louis engaged himself to Cecile Braun, and the two parted without a doubt about their uncertain future. They had each other, and that was enough.

Never did a man have more fun doing the things he wanted to do

By this time Louis had almost forgotten that he ever intended to be a doctor. He and Alex went off to the University of Munich where Louis did such brilliant work in natural history that, instead of getting an M.D., Louis was presented with the degree of doctor of philosophy. At twenty-three he collected the M.D. to please his mother, but now he was a distinguished naturalist and no kind of a degree could deflect him.

Yet having a medical degree, and the necessity of earning a living, the next move seemed to be toward collecting some patients. But no patient must be allowed to interfere with his research in his laboratory. He decided to live at home where it cost little, and where he could easily deflect patients if they were so unwary as to bother him.

But no backwater could hold Louis for long. And as ever, his undeviating intentions found a way to drive him on his way. Pastor Christinat, a good friend of Pastor Agassiz, caught the fire of the brilliant young Louis and handed him the fare to Paris. And in payment Papa Christinat was to become the trusted and dear friend of Louis as long as he lived.

Yet even then Louis travelled to Paris by way of Carlsruhe where poor Cily still waited in the hope that she might be preferred to fishes. Such a good time he had that it took a strong letter from his mother to send him on his way. But small thought he had of Cily when soon after his arrival the great scientist Cuvier delivered over to him the seal of his trust, his prized portfolio of fossil fish drawings. Small thought for anything except his profound gratitude and his determination to be worthy of the gift.

Poverty dogged him, and even in Paris poverty can reach an unbearable stage. His mother urged his return. But Alex Braun was in town, another Little Academy of eager young scientists were meeting in Louis's rooms, and as ever help came at the last despairing moment. The great Alexander von Humboldt, who had become his warm friend, sent him one thousand francs, which gave Louis a wonderful walking tour in Normandy as well as his chance to stay in Paris. Some special guardian angel seemed to keep cash on hand for Louis Agassiz.

Louis worked hard on the relation of living fishes to fossil fishes, and made a real contribution of their relation and classification. He stayed there a year, and no moment of that rich and full year was wasted. But now at twenty-five he must earn a living, and Louis went back to Neuchatel, the home of his boyhood, where he joined the University staff at a salary of four hundred dollars.

Never had the university known such a teacher before. He swung the boys and the townspeople before him in a great surge of interest in natural history. He flung open doors of knowledge to them which did not seem knowledge but high excitement of discovery. As in those early days of his childhood, eager followers were always at his heels. And he liked it. Never was he more in his element than when he was sharing his discoveries. He was, indeed, a born teacher!

Now with such a well-paid job, and so much appreciation of his work, Louis felt that it was time for marriage. Cily agreed with him for she had waited long. She was twenty-four now, high-strung, and utterly unfitted to be the wife of the rash Louis, or to share his turbulent life. Her brother, Alex, fond as he was of Louis, tried to dissuade her, but Cily had not waited all those years for nothing. She married him, and when in high delight he carried her back to Neuchatel she was bitterly homesick. Poor Cily had to find out what it was to marry a genius. Time dragged for her, but for Louis it raced him toward new goals.

His first number of his *Poissons Fossiles* had come out, and had brought him recognition from England, where he just missed meeting Darwin who had sailed away for five years. Those two young men should have met. They had much to thresh out. They might indeed have influenced each other's conclusions. But Louis missed little else! He flung himself into this life with his usual exuberance, and came away determined to found, some day, a museum where a man could find what he needed without travelling the world over. And he did!

But before he founded that great museum at Harvard he had a long way to go. And he travelled most of that long distance to Cambridge, curiously enough, by way of mountains. A man must have a scholarly reputation for Harvard to notice him, and Agassiz won his through his work with these Swiss mountains, which might easily, to a different temperament, have seemed a lonely, empty prison. As indeed, they did to poor Cily with her three small children to rear!

Here in the mountains Louis discovered fossils of small sea animals, star fish, sea urchins, sea lilies, which later he was to know stirring about alive on the shore of Nahant. Yet here they had been, and here the sea must have been. They were to Louis evidence of the strata of the earth. He collected them, talked about them to his classes and to any scientists who would listen. His publications, for which nobody seemed able to pay, brought him invitations and medals from European scientists, which he accepted, always leaving Cily at home to care for her family.

He flung himself with tremendous excitement into the theory of the Ice Age and found evidence of its soundness all through his mountains. He saw the earth covered by a slow-moving sheet of ice, and by building his laboratory hut on the surface of a glacier, saw it gradually move away and disappear. Fortunately, not while he and his companions were in it. Neuchatel was a perfect laboratory for Louis Agassiz.

With his salary raised from four to six hundred dollars, he felt rich enough to fill his house with assistants, very pleasant for him, but hard on Cily. When Pastor Agassiz died, and his wife Rose was left alone, she came to Neuchatel to help run the crowded household. Cily, with great relief, took her babies and went home to Carlsruhe. For the first time Louis knew a home which was orderly and run for his own service. No wife could have managed it thus, but a mother could.

He built his own printing establishment with many men at work in it; he published twenty volumes so fine that no one could afford to buy them; he used every resource which Neuchatel could offer him, establishing the Ice Age beyond refutation. Now he was through with Neuchatel. He must have room to grow. With no money to pay his fare, he decided to go to America.

As often happens when the desire is stronger than the means

of satisfying it, the way was opened for Louis to do what he intended to do, anyway. His old friend Humboldt interested the King of Prussia who offered him a grant of fifteen thousand francs to visit America.

Louis set his house in order, and it is no wonder that it took him nearly a year to do it. He parted from his friends and neighbors, sharing deeply their sorrow, and forgetting them at once in his ardent search of the future. He was a man of genius who could not bind himself to the past.

So here he was at thirty-nine, off for America with its unknown and endless possibilities for a scientist. Perhaps he could even send for Cily and the children when he was established. He visited Paris and England on the way, and was greeted by scientists of renown, now his warm friends. He boarded a steamer for Boston, leaving behind him all security and looking ahead to no certainty.

The voyage was rough and the ship was nearly lost. The man of the mountains was tossed about by the sea without mercy. But withal he managed to make friends who taught him enough of our language to ease his entrance to our country. He walked along the Boston streets, carrying his bags, savoring the strange place, until he came upon the house for which he searched, the home of John Lowell. Louis might be here only for a year's visit, but he made a friend for a lifetime. And a friend who knew what he needed and how to help him to get it.

America needed a Louis Agassiz, and had sense enough to know it. The country was young and concerned with establishing itself. We knew that we had rich resources in the earth, and needed wisdom to guide us in their use. Agassiz was the soundest authority on geology who could have come our way. We felt sure, especially in New England, that every man, woman, and child should have an education. Of course a good many couldn't take it, but that we hadn't found out yet. And here was a renowned and inspired teacher at our very doors. With no war in the offing, we had for the first time the money and the desire to discover something about the arts and sciences. Here was Agassiz, a contributor to European science, who could show us how to make contributions of our own. And withal a man whom nobody could help liking.

Louis Agassiz may have seemed to come empty-handed to this country, but his offerings were beyond price, and he gave of them generously. The Lowell Institute was Boston's idea of education for everybody, and Louis captured its audiences in spite of his lack of English. They waited, breathless, while he searched for the right word, and applauded when he found it. He talked *with* them, not *at* them. Never did they have more fun with learning! The new scientific school at Harvard kept an eye on him.

From the moment he landed, he began collecting specimens with, as usual, no place to house them. He also collected assistants with, as usual, no money to pay them. But small items like this never troubled him. He got himself a little house in East Boston with the harbor in its back yard where he had his helpers, dredged and collected, and lived in complete disorder.

As ever, someone was ready to take charge of his troubled affairs. Papa Christinat wrote that, through politics, he was exiled from his church, and that he would run Louis's household, which he did in an amazing fashion most satisfactory to the members of it. And this left Louis free to go on long research explorations. A good arrangement all around!

The outcome of his year's visit was inevitable. Harvard wanted him and would pay him fifteen hundred dollars if he would accept the chair of zoology and geology. Not a small assignment! But Louis Agassiz could not only hold down his chair, but carry on an endless number of projects besides. There was no end to his energy in this fulfillment of his life. Both he and Harvard took on new vitality.

It was not all fair sailing. It never was with Louis. His utter disregard of money except as something to spend for his work, his reckless collection of assistants who were bound to quarrel with him and about him, his old traits of boyhood still had their sway. But Louis usually managed to escape by attacking some fresh project which took him away from the turmoil. Papa Christinat managed his new house in Cambridge, and he could always come back to it when the storm was over.

But one blow which fell upon him was final. Cily died. She could rest in peace now. But on Louis, for the first time, fell the responsibility of his children. His mother took charge of the daughters, and young Alexander stayed with the Brauns. But these arrangements were temporary.

In the spring of 1850, Louis found his way out of his perplexities in as wise a step as he ever took. Through his good friends, the Feltons, he met their sister, Elizabeth Cary, who had all of the wisdom and balance which Louis needed. They loved each other quietly and deeply, and when he married her the house in Cambridge became a home, perhaps the first home of his own. Young Alexander came to live with him, and then the two girls, Ida and Pauline. Elizabeth treated them as her own, as indeed they were, for she loved them and set them on their pleasant ways. Louis had not known that his life could be so serene.

With his middle years set in such pleasant places, it would have seemed natural for Louis to take on the quiet complacency of that time of life. Not Louis Agassiz! For him such comfort gave fresh impetus to new effort. Peace was good to come back to, but outside of it were undiscovered areas of the earth waiting for his attention. And he gave it without stint.

It is not often given to a man to reap recognition of his work in his lifetime which becomes so heightened that he can find in it, as long as it lasts, new ways to add to its glory. Agassiz had always longed for a sea voyage of his own. Our government placed at his service a vessel to explore the reefs and keys of Florida, and to enable him, on the side, to study coral and collect it.

Europe begged him to return. He had much ado to convince Zurich and Paris that he meant to stay right where he was, in America. When he finally made a visit back to his Swiss mountains to bring his family to his dear mother, he had to stop on the way for medals and honors. But none could move him as did the greeting of Rose Agassiz.

For sixteen months he explored the Amazon River and its valley to discover new truths about the distribution of species, and glacial tracks. He took a vacation to look over the copper mines of Lake Superior, and formed the nucleus of a great fortune for the Agassiz family, though for himself he had small use for money except to spend it on his projects.

The great project which had beckoned him all his life was the establishment of a museum. And with every available, and unavailable, place crammed full of his specimens he certainly needed one! He got it, too. The legislature, private contributors, the college, all poured money into his hands. The Museum of Comparative Zoology was built, staffed, and filled with invaluable specimens, and it was always called the Agassiz Museum, as it should be. Nothing but Agassiz's headlong determination could have built it.

He got himself an island in Buzzards Bay called Penikese, and there he gathered scientists, and those who would know science, and began that great educational contribution of summer schoolwork which has so lightened and enriched the lives of young workers, and has shown teachers that science is not an assignment in a book, but a piece of life to be studied from living parts of it.

In all this activity the man never lost sight of other men around him. There in Cambridge he spent high hours with the great men of his time. When the Saturday Club celebrated his fiftieth birthday with a dinner, there sat around the table men whose equal we should find it hard to produce. All his friends. Whittier, Longfellow, Lowell, Hawthorne, Holmes, Motley, Parker, a roll call of our poets and scholars, and every man with his gift of verse and wit at the table. Thoreau would not come from Walden for a party, but he and Agassiz hunted turtles together. Everybody knew this great naturalist, Louis Agassiz, whom our country had taken over for its own.

So the years went by until he was sixty-six, years so ripe and full of rich return that Louis must have hated to leave them. But he left them with the knowledge that he had filled them with new life for others to go on with. No man could ever finish his work in a lifetime, but there would be fresh minds whose vigor would rise from it. That was as Louis Agassiz would wish.

His son, Alexander, devoted his life to the science which was his heritage. His dear wife, Elizabeth, carried on his educational ideas at Radcliffe, and helped his children to good lives. His friends and students missed him as a man could rarely be missed. But no one could be sad about Louis Agassiz. It is not given to many a man to fulfil his life with the rewards which are his because he has worked for them and enjoyed every step of the way.

Stephen Vincent Benét

DANIEL WEBSTER

ILLUSTRATED BY *John Merryweather*

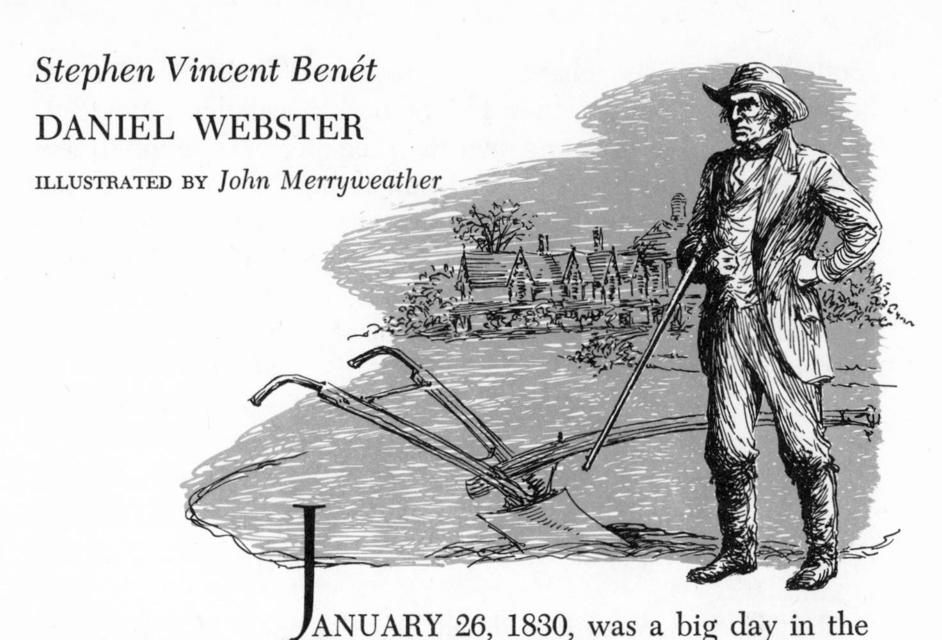

JANUARY 26, 1830, was a big day in the United States Senate. We believed then, as we believe now, in thrashing issues out in public, not in settling them behind closed doors—and a very big issue indeed was before the nation. In the space of a man's lifetime, we had grown from a loose confederation of squabbling colonies to a Union of sovereign states. But how sovereign were these states? Was the Union more important than the states or were the states more important than the Union? Could a state refuse to obey laws passed by the federal government for the general good? Was a man an American first and a Virginian or a New Hampshireman second, or was it the other way around? The country was split and divided on the question.

Senator Robert Y. Hayne of South Carolina had spoken, and spoken well for his side of the argument. A proud man, from a proud and gallant state, he asserted the rights of his state. South Carolina could nullify federal laws if she chose, withdraw from the Union itself if she chose. Now, for the second time in the great debate, a swarthy, burning-eyed man—"Black Daniel" of Massachusetts—Daniel Webster—rose to reply.

"I have not allowed myself, sir, to look beyond the Union, to see what might lie hidden in the dark recess behind. I have not coolly weighed the chances of preserving liberty when the bonds that unite us together shall be broken asunder. I have not accustomed myself to hang over the precipice of disunion to see whether, with my short sight, I can fathom the depth of the abyss below; nor could I regard him as a safe counsellor in the affairs of this government whose thoughts should be mainly bent on considering, not how the Union may be best preserved but how tolerable might be the condition of its people when it is broken and destroyed . . ."

The great voice rose and fell—the packed audience in the Senate Chamber listened.

"No such miserable interrogatory as 'What is all this worth?' . . . but everywhere, spread all over in characters of living light . . . Liberty *and* Union, now and forever, one and inseparable!"

The last sentence came down like the crash of a breaker. And, when the applause was over, Daniel Webster went home to his house, for he was tired. But his words about the Union were to go all over the Union. They were to go out to the Indiana frontier and touch the mind of a youngster named Abraham Lincoln. They were to make the United States seem worth living for, and dying for, to hundreds and thousands of men whom Webster never even saw. They were to be among the great words that have made and sustained this nation. And they are an answer still to all the divided and faint-hearted who look around them and quaver, "What is all this worth?"

So what sort of man was it who said these words? Did he know his country and his people—did he know what he was talking about?

He was farmer, orator, fisherman, lawyer, statesman. He was a frail boy who grew into a strong man. "This is our Yankee Englishman; such limbs we make in Yankee land." Born on a New Hampshire farm of hard-bitten, resolute stock, educated at Phillips Exeter Academy and Dartmouth College, he was in the House of Representatives at thirty-one, and, till he died at seventy, he was one of the great men of the country. He was the greatest orator of his day, one of the greatest lawyers of his day. He was secretary of state—everything but president—and a bigger man than many presidents. But that does not say enough.

First, last, and all the time, Daniel Webster was a good neighbor. And that wasn't a political pose—it was in his blood. He liked growing things and raising things and helping other people grow them and raise them. Nobody who came to him in trouble went empty-handed away. On his big farm at Marshfield, Massachusetts, he raised fine sheep and fine cattle and fine horses. He had a ram named Goliath, a Hungarian bull named King Stephen—and he used to say that there was a lot more sense in King Stephen's off hoof than there was in the heads of some United States senators. When his favorite horses died, he had them buried standing up with their shoes still on, because he thought that did them honor. But the big farm had been poor land when he first got it—he nursed it along and improved it till it got to be a place that people came to see. He'd get up before daybreak to talk and plan and argue with his hired men—and he didn't think of them as anything but men just because they were hired. If anyone had tried to say that he belonged to one class because he made money and the hired men to another because they worked for wages, that man would have got a beautiful dressing-down from Daniel Webster.

So he became to his neighbors, and to New England, the good giant, the man you could count on, the famous orator who was never too busy to help out a neighbor, the man whose voice could roll out like thunder over Monadnock but the human man who liked Medford rum and good living, the man who could whip a trout stream or an enemy with equal skill. They talked about his fishing rod, Old Killall, and his shotgun, Wilmot Proviso—and when he walked into the depot, to take the train for Washington, everybody in the depot stood up. It takes a good deal to make New Englanders stand up, but they did it for Daniel Webster. They don't do it for many people now.

He had reverses and troubles. He spent money as freely as he made it. He used to say that good lawyers "lived well, worked hard, and died poor." He wanted sons to carry on his name, but his sons died. He never attained the greatest ambition of his

life—smaller men, Polk, Tyler, Fillmore, were made president and he was not. But reverses and troubles could not break him. His last great speech, the Seventh of March speech, supporting Henry Clay's compromise, was bitterly attacked by his own people of New England—they thought he was trying to compromise with slavery when what he was trying to do was to seek for a peaceful solution for the differences between North and South. But that did not break him either—he had always put the Union first, even above New England, and he said what he thought was right. When he died, in 1852, New England felt differently. They knew a great oak was down. "A mournful voice went up from every house, 'The pride of our nation has fallen—our great neighbor and townsman is no more!' " And that would have satisfied Daniel—to be talked of as neighbor and townsman, not just as a great man.

What did he do, through his long busy fighting life, so crowded with fame and action, with law cases and treaties, country neighbors and foreign ambassadors, orations that men still read, and fishing in Plymouth Bay? He did one central thing. He set up and affirmed in men's minds the idea of the United States, not just a haphazard, temporary league or a partnership between states to be dissolved at their convenience, but as an entity, a deep reality, a living thing that deserved and must have the deepest devotion of every American. He looked beyond his time to do that, he looked beyond his section and the place where he was born. We take that idea for granted, now—we would not take it for granted if men like Webster had not lived for it and fought for it. But with Union must go liberty, forever and ever; with Union must go good-neighborliness and humanity. Webster knew that if men wanted a great, free nation they had to work for it and pay for it and get behind it, just as he and his neighbors at Marshfield worked to make their poor ground into good ground. And that is why his great speeches are still remembered—and the memory of the man with a mouth like a mastiff, a voice like thunder, and eyes like burning anthracite still haunts the New England seacoast and the New Hampshire hills.

CHRONOLOGY

1451–1506	Christopher Columbus
1452–1519	Leonardo da Vinci
1475–1564	Michelangelo
1477–1576	Titian Vecelli
1491–1557	Jaques Cartier
1564–1616	William Shakespeare
1564–1642	Galileo
1599–1641	Antonio Van Dyck
1685–1759	Georg Frederick Handel
1706–1790	Benjamin Franklin
1712–1759	Louis Joseph, Marquis de Montcalm
1732–1799	George Washington
1736–1799	Patrick Henry
1738–182–	Benjamin West
1743–1826	Thomas Jefferson
1756–1791	Wolfgang Mozart
1770–1827	Ludwig van Beethoven
1780–1851	John Audubon
1782–1852	Daniel Webster
1805–1875	Hans Christian Andersen
1807–1873	Louis Agassiz
1807–1870	Robert Edward Lee
1807–1882	Henry Wadsworth Longfellow
1809–1865	Abraham Lincoln
1812–1870	Charles Dickens
1822–1892	Alexander Mackenzie
1823–1915	Jean Henri Fabre
1832–1888	Louisa May Alcott
1832–1898	Lewis Carroll
1835–1910	Mark Twain
1847–1931	Thomas Alva Edison
1850–1894	Robert Louis Stevenson
1853–1911	Howard Pyle
1858–1919	Theodore Roosevelt
1858–1943	Booker Taliaferro Washington
1860–1935	Jane Addams
1864–1943	George Washington Carver
1867–1934	Marie Curie
1867–1912	Wilbur Wright
1871–1948	Orville Wright
1874–1937	Guglielmo Marconi
1875–	Albert Schweitzer
1880–	Helen Keller
1902–	Charles Lindbergh
1908–	Marian Anderson
1926–	Elizabeth II

Index

MICHELANGELO

THOMAS EDISON

LEONARDO DA VINCI

GALILEO

HELEN KELLER
BENJAMIN FRANKLIN

JANE ADDAMS